SUPPORTED EMPLOYMENT FOR PERSONS WITH DISABILITIES
Focus on Excellence

SUPPORTED EMPLOYMENT FOR PERSONS WITH DISABILITIES
Focus on Excellence

Edited by

Paul Wehman, Ph.D., and
John Kregel, Ed.D.

Virginia Commonwealth University
Richmond, Virginia

 HUMAN SCIENCES PRESS, INC.

Library of Congress Cataloging in Publication Data

Supported employment for persons with disabilities: focus on excellence.

Includes index.
1. Vocational rehabilitation—United States. 2. Handicapped—Employment—United States. 3. Handicapped—Services for—United States. I. Wehman, Paul. II. Kregel, John, Ed. D.
HD7256.U5S87   1989   362'.0425   88-9033
ISBN 0-89885-446-6

© 1989 Human Sciences Press, Inc.
A Subsidiary of Plenum Publishing Corporation
233 Spring Street, New York, N.Y. 10013

Printed in the United States of America

CONTRIBUTORS

Thomas Baffuto, Project HIRE, Association of Retarded Citizens of New Jersey, North Brunswick, New Jersey

P. David Banks, Rehabilitation Research and Training Center, Virginia Commonwealth University, Richmond, Virginia

Philip E. Bourbeau, Supported Employment Resource Project, Oregon Health Sciences University—UAP, Portland, Oregon

Jeaninne Strom Boyer, Association for Habilitation and Employment of the Developmentally Disabled, Inc., Lemoyne, Pennsylvania

Rocco Cambria, Association for Habilitation and Employment of the Developmentally Disabled, Inc., Lemoyne, Pennsylvania

Elizabeth Evans Getzel, Community Services Assistance Center, Virginia Commonwealth University, Richmond, Virginia

Katherine J. Inge, Rehabilitation Research and Training Center, Virginia Commonwealth University, Richmond, Virginia

Patricia D. Juhrs, CSAAC Training Institute, Community Services for Autistic Adults and Children, Rockville, Maryland

John Kregel, Rehabilitation Research and Training Center, Virginia Commonwealth University, Richmond, Virginia

Eileen Latimer, Central Adult Training Center, Cuyahoga County Board of Mental Retardation/Developmental Disabilities, Cleveland, Ohio

Thomas Major, Adult Services Program, New Jersey Division of Developmental Disabilities, Trenton, New Jersey

Ernest J. Markovic, Jr., Central Adult Training Center, Cuyahoga County Board of Mental Retardation/Developmental Disabilities, Cleveland, Ohio

Kathleen Marshall, Rehabilitation Research and Training Center, Virginia Commonwealth University, Richmond, Virginia

Helen M.D. Metzler, Rehabilitation Research and Training Center, Virginia Commonwealth University, Richmond, Virginia

John J. Miller, Association for Habilitation and Employment of the Developmentally Disabled, Inc., Lemoyne, Pennsylvania

Larry Naeve, CITY Education and Employment Services, La Canada, California

Anne O'Bryan, EAS, 123 North Pitt Street, Suite A-210, Alexandria, Virginia

Wendy Parent, Rehabilitation Research and Training Center, Virginia Commonwealth University, Richmond, Virginia

Larry E. Rhodes, Specialized Training Program, University of Oregon, Eugene, Oregon

Martha Larus Rice, Rehabilitation Research and Training Center, Virginia Commonwealth University, Richmond, Virginia

Daniel Rossi, Association for Habilitation and Employment of the Developmentally Disabled, Inc., Lemoyne, Pennsylvania

Janet Segrott, Association for Habilitation and Employment of the Developmentally Disabled, Inc., Lemoyne, Pennsylvania

John Seyfarth, Division of Educational Studies, Virginia Commonwealth University, Richmond, Virginia

Michael S. Shafer, Rehabilitation Research and Training Center, Virginia Commonwealth University, Richmond, Virginia

Marcia Datlow Smith, CSAAC Training Institute, Community Services for Autistic Adults and Children, Rockville, Maryland

Brian Sobczak, Central Adult Training Center, Cuyahoga County Board of Mental Retardation/Developmental Disabilities, Cleveland, Ohio

Lee Valenta, Washington Supported Employment Initiative, Seattle, Washington

Linda C. Veldheer, Developmental Disabilities Program, Virginia Department of Mental Health, Mental Retardation, and Substance Abuse Services, Richmond, Virginia

Paul Wehman, Rehabilitation Research and Training Center, Virginia Commonwealth University, Richmond, Virginia

Wendy Wood, Community Futures, Inc., Richmond, Virginia

PREFACE

In this book we have brought together a number of papers and research studies that highlight the major features of supported employment and transition. Persons with severe disabilities are asking for higher quality services. They are also asking for those services to be better coordinated between different local and state agencies than has traditionally been the case. Furthermore, there are greater expectations that agencies will deliver services that they promise in a more effective fashion. Supported employment is a new method of vocational service delivery that clearly addresses these needs and concerns. Integration at the work site with employment into real jobs that provide decent pay are key elements of supported employment. Long-term permanent staff commitment to job retention is also a cornerstone of supported employment.

The purpose of this book is to present a series of meaningful readings that share the best knowledge available in supported employment. Most of these chapters are original work on specialized topics. Transition from school to work is also included because so many students with disabilities are now exiting special education programs and many of them will need specialized vocational services.

Transition and supported employment are two different entities. Transition is a process of moving from school to adult life. Supported employment is an outcome, that of paid work with long-term staff support in real work settings. Special education students with severe handicaps may possibly exit into supported employment arrangements if their local communities have such resources available.

It is our hope that readers of this volume will develop an increased understanding of the major supported employment models as well as the results of recent research in the field. A special focus is provided on portraying exemplary local programs that do not have research or university affiliation but which have been highly effective in implementing successful employment programs. Finally, there is a section on transition from school to work which provides a sense of the significant issues involved in preparation for supported employment and adult living.

This book is for service providers in education, mental health, mental retardation, developmental disabilities, social work, and psychology. We believe that faculty and students in these disciplines can benefit as well. We are indebted to the numerous contributors to this volume who willingly gave of their time and work to make this a successful project. Also, our many colleagues at the Rehabilitation Research and Training Center helped shape our thinking on what topics should go into this book. We are most appreciative of the intellectual stimulation they provide us. Finally, a very special thanks goes to Rachel Conrad, Brenda Robinson, and Jan Smith for the typing, organizing, and technical work involved in bringing the manuscript to fruition. Their cheerful and uncomplaining attitude is greatly appreciated.

P.W.
J.K.

CONTENTS

II. SUPPORTED EMPLOYMENT: RESEARCH ANALYSIS AND POLICY

III. SUPPORTED EMPLOYMENT: LOCAL AND STATE IMPLEMENTATION

IV. TRANSITION: RESEARCH INTO PRACTICE

PART I

SUPPORTED EMPLOYMENT
Individual Models

CHAPTER 1

AN INTRODUCTION TO
SUPPORTED EMPLOYMENT

Michael S. Shafer

There is little doubt that the development of supported employment and its authorization by the federal government represents a basic, fundamental shift in the social policy of this
country. Similar to the deinstitutionalization movement of the
1960s and the public special education movement of the 1970s,
the supported employment movement of the 1980s is producing widespread philosophical and structural changes in the
manner in which rehabilitative services are provided to persons
who are handicapped.

Philosophically, the importance of productive work as a
means of achieving social equality and financial independence
has now been recognized to apply to individuals with severe
handicaps (Bellamy *et al.*, 1984). Structurally, the process of
achieving productive labor has altered from determining one's
potential for employment to identifying and providing the
supports one needs to engage in productive labor.

To appreciate the significance of these changes, it is important to recognize and understand the variables that lead to

Michael S. Shafer ● Rehabilitation Research and Training Center, Virginia
Commonwealth University, Richmond, Virginia.

the initial development of what we now call supported employment. Supported employment would not have been possible without significant advances in behavioral technology that occurred during the 1960s and 1970s. These advances, it must be noted, were due in part to demands created by the major policy changes regarding institutionalization and public special education. As a result of these policy initiatives, enhanced efforts were mounted to develop, demonstrate, and diffuse a technology allowing for more effective placement and training of persons with handicaps in natural, community-based residential and educational settings.

Unfortunately, the technological advances that occurred within the context of residential and educational settings did not occur in equal proportion within the employment context. While mainstreaming, integrated schools, and community-based group homes developed, segregated sheltered workshops and day activity centers came into existence. As such, the supported employment initiative to which we are currently witness may be considered a natural, if not mandatory, extension of these earlier initiatives.

Within the context of this emerging supported employment initiative this chapter will examine the essential philosophical elements that support that initiative; provide a general overview of the current models of supported employment; and identify the common operational variables which these different models share in common. Subsequent chapters will expand upon this discussion, providing a more detailed analysis of the essential elements of quality supported employment services.

UNDERLYING PHILOSOPHY

Three philosophical goals or tenets may be identified that define the values inherent in supported employment. First, supported employment is based upon the philosophy of zero exclusion or zero reject (Bronicki & Turnbull, 1987; Brown *et al.*, 1977; Wehman, in press). This concept stipulates that *all* individuals, regardless of the severity of their handicap, are capable of engaging in meaningful and remunerative vocational activity and therefore should be provided appropriate vocational rehabilitative services.

A second philosophical tenet of supported employment is that individuals with severe handicaps should be provided only with rehabilitative services that support the opportunity to engage in meaningful and socially valued vocational activity (Bellamy et al., 1984; Wehman & Moon, 1987). Obviously, wages that are commensurate with those paid to nonhandicapped individuals provide one of the more valid indicators of the value that society places upon specific vocational activity. Supported employment services are based upon the goal of providing individuals with opportunities to engage in meaningful work with support in real work settings so that they may earn wages that are meaningful and likely to enhance the quality of their lives.

A third philosophical goal of supported employment is that employment opportunities should be made available only in integrated settings in which nonhandicapped individuals are also employed (Brown et al., 1984). This concept implicitly denies the legitimacy of sheltered workshops and other rehabilitation facilities in which clients with handicaps are served in settings segregated from other individuals who are not handicapped. Supported employment provides services to clients in regular integrated work sites such as restaurants, factories, shopping malls, and other community settings in which nonhandicapped individuals predominate, either as customers, coworkers, or supervisors.

MAJOR MODELS OF SUPPORTED EMPLOYMENT

Numerous models of supported employment have been described in the literature ranging from supported competitive employment (Rusch, 1986; Vogelsberg, 1986; Wehman, 1981; Wehman & Hill, 1985; Wehman & Kregel, 1985), supported jobs (Mank, Rhodes, & Bellamy, 1986), enclaves (Rhodes & Valenta, 1985a), mobile work crews (Bourbeau & Wilkinson, 1983) and benchwork models (O'Bryan, 1985). Each of these models provides employment services to clients in regular community-based settings where they receive ongoing support and training. However, these models may be distinguished from one another by several features.

SUPPORTED COMPETITIVE EMPLOYMENT

This model provides placement into regular employment situations on an individual basis such that only one client is employed at the same place of employment (Wehman & Kregel, 1985). Due to this placement orientation, the opportunity for integration and social interaction with nonhandicapped individuals is greatly enhanced (Shafer, 1986). Clients are typically placed into entry-level service occupations where they will earn the federally required minimum hourly wage or more. These wages are paid directly to the client from the employer, in contrast to the indirect payment mechanisms that are characteristic of other supported employment models. Employment specialists or job coaches (Wehman & Melia, 1985) accompany clients to their employment sites and serve as trainers and advocates.

Employment specialists serve a variety of functions for clients at their job sites. These functions include training clients to perform their work tasks, assisting clients to perform tasks that they have not learned to perform, advocating on behalf of the clients with employers and co-workers, and training clients to perform a variety of skills related to work, such as using public transportation, maintaining proper personal hygiene, and engaging in appropriate social interactions with co-workers and employers. Employment specialists will gradually reduce the intensity of their training procedures and the amount of time that they spend at the employment site as clients become proficient in the performance of all work-related behaviors. The process by which employment specialists reduce their involvement at job sites is commonly referred to as "fading" (Moon et al., 1986). Eventually, employment specialists will be present at employment sites on a relatively infrequent basis; but will nonetheless be available to reenter the job site and provide intensive training again as needed.

The population with whom supported competitive employment has been demonstrated has primarily consisted of individuals with moderate to severe levels of mental retardation (Bates, 1986; Moss, Dineen, & Ford, 1986; Vogelsberg, 1986; Wehman, 1986), although recent endeavors have also extended this service model to persons with traumatic brain injury (Kreutzer & Morton, in press) and cerebral palsy (Pietruski, Everson, Goodwyn, & Wehman, 1985). Wehman and his colleagues have provided numerous reports regarding the characteristics of clients that they have provided with supported competitive employment services since 1978 (Wehman et al., 1982; Wehman, Hill, Wood, & Parent, 1987). The characteristics of 186 clients placed into supported competitive employment were recently summarized in a report by Wehman and his colleagues (Rehabilitation Research and Training Center, 1986). That report indicated that 52 percent of the clients served were moderately mentally retarded, while the median IQ for the entire client population was 49. The average monthly gross salary for clients after placement into supported competitive employment was $436.

Supported Jobs

A second model of supported employment is referred to as supported jobs (Mank et al., 1986). This model is similar to supported competitive employment because clients are individually placed into regular, entry-level employment positions where they receive intensive training, support, and ongoing assistance from employment specialists. Similarly, the amount of training and assistance that is provided by employment specialists is gradually reduced to about 1 hour of support daily (Mank et al., 1986).

Clients in supported jobs are paid less than the federal minimum wage due to their low productivity, and are not paid directly by the employer. These wages are paid by the service agency that negotiates placements with host companies. These companies in turn pay the service agency for the work performed by the clients. Mank et al. (1986) reported that clients earned an average of $210 per month while working 4 to 6 hours daily.

ENCLAVE

The enclave model (also referred to as work stations in industry) is a third form of supported employment (Mank *et al.*, 1986; Rhodes & Valenta, 1985a). Enclaves can be distinguished from supported competitive employment and supported jobs by two critical variables. First, this model places a *group* of clients, rather than *individual* clients, into a single company. Generally, no more than five to eight persons will be placed within the same enclave. A second distinguishing feature of this model is that the training and support services of the employment specialist are continuously provided and no attempt is made to reduce the intensity or frequency of these services, as in the preceding models.

Enclaves are typically located in manufacturing firms, such as electronic assembly plants, woodworking or furniture-making shops, textile mills, and other industrial settings. Enclave clients are paid a subminimum wage that is based upon their productivity. These wages are paid by the service agency that contracts with the host company and provides the employment specialist.

Rhodes and Valenta (1985a) reported on the operations of an enclave operated in a biomedical electronic company in the Pacific Northwest. Six individuals labeled severely mentally retarded, with IQs ranging between 33 and 45, were employed in production-line positions. These individuals were provided with constant and continuous supervision from an employment specialist and a model worker who was provided by the host company. Average monthly gross wages for these workers were reported to be $295 after 8 months of employment.

The opportunity for social interaction and integration with nonhandicapped individuals is a critical issue in the operation of enclaves. Rhodes and Valenta (1985a) noted that their clients were located within the general assembly area of the company and that they took their lunch break at the same time and in the same location as the other employees in the company. Social contacts were also reported to have occurred through company-sponsored picnics and other social events and through spontaneous interaction between the managers and employees of the company and the enclave clients.

MOBILE WORK CREW

A fourth model of supported employment is known as a mobile work crew (Bourbeau & Wilkinson, 1983; Mank *et al.*, 1986). A mobile work crew consists of a small crew (e.g., four to seven) of clients who are transported to a variety of job sites and are under the constant supervision of an employment specialist or crew leader. These crews generally provide grounds or building maintenance services to local businesses or individuals.

Clients served in mobile work crews typically are paid subminimum wage by the service agency that contracts for jobs and provides transportation and employment specialists for the workers. Workers with severe handicaps, mild sensory impairments, and some behavioral problems have been reported successfully employed in this model. Workers with severe physical disabilities or significant behavioral challenges (such as aggression, self-injury, or property destruction) are reportedly poor candidates for this model because only one employment specialist is available to supervise the workers (Mank *et al.*, 1986). Monthly gross wages have been reported to range between $130 and $185 per client.

Inherent opportunities for integration and social integration with nonhandicapped individuals are lacking in this model because mobile crews do not operate from one existing host company where nonhandicapped co-workers are present. As a result, these crews must maximize the use of community services, such as restaurants and fast food establishments, to provide workers with opportunities to integrate with nonhandicapped individuals (Mank *et al.*, 1986).

BENCHWORK/ENTREPRENEURIAL MODEL

A fifth model of supported employment is the benchwork model, which typically operates as a small, specialized business that employs 15 or fewer clients (Mank *et al.*, 1986; O'Bryan, 1985). These clients will receive constant and continuous training and supervision by employment specialists who maintain a staff-to-client ratio of 1:5 (Mank *et al.*, 1986). Generally, benchwork models are located within a building or shop and will employ clients to perform highly specialized and specific tasks, such as preparing or assembling electronic cables and circuit boards (O'Bryan, 1985). The tasks required of benchwork clients are contract jobs that the service agency has secured with large electronics firms or other industrial concerns. Generally, benchwork programs will specialize in only one type of contract work (e.g., electronics) and will minimize the number of different tasks or jobs that clients perform.

This model is particularly well suited for individuals with severe and profound levels of mental retardation, due to the specialization of work that is performed by the workers. Benchwork programs are also appropriate for individuals with significant behavior challenges (aggression) due to the high concentration of staff. Clients employed in benchwork programs average wages of $110 monthly (Boles, Bellamy, Horner, & Mank, 1984). Opportunities for integration and social interaction with nonhandicapped individuals is limited due to the segregated nature of this model. Opportunities for integration can be enhanced by locating these programs near community business facilities, such as banks, restaurants, or business districts, and providing community integration training to clients before or after work and during their lunch break (Mank *et al.*, 1986).

COMMON COMPONENTS OF SUPPORTED EMPLOYMENT

The preceding discussion of the major supported employment models highlighted the differences between these models. These differences consist of placement orientation (individual client placement versus group placement), level of wages paid to clients (above federal minimum wage versus subminimum wage), the manner in which wages are paid (directly from the employer versus indirectly through the service agency), and the existing opportunity for integration and social interaction with nonhandicapped individuals (existing opportunities available versus opportunities needing to be provided). In spite of these various differences among the supported employment models, several operational factors have been identified in the literature that represent critical features of effective supported employment programs. These factors include: marketing and development, systematic instruction, long-term support, and outcome evaluation.

MARKETING AND DEVELOPMENT

The ability to develop meaningful and socially valued work opportunities for individuals with severe handicaps is contingent upon the ability to identify and respond to the needs of the private sector business community. This community must be perceived as a diverse group of consumers for whom supported employment services can provide unique and monetarily valued services (Shafer, Parent, & Everson, in press). Supported employment developers, regardless of their specific orientation, must first assess the needs within their localities and determine effective means by which these needs can be met through one of the various supported employment models.

One process by which these needs can be identified is a "community job market screening" which assists supported employment developers to identify the labor needs of a community, the specific type and frequency of job openings that are available, and the major employers or companies who appear to experience the most significant need (Moon *et al.*, 1986). While community job market screenings are most applicable in supported competitive employment, the underlying concepts are universally applicable to all supported employment programs. For example, supported competitive employment that is dependent upon a service-oriented economy will do poorly within a primarily industrial or rural community. Similarly, industrial-dependent enclaves will fare poorly in localities that do not have a strong industrial base.

In addition to identifying and responding to the needs of the business community, it is also important to assess the ability of the business community to meet the needs of the supported employment program. Rhodes and Valenta (1985b) identify three criteria that should be used to evaluate the appropriateness of potential host companies when developing enclaves. These criteria include: size and stability, image and culture, and the presence of committed individuals. Large and more stable companies will generally provide better opportunities for enclaves. Additionally, companies that portray themselves as leaders within the community or that have progressive personnel programs typically will be more flexible and open to the concept of enclaves and, as a result, more likely to have committed individuals within the company willing to support the enclave's development and operation.

JOB-SITE SUPPORT AND SYSTEMATIC INSTRUCTION

Providing clients with support and systematic instruction at the place of employment represents one of the cornerstones of supported employment. This training is ideally provided by an experienced rehabilitation professional, known as a job coach or employment specialist (Wehman & Melia, 1985). Following the placement of a client into a supported employment position, training will be provided throughout the working day. In individual placement models, such as supported competitive employment and supported jobs, this training will gradually be reduced through the process of fading. In contrast, group employment models make no attempt to reduce the training or employment site presence of employment specialists. In these models, employment specialists are consistently present at the employment site and provide continuous monitoring and training to clients as needed.

Employment specialists will provide training primarily for the social-vocational survival skills (Rusch, 1979) that have been identified through a detailed analysis of the position for which the client is employed (Moon *et al.*, 1986). Social-vocational survival skills are defined as the social and vocational behaviors and competencies that are required of individuals to survive (e.g., remain employed) in a particular employment setting (Rusch, 1979).

Long-Term Support

The continued provision of support and services to clients long after they have been placed into employment represent another common characteristic of all supported employment models. In supported competitive employment, this long-term support is provided by maintaining a program of ongoing client assessment and evaluation that may include written employer evaluations of the client's performance and direct observation of the client at the job site (Wehman & Kregel, 1985). Based upon the information obtained by this ongoing assessment, employment specialists can identify and respond to potential job-threatening situations by providing retraining or counseling to the client.

In group placement supported employment models, ongoing support is provided continuously and, as a result, ongoing assessment and communication with host companies and customers is more routine. In benchwork models, this ongoing support is maintained by remaining responsive to customer specifications and retraining clients as needed (O'Bryan, 1985). In mobile work crews and enclaves, ongoing support is maintained by remaining cognizant of the production and quality standards of the customer or host company, and providing services to clients that will ensure that these standards are met. Additionally, within supported employment models that accommodate individuals who exhibit aggressive, self-injurious, or other disruptive behavior, ongoing support is provided to assist clients in maintaining their productivity and developing and maintaining more socially appropriate forms of behavior (O'Bryan, 1985).

Outcome Oriented

A final component of supported employment services is the careful attention to *outcomes* rather than *processes* associated with these services (Bellamy *et al.*, 1986; Schalock & Hill, 1986). Outcomes realized by the clients of supported employment may include improvements in quality of life (Inge, Hill, Shafer, & Wehman, 1987), community integration (Wehman & Hill,

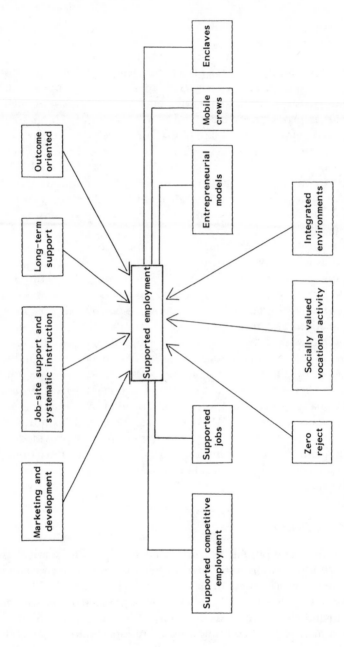

Figure 1. Philosophical tenets and common elements of supported employment.

1981; Bellamy *et al.*, 1980), and financial growth (Hill *et al.*, 1987; Schneider *et al.*, 1982). Similarly, outcomes identified as financial benefits and costs have also been evaluated as they affect service agencies that provide supported employment services (Hill *et al.*, 1987; Schalock & Hill, 1986). Collectively, the evaluation of monetary and nonmonetary outcomes of supported employment serve to legitimize these services by demonstrating the clinical effectiveness and financial efficiency of these services. (See Figure 1.)

SUMMARY

This chapter has attempted to provide a historical context within which supported employment and the process of transition may be viewed. Quite obviously, supported employment as a social policy is quite young and vulnerable to modification and compromise. This vulnerability is already evidenced as supported employment services are initiated that serve individuals who are not severely handicapped and that fail to improve the social equality or financial independence of those served.

In summary, supported employment demands excellence. The individuals to be served by supported employment deserve nothing less. The business community upon which the posterity of supported employment depends will accept nothing less.

ACKNOWLEDGMENTS. This chapter was supported in part by Grants G008635235 and G008301124 from the National Institute on Disability and Rehabilitation Research, U.S. Department of Education. The opinions expressed in this chapter are solely those of the author and no endorsement from the Department is to be assumed. I would like to acknowledge the comments and feedback provided by Fred Orelove, Paul Wehman, John Kregel, John Seyfarth, and Ralph Hambrick on an earlier version of this manuscript.

REFERENCES

Bates, P. E. (1986). Competitive employment in Southern Illinois: A transitional service delivery model for enhancing competitive employment outcomes for public school students. In F. R. Rusch (Ed.), *Competitive employment issues and strategies* (pp. 51–64). Baltimore: Paul H. Brookes.

Bellamy, G. T., Rhodes, L. E., & Albin, J. M. (1986). Supported employment. In W. E. Kiernan & J. A. Stark (Eds.), *Pathways to employment for adults with developmental disabilities* (pp. 129–138). Baltimore: Paul H. Brookes.

Bellamy, G. T., Rhodes, L. E., Wilcox, B., Albin, J. M.,. Mank, D. M., Boles, S. M., Horner, R. H., Collins, M., & Turner, J. (1984). Quality and equality in employment services for adults with severe disabilities. *Journal of the Association for Persons with Severe Handicaps, 9*(4) 270–277.

Bellamy, G. T., Sheehan, M. R., Horner, R. H., & Boles, S. M. (1980). Community programs for severely handicapped adults: An analysis. *Journal of the Association for Persons with Severe Handicaps, 9*(4), 270–277.

Boles, S. M., Bellamy, G. T., Horner, R. H., & Mank, D. M. (1984). Specialized training program: The structured employment model. In S. C. Paine, G. T. Bellamy, & B. Wilcox (Eds.), *Human services that work: From innovation to standard practice* (pp. 181–205). Baltimore: Paul H. Brookes.

Bourbeau, P. E., & Wilkinson, K. R. (1983). *Mobile maintenance model operations manual.* Eugene: University of Oregon.

Bronicki, G. J., & Turnbull, A. P. (1987). Family-professional interactions. In M. E. Snell (Ed.), *Systematic instruction of persons with severe handicaps* (3rd ed.) (pp. 9–36). Columbus, OH: Charles E. Merrill.

Brown, L., Shiraga, B., York, J., Kessler, K., Strohm, B., Rogan, P., Sweet, M., Zanella, K., VanDeventer, P., & Loomis, R. (1984). Integrated work opportunities for adults with severe handicaps: The extended training option. *Journal of the Association for Persons with Severe Handicaps, 9*(4), 262–269.

Brown, L., Wilcox, B., Sontag, E. Vincent, B., Dodd, N., & Gruenewald, L. (1977). Toward the realization of the least restrictive educational environments for severely handicapped students. *The AAESPH Review, 2*(4).

Hill, M. L., Banks, P. D., Handrich, R. R., Wehman, P. H., Hill, J. W., & Shafer, M. S. (1987). Benefit-cost analysis of supported competitive employment for persons with mental retardation. *Research in Developmental Disabilities, 8*, 71–89.

Inge, K. J., Hill, J. W., Shafer, M. S., & Wehman, P. H. (1987). Positive outcomes of competitive employment: Focus upon parental concerns. In P. H. Wehman, J. Kregel, M. S. Shafer, & M. L. Hill (Eds.), *Competitive employment for persons with mental retardation: From research to practice.* Vol. II (pp. 233–253). Richmond: Virginia Commonwealth University, Rehabilitation Research and Training Center.

Kreutzer, J., & Morton, M. V. (in press). Supported employment for persons with head injury. In P. Wehman & S. Moon (Eds.), *Vocational rehabilitation and supported employment.* Baltimore: Paul H. Brookes.

Mank, D. M., Rhodes, L. E., & Bellamy, G. T. (1986). Four supported employment alternatives. In W. E. Kiernan & J. A. Stark (Eds.), *Pathways to employment for adults with developmental disabilities* (pp. 139–153). Baltimore: Paul H. Brookes.

Moon, M. S., Goodall, P., Barcus, M., & Brooke, V. (1986). *The supported work model of competitive employment for citizens with severe handicaps: A guide for job trainers.* Richmond: Virginia Commonwealth University, Rehabilitation Research and Training Center.

Moss, J. W., Dineen, J. P., & Ford, L. H. (1986). University of Washington employment training program. In F. R. Rusch (Ed.), *Competitive employment issues and strategies* (pp. 77–85). Baltimore: Paul H. Brookes.

O'Bryan, A. (1985). The STP benchwork model. In P. McCarthy, J. Everson, S. Moon, & M. Barcus (Eds.), *School-to-work transition for youth with severe disabilities* (pp. 183–194). Richmond: Virginia Commonwealth University, Project Transition Into Employment.

Pietruski, W., Everson, J., Goodwyn, R., & Wehman, P. (1985). *Vocational training and curriculum for multihandicapped youth with cerebral palsy.* Richmond: Virginia Commonwealth University, Project Vocations in Technology.

Rehabilitation Research and Training Center. (1986). *From research to practice: The supported work model of competitive employment* (Newsletter), *3*(2). Richmond: Virginia Commonwealth University, Rehabilitation Research and Training Center.

Rhodes, L., & Valenta, L. (1985a). Industry-based supported employment: An enclave approach. *Journal of the Association for Persons with Severe Handicaps, 10,* 12–20.

Rhodes, L. E., & Valenta, L. (1985b). Enclaves in industry. In P. McCarthy, J. Everson, S. Moon, & M. Barcus (Eds.), *School-to-work transition for youth with severe disabilities* (pp. 127–151). Richmond: Virginia Commonwealth University, Project Transition Into Employment.

Rusch, F. R. (1979). Toward the validation of social/vocational survival skills. *Mental Retardation, 17,* 143–144.

Rusch, F. R. (Ed.). (1986). *Competitive employment issues and strategies.* Baltimore: Paul H. Brookes.

Schalock, R. L., & Hill, M. L. (1986). Evaluating employment services. In W. E. Kiernan & J. A. Stark (Eds.), *Pathways to employment for adults with developmental disabilities,* (pp. 285–302). Baltimore: Paul H. Brookes.

Schneider, K., Rusch, F. R., Henderson, R., & Geske, T. (1982). *Competitive employment for mentally retarded persons: Costs vs. benefits.* Champaign: University of Illinois, Office of Career Development for Special Populations.

Shafer, M. S. (1986). Providing follow-up services after placement: The utilization of coworkers. In F. R. Rusch (Ed.), *Competitive employment: Issues and strategies* (pp. 215–224). Baltimore: Paul H. Brookes.

Shafer, M. S., Parent, W., & Everson, J. M. (in press). Employers and supported employment: The need for responsive marketing by supported employment providers. In P. Wehman & M. S. Moon (Eds.), *Vocational rehabilitation and supported employment.* Baltimore: Paul H. Brookes.

Vogelsberg, R. T. (1986). Competitive employment in Vermont. In F. R. Rusch (Ed.), *Competitive employment issues and strategies* (pp. 35–49). Baltimore: Paul H. Brookes.

Wehman, P. (1981). *Competitive employment: New horizons for severely disabled individuals.* Baltimore: Paul H. Brookes.

Wehman, P. (1986). Supported competitive employment for persons with severe disabilities. *Journal of Applied Rehabilitation Counseling, 17*(4), 26–30.

Wehman, P. (in press). Supported employment: Toward zero exclusion of persons with severe disabilities. In P. Wehman & S. Moon (Eds.), *Vocational rehabilitation and supported employment.* Baltimore: Paul H. Brookes.

Wehman, P., & Hill, J. (1981). Competitive employment for moderately and severely handicapped individuals. *Exceptional Children, 47*(5), 338–345.

Wehman, P., & Hill, J. W. (Eds.). (1985). *Competitive employment for persons with mental retardation: From research to practice,* Vol. 1. Richmond, VA: Virginia Commonwealth University.

Wehman, P., Hill, M., Goodall, P., Cleveland, P., Brooke, V., & Pentecost, J. H. (1982). Job placement and follow-up of moderately and severely handicapped individuals after three years. *Journal of the Association for Persons with Severe Handicaps, 7,* 5–16.

Wehman, P., Hill, J. W., Wood, W., & Parent, W. (1987). A report on competitive employment histories of persons labeled severely mentally retarded. *Journal of the Association for Persons with Severe Handicaps, 12*(1), 11–17.

Wehman, P., & Kregel, J. (1985). The supported work model: Toward job placement and retention of severely handicapped workers. *Journal of the Association for Persons with Severe Handicaps, 10*(1), 3–11.

Wehman, P., & Melia, R. (1985). The job coach: Function in transitional and supported employment. *American Rehabilitation, 11*(2), 4–7.

Wehman, P., & Moon, M. S. (1987). Critical values in employment programs for persons with developmental disabilities: A position paper. *Journal of Applied Rehabilitation Counseling, 18*(1), 12–16.

CHAPTER 2

THE SUPPORTED WORK MODEL OF COMPETITIVE EMPLOYMENT
Illustrations of Competence in Workers with Severe and Profound Handicaps

Paul Wehman, Wendy Parent, Wendy Wood, John Kregel, and Katherine J. Inge

Supported employment involves paid work in integrated work settings. Unlike other rehabilitation models, permanent long-term follow-along staff support is provided to workers in order to enhance job retention. The target population upon which supported employment programs are designed to focus comprises those individuals who are severely handicapped and who have been traditionally excluded from competitive employment. The Rehabilitation Act Amendments of 1986 provide for a discretionary supported employment grant program, through which 27 states are currently funded to convert their adult service systems from center-based programs emphasizing preparatory activities to industry-based employment. In addi-

Paul Wehman, Wendy Parent, John Kregel, and Katherine J. Inge ● Rehabilitation Research and Training Center, Virginia Commonwealth University, Richmond, Virginia.   *Wendy Wood* ● Community Futures, Inc., Richmond, Virginia.

tion, the Amendments of 1986 also provide for Title VI-C which is a formula-based program to all states for the purpose of stimulating new supported employment programs.

The past several years have shown promising developments for persons who in the past have not had a fair opportunity to work. Many new supported employment programs are beginning and some are quite good. Almost universally, however, there continues to be a serious omission of persons who are truly severely handicapped in many of these programs. Although supported employment programs were initially created with the principle of not excluding any person regardless of severity of handicaps, there has been a tendency for service providers, especially those providers with very little experience, to take those persons who are not the most challenging. Hence, as one reviews the progress over the past 5 years, on the one hand, an excellent development has been the emergence of dozens of good local programs moving clients from nonproductive day activity programs to paid integrated employment. However, it is also clear that those persons with severe and profound mental retardation, significant autism, severe sensory impairments, and multiple physical handicaps still are not participating in this movement as much as they could be.

There are at least two major reasons for this lack of participation. The first is that many service providers generally do not believe that people with truly severe handicaps can perform meaningful paid work. Sufficient demonstrations of their potential for employment have not occurred in enough communities and, therefore, high levels of skepticism continue to exist. The second reason revolves around the fact that even those providers who believe employment is possible do not know how to implement such programs with challenging clients.

To this end, we have developed a paper which provides a close look at four young adults, three with severe mental retardation and one with autism, all of whom are competitively employed. We have selected these persons on the basis of the difficulty involved in their placement, training, and job retention; also, all four have been working for different lengths of time, which will portray a cross-section of problems and costs associated with implementation. All individuals were employed using a supported competitive employment model. That model as it was implemented is described as follows.

SUPPORTED COMPETITIVE EMPLOYMENT MODEL

In earlier publications the supported work model of competitive employment has been described in some detail (Moon, Goodall, Barcus, & Brooke, 1986; Wehman & Kregel, 1985). It is important to note that we distinguish this model from competitive employment which occurs *without* long-term follow-along support. Job placement into competitive employment without long-term support has traditionally been provided by vocational rehabilitation counselors to mildly handicapped clients.

We are also distinguishing this model from supported jobs (e.g., Mank, Rhodes, & Bellamy, 1986), a model which provides for individualized placement into integrated work settings, but often at less than minimum wage. Finally, we do not consider individual placements into work settings without pay *as employment*. Volunteer work experience can be very meaningful, especially for school-age students; but it is *not* competitive employment.

Supported competitive employment, also known as the supported work model of competitive employment, has five key features: (1) job development, or the location of appropriate jobs; (2) job placement, or the appropriate matching of the person to the job; (3) job-site training, which involves on-site skill training by the staff person assigned to the new worker; (4) assessment, which is an ongoing process to determine how the new worker is performing; and (5) job retention, which involves advocacy and procedures to ensure long-term job maintenance. All of these program elements are important to the successful implementation of this model; however, there are three factors that deserve special attention.

First, almost 10 years of experience has taught those familiar with this model (e.g., Rusch, 1986; Vogelsberg, 1985; Wehman, 1986) that an appropriate matching of a difficult-to-place person to the "right" job is crucial. As was noted in an earlier report (Wehman, Hill, Wood, & Parent, 1987), astute job development and placement can save hundreds of hours of onsite training after employment. Second, the more difficult the person to work with, the greater skill in training expertise the employment specialist must have. This will often hold true with populations of clients who have experienced very poor training in their school years. Third, long-term commitment to ensure employment and replacement as needed is a very different approach than has traditionally been available. Yet it is precisely this feature of the model that makes it most attractive to businesspersons, parents, and clients themselves. To refuse to make this commitment dilutes drastically the power of the model.

In the four case studies which follow, the major elements described above will be portrayed. Following these presentations is a general discussion section which looks at each of these chronological cases in a larger perspective.

ILLUSTRATIONS OF EMPLOYMENT COMPETENCE IN WORKERS WITH SEVERE AND PROFOUND HANDICAPS

CASE #1: LARRY (1978)

Employee Characteristics

Larry was labeled severely mentally retarded with measured intelligence or an IQ of 27 in a report obtained from his mother in 1978. At this time, he was 23 years of age and was participating 5 days per week in an adult activity center located in a church basement. Larry is nonverbal and communicates through animated sounds, gestures, and pointing. He exhibits basic self-care skills but no academic skills whatsoever. During initial observations and meetings with Larry in 1978, he displayed a number of socially immature behaviors, such as high-pitched giggling and making strange noises. He was quiet and seldom initiated interactions with others.

Larry had gone to a special school during his special education years. He had not obtained any systematic community living or employment skills, since the school followed a developmental curriculum. His parents were very happy that he was able, once school was over, to gain entry into the local activity center. Neither vocational rehabilitation or the sheltered workshop had considered him eligible for their services due to the perceived severity of his intellectual impairments.

Employment Record

Larry is employed at a medium-sized private university where he works in a food service position. His job includes busing tables, cleaning the floor, refilling condiments and salt-and-pepper shakers, and general food service utility work. He works 32 hours per week at a pay rate of $4.80 per hour. He also receives full fringe benefits. This is only a 9 month-a-year job, so Larry does not work during the summer. This is one of numerous food service jobs at the university. Larry has only missed 8 days of work in the 8½ years that he has been employed. His mother takes him to work every day and he is generally well liked by students and faculty who patronize the cafeteria. While there have been a number of different co-workers and supervisors during Larry's employment, he has managed to get along well with most of them.

Problems Presented and Nature of Intervention

The employment specialist used a system of least instrusive prompting (Snell, 1987) to teach Larry the skills required to perform the job. In addition, the employment specialist monitored the percent of Larry's on-task behavior to assess his independent work performance. Systematic instruction has consistently been used to help Larry overcome the different challenges of his job. After 4 months of training, the employment specialist's time at the job site was gradually reduced. Larry's work performance continues to be assessed by supervisor evaluations, parent feedback, job-site visits, and task analytic data. Each year, the employment specialist provides ad-

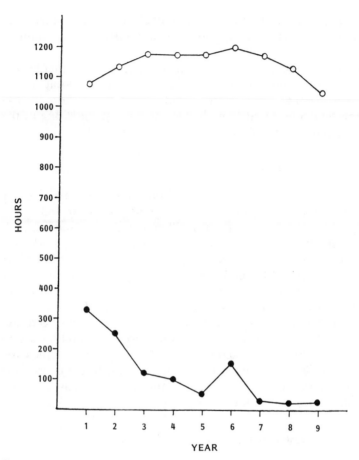

Figure 1. Annual staff intervention hours and hours worked: Worker #1—
Larry. Key: ●——● = intervention hours; ○——○ = hours worked.

ditional training on the job tasks after Larry returns from
his summer break. The supervisor reports that his main problem after summer vacation is a decrease in Larry's stamina.
The total intervention time after 97 months of employment is
1,122 hours. Figure 1 illustrates the decreasing amount of staff
intervention hours required for Larry annually since 1978.

Larry's employer has requested trainer intervention peri-
odically over the last 8 years. The supervisor has reported that,

at different times, Larry was not responding to supervision, exhibiting immature behaviors, taking lunch and break at incorrect times, not attending to tasks consistently, and making inappropriate noises. Each time, a trainer intervened and used behavioral training strategies and reinforcement to reduce the behaviors and to improve work performance.

After 6 years on the job, the employer received complaints from the customers because of Larry's inappropriate sounds. Baseline data determined that the behavior occurred as frequently as 50 times per hour. Strategies to reduce the behavior previously had included verbal reprimands and reinforcement. An intervention program was implemented using a differential reinforcement strategy (DRO) and suspension consequence with the goal of reducing the behavior to five occurrences in a 2-hour period. Larry was driven home if the behavior occurred more than five times during that time interval. As the behavior decreased, the criterion was increased by 30-minute increments. This program was effective in eliminating the problem. A detailed summary of the behavior management program can be obtained from the first author.

More recently, Larry's supervisor evaluations have indicated that his appearance was not acceptable. Specifically, Larry's pants were not fitting properly and his shirttail was hanging out. The employment specialist instructed Larry on how to tuck in his shirt and to tighten his belt. His mother purchased suspenders, which were a fashionable solution for correcting the employer's dissatisfaction with his appearance.

Outcome Measures

After 105 months of employment with the same employer, Larry has earned $34,929 in wages and paid $8,033 in taxes. His family reports that working has "helped Larry more than anything in the world." Larry's most recent employment evaluation rated his overall performance as satisfactory and the employer stated that "he does the amount of work of two people." Ongoing assessment data indicate that Larry is able to adapt to change and respond to supervision more easily now than when he was first hired. The employment specialists, fam-

ily members, and co-workers all report that Larry is currently
very outgoing socially and friendly to others.

CASE #2: TAYLOR (1985)

Employee Characteristics

Taylor is a 22-year-old male who has been assessed by
school psychologists as having severe mental retardation (IQ
score of 24) according to his scores on standardized intelligence
tests. Medical records report that he has Trisomy 21 with ven-
tricular septal defect, a serious cardiac defect. Taylor takes
heart medication daily and is not allowed to lift over 25 pounds
or work in excessive heat. He has no sensory or motor impairments and is reported to be overweight. His speech is unclear
and difficult to understand. Psychological evaluations indicate
significant deficits in language development.

Taylor has lived with his family for 9 years, and prior to
that, lived in a residential institution for persons with severe
and profound mental retardation. His educational program
since leaving the institution has been a self-contained classroom
in an integrated high school. Taylor's school curriculum provided community-based training in janitorial and food service
jobs at a local manufacturing center, supply center, and the
school cafeteria. His training included dusting, busing tables,
sweeping, operating a dish machine, trash disposal, mopping,
and pot-scrubbing. His teachers report that he can perform the
tasks correctly although he works at a slow rate.

Employment Record

With the help of a special university project and local
school personnel, Taylor was placed as a dishwasher at a restaurant 8 months before his graduation. He was hired to work
16 hours a week on Friday and Saturday nights. His schedule
increased to approximately 20 hours a week after 5 months.
Taylor was paid $3.50 an hour from the first day of employ-
ment. Additional benefits include medical insurance, a free

meal, and a bonus incentive plan. Taylor has received one bonus check of $100 for working 500 hours. His family transports him to and from work.

Taylor's job includes operating a dish machine, putting dishes away, sweeping, mopping, and emptying trash. A copy of a detailed task analysis of daily activities used for training necessary job skills is found in Table 1. After one year of employment, the supervisor changed Taylor's job tasks to wrapping potatoes for baking, making french fries, operating a dish machine, and emptying trash. Two other dishwashers work during the same hours, and Taylor assists them as needed. The supervisor and co-workers trained Taylor to perform the new job tasks without assistance from the employment specialist.

Problems Presented and Nature of Intervention

Taylor was trained by the employment specialist to perform the job tasks, to use the time clock, to order his meal at break time, and to socialize appropriately with co-workers. As the task analytic data indicated that Taylor was completing the job to the company's standards, the employment specialist gradually reduced her time on the job site. Initial training during the first month required 89 hours of trainer intervention time. The employment specialist began fading during the second month, and reduced her time to one hour per shift during the third month. The total intervention time after 21 months of employment is 174 hours. Figure 2 shows the decrease of staff time required over this period as well as the number of hours worked each quarter. Taylor continues to receive ongoing follow-along services by the employment specialist. His work performance is monitored by job-site visits, supervisor evaluations, and phone calls to the family.

Taylor's supervisor evaluations during the first 2 months on the job reported that he needed improvement in speed and consistency. The employment specialist used behavioral training strategies to improve his production rate before fading from the job site. Two additional supervisor evaluations reported that he was frequently tardy and absent. The employ-

Table 1. Individualized Task Analysis and Special Training Strategies

Trainee: Taylor Employment specialist: Sheila M.		Job site: Western Sizzlin Restaurant Job title: Dishmachine Operator
Approximate time	Task performed	Task analysis—diagrams— special training techniques
4:55– 5:00 P.M.	1. Put on uniform.	1a. Put on apron and tie. b. Put on hat.
	2. Punch time card.	2a. Locate card in rack. b. Locate "in" on card. c. Line "in" up with red nozzle on clock. d. Pull black lever to clock in.
5:00– 7:00 P.M.	3. Load dishes onto racks.	3a. Pick up plates, hold in left hand. b. Shake apart, put in rack. (Black behind silver in same row.) c. Repeat until all black plates are removed from table. d. Remove salad plates, bowls from bus pan. e. Put dishes in rack. f. Repeat d and e until rack is full.
	4. Place full rack over sink. Rinse with hose.	4a. Lift rack and carry to sink area. b. Use water hose to rinse dishes.
	5. Load dishes onto racks.	5. Repeat step 3.
	6. Place full rack over sink.	6. Repeat step 4. If busy, it is better to load rack, place over sink area, and spray both racks at one time.
	7. Put 2 racks into dish machine.	7. Take racks over sink and push or slide into dish machine.
	8. Close machine door.	8. Take handle with hand and pull door completely down.
	9. Turn on dish machine.	9a. Use index finger and push white button to the right. b. Hold for approximately 2–3 seconds. c. Release button.
	10. Load glasses, cups, and soup bowls.	10a. Remove glasses, cups, or soupbowls from buspan. b. Carry and load into racks located above sink area.

Table 1 (*Continued*)

Approximate time	Task performed	Task analysis—diagrams—special training techniques
		c. Repeat a and b until the racks become full. (This is to be done throughout the loading process. It may be an hour before the rack is full.)
	11. Put glasses, cups, etc. into dish machine.	11a. When one of the racks is filled with glasses, cups, or soup bowls, put in dish machine.
		b. Repeat step 7.
	12. Close machine door.	12. Repeat step 8.
	13. Turn machine on.	13. Repeat step 9.
6:00– 7:00 P.M.	14. Continue loading racks with dirty dishes.	14. Repeat steps 3–13.
	15. If caught up on work (loading), wash pans and plastic containers.	15a. Go to sink and remove dirty pans.
		b. Bring pans to work area near sink.
		c. Spray with water hose the inside of pans.
		d. Scour with green pad if needed. (This is to loosen food only.)
		e. Put pans on flat rack.
		f. Slide through dish machine. (Make sure 2 racks are in the machine before turning on.)
		g. Turn machine on. Repeat step 9.
	16. Wash silver.	16a. When silver rack bottom is covered with knives, forks, and spoons, carry rack to sink.
	16a. Locate push cart.	
		b. Rinse with hose.
		c. Push rack of silver in dish machine. Make sure 2 racks of dirty dishes are in machine.
		d. Turn machine on. Repeat steps 8 and 9.
8:00– 9:00 P.M.	17. Catch clean dishes.	17a. When machine cuts off, lift machine door.
		b. Pull out 2 racks of dishes.
		c. Stack dishes at end of counter (bowls, etc.).

(*continued*)

Table 1 (Continued)

Approximate time	Task performed	Task analysis—diagrams— special training techniques
	18. Catch clean silver.	18a. Pulls rack with silver out of machine. b. Pour silver on counter. c. Sorts knives and put into round containers. d. Sorts forks and put into round containers. e. Sorts spoons and put into round containers. f. Sorts soup spoons and puts into container.
	19. Wash silver second time.	19. When silver containers become at least half full, push silver back into machine and wash again. (2 racks needed in machine.)
	20. Load clean dishes onto push cart.	20a. When caught up, put black plates on top of cart. b. Put smaller dishes on second and bottom rows. c. Continue until all clean dishes are on cart.
	21. Carry clean dishes to front line and store.	21a. Push loaded cart to front (grill area). b. Unload black plates first. Place on top of counter behind grill. c. Repeat b for remaining dishes. Red plates, potato plates, salad bowls, small bowls along under table behind french fry area. Salad plates belong on counter beside desserts.
	22. Load glasses, bowls, etc.	22. If down time, repeat step 10.
9:00– 9:30 P.M.	23. BREAK a. Order meal, continue to work, then punch out.	23a. Order meal at cashier stand. b. Carry meal ticket to order desk. c. Go to time clock, locate time card. d. Locate "out" on card just under the punched "in" 5:00.

Table 1 (Continued)

Approximate time	Task performed	Task analysis—diagrams—special training techniques
		e. Line "out" up with red nozzle on clock.
		f. Pull black lever to clock out.
		g. Go to very back of restaurant and eat meal.
9:30 P.M.	24. Punch in.	24. Follow step 2. Punch directly under time he punched out.
9:30 P.M. – Closing	25. Load and/or catch dishes, pans, silver, plastic containers.	25. Follow steps 3–22.
	26. Sweep visible trash from floor.	26a. Use broom to collect debris.
		b. Use dustpan to collect debris.
		c. Discard in trash can.
	27. Put detergent and water in bucket.	27a. Put 2 cups of detergent in bucket.
		b. Use hose to fill bucket with water.
	28. Scrub floor with scrub brush and Tide solution.	28a. Start in prep area, dip brush in solution.
		b. Pull out and scrub floor.
		c. Repeat a and b when brush becomes dry.
		d. Continue until floor is completely scrubbed.
	29. Hose floor down.	29. Repeat step 27.
	30. Remove excess water from floor with squeegee.	30a. Use squeegee to push excess water into floor drain.
		b. Repeat until prep and dish room are finished.
11:00 P.M. on Thurs.; 12:00 noon– 12:30 P.M. on Fri. & Sat.	31. Before leaving, all pans and dishes must be washed and put away.	31. Repeat steps 3–22.
	Make sure dish room is clean before leaving	

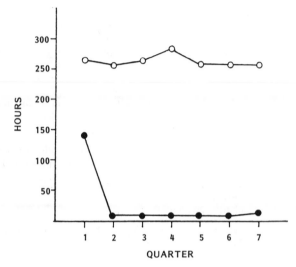

Figure 2. Quarterly staff intervention hours and hours worked: Worker #2—Taylor. Key: ●——● = intervention hours; ●——○ = hours worked.

ment specialist identified the problem as a change in scheduling which resulted in an increase in Taylor's hours. Taylor's employer verbally notified him of the change. To prevent future occurrences, arrangements were made so that the employer would send a note home to the family notifying them of schedule changes.

After Taylor had been employed for 11 months, the employment specialist made a follow-along visit to the job site and observed him lifting potato boxes weighing 50 pounds. Co-workers reported that they volunteered to provide assistance but that Taylor repeatedly initiated the task independently. After lifting the boxes, Taylor would grasp his chest and close his eyes. The co-workers and supervisors would respond by asking Taylor if he was all right and suggesting he take a break. The employment specialist intervened and modeled initiating asking for assistance as the opportunity to lift the boxes occurred. Reinforcement was provided by the co-workers and employment specialist for requesting assistance. After several weeks of training, the behavior was eliminated.

Outcome Measures

Taylor has earned over $6,513 in wages and has paid $1,498 in taxes after 21 months of employment. Since Taylor has been employed he has lost over 8 pounds, a significant improvement. His family, teachers, and employment specialist state that his immature social behaviors are reduced. Taylor's family reports that he is allowed to stay home alone now, which was not permitted before he began working. Assessment data indicate that Taylor's work rate has increased from a slow to an average pace. In addition, the performance evaluations show that Taylor adapts to task changes more easily since the beginning of his employment. The employer consistently rates Taylor's work performance positively on supervisor evaluations, and states that "he reduces the tension in the kitchen."

CASE #3: MARY (1985)

Employee Characteristics

Mary is a 24-year-old female who has been labeled severely mentally retarded with an IQ of 35 according to scores on standardized intelligence tests. She communicates with others in short phrases that are difficult to understand. In the past Mary has exhibited immature behaviors in social situations, such as giggling, acting silly, wringing her hands, and looking at the floor. School evaluations report that Mary has been observed to frequently rock her body, especially when she became upset. She is eager to please others and withdraws into silence when criticized or corrected.

Mary resides in a supervised apartment with one roommate and a residential counselor. She is independent in self-care and grooming skills. Mary shares responsibility for keeping the apartment clean, grocery shopping, and preparing meals, which she completes with supervision.

Mary attended a self-contained classroom in an integrated high school. Her Individualized Education Plan goals during her last years in school focused on the areas of leisure/recreation, clothing maintenance, housekeeping, and work adjust-

ment skills. She received community-based training as a cook's
assistant in the cafeteria of a local factory. Her vocational training included mopping, sweeping, operating a dish machine,
food preparation, trash disposal, busing tables, and restroom
cleaning. Her teachers reported that Mary is a good worker
and learns tasks quickly with visual and verbal prompting.
Mary stated that she enjoys working and wanted a job when
she finished school.

Employment Record

Mary was referred for supported competitive employment
services by her vocational rehabilitation counselor during her
last year in school. An employment specialist located a position
as a Softline Hanger in a department store. Initially, Mary
worked 16 hours a week and earned $3.35 an hour. After 6
months, Mary's hours increased to 20 per week and she received a 20-cent-per-hour raise. Additional benefits includ∶
paid holidays, one paid personal day per year, and a 10 percent employee discount. The residential counselors provide
transportation to and from the job.

Mary works in the stockroom with 10 other employees and
one other co-worker in the same position. Her job includes
sorting and opening packaged clothing, hanging the clothing
on correct hangers, and emptying the trash. The job requires
discriminating between 15 types of hangers that differ in size,
shape, and color. A copy of the task analysis used for training
the job duties is provided in Table 2.

Problems Presented and Nature of Intervention

The employment specialist used behavioral training strategies to teach the skills required to perform the job. The trainer
recorded the frequency and level of prompts on each sorting
task as Mary was learning to complete the job skills. After 6
weeks of initial training, the employment specialist began reducing her time on the job site as Mary demonstrated proficiency. Intervention time totaled 83 hours and 30 minutes
for the first 6 weeks, 13 hours and 15 minutes for the next 2

Table 2. Individualized Task Analysis and Special Training Strategies

Trainee: Mary	Job site: Bradlees Department Store
Trainer/advocate: Terri M.	Job title: Softline Hanger

Approximate times	Task performed	Task analysis—diagrams— special training techniques
2:00– 5:55 P.M.	Clock-in	A. 1. Locate time card. 2. Put arrow on first "in" position. (Shift to the right/left as necessary.) 3. Put card in clock. 4. Push card till machine clicks. 5. Remove card from clock. 6. Put card back in appropriate area.
	Set up workstation	B. 1. Go to work area. 2. Locate clothes to be hung. a. At workstation b. Ask Betty or Norma. 3. Hang up clothes.
	To hang shirts and sweaters	C. 1. If necessary, remove item from box. 2. Choose appropriate hanger (see chart): a. Color b. Size c. Pad, if needed 3. Gather several appropriate hangers and put in accessible place. 4. Remove plastic and dispose. 5. Remove existing hanger and dispose. 6. Hang on appropriate hanger. 7. Check top seams and neatness of garment on hanger. 8. Place completed item on rolling rock (put some colors together). 9. Repeat steps 1–8 until all shirts/sweaters are hung.
	To hang pants	D. 1. If needed, remove item from box. 2. Choose appropriate hanger (see chart): a. Color b. Size

(continued)

Table 2 (Continued)

Approximate times	Task performed	Task analysis—diagrams— special training techniques
		3. Gather several appropriate hangers and put in accessible place.
		4. Determine whether to hang "open" or "closed" (see note #2).
		5. Remove plastic and dispose.
		6. Remove existing hanger and dispose.
		7. Hang pants appropriately: a. Centered on hanger b. Open or closed
		8. Hang completed item on rolling rack (put some colors together).
		9. Repeat steps 1–8 until all pants are hung.
		E.
	To hang coats and jackets	1. If needed, remove item from box/cart.
		2. Choose appropriate hanger (see chart): a. Color b. Size c. Bowed or not d. Hollow or not
		3. Gather several appropriate hangers and put in accessible place.
		4. Remove plastic and dispose.
		5. Remove existing hanger and dispose.
		6. Hang coat correctly and neatly.
		7. Place completed item on rolling rack.
		8. Repeat steps 1–7 as necessary.
		F.
	To hang pant and skirt sets	1. Remove item from box, if necessary.
		2. Choose appropriate hanger (see chart): a. Pad, if necessary b. Size
		3. Gather several appropriate hangers and put in accessible place.
		4. Remove plastic and dispose.
		5. Remove pant/skirt.
		6. Hang correctly (see section D).
		7. Remove upper garment and dispose hanger.
		8. Hang correctly (see section C).

Table 2 (*Continued*)

Approximate times	Task performed	Task analysis—diagrams— special training techniques
		9. Place completed item on rolling rack.
		10. Repeat Steps 1–9 as necessary.
		G.
	To hang dresses and robes	1. Choose appropriate hanger (see chart):
		a. Color
		b. Pad, if needed
		c. Size
		2. Gather several hangers and place in accessible place.
		3. Remove plastic and dispose.
		4. Remove existing hanger and dispose.
		5. Hang garment correctly.
		a. Check neatness
		b. Check shoulder seams
		6. Place completed item on rolling rack.
		7. Repeat steps 1–6, as necessary.
		H.
	To hang skirts	1. Choose appropriate hanger: (see chart).
		a. Size
		2. Remove plastic and dispose.
		3. Remove existing hanger and dispose.
		4. Hang garment correctly.
		a. Centered on hanger
		b. Check neatness
		5. Place completed item on rolling rack.
		6. Repeat steps 1–5 as necessary.
		I.
5:55 P.M.	Cleanup	1. Straighten area.
		2. Pick up trash in area.
		3. Put trash can contents and empty boxes in compactor.
		J.
6:00 P.M.	Checkout	1. Locate time card.
		2. Put arrow on first "out" position (shift to right/left as necessary).
		3. Put card in clock.
		4. Push card until machine clicks.
		5. Remove card.
		6. Replace card back in appropriate place.

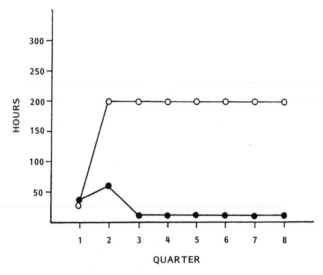

Figure 3. Quarterly staff intervention hours and hours worked: Worker #3—
Mary. Key: ●——● = intervention hours; ●——○ = hours worked.

weeks, and 1 to 4 hours monthly thereafter. Figure 3 illustrates
the intervention time provided to Mary and the hours she
worked quarterly. The employment specialist continues to assess Mary's work performance by visiting the job site, obtaining
supervisor evaluations, and communicating with the residential
counselors.

The employment specialist trained social skills at the job
site by modeling appropriate interactions and verbally coaching
Mary to interact with her supervisor and coworkers. Supervisor
evaluations report that communication with Mary is not a problem. Mary gets along well with her coworkers and socializes
more frequently with one individual in particular. After 9
months on the job, the employer called the employment specialist following a report by this coworker that Mary was "de-
pressed" and "withdrawn." It was revealed that Mary did not
like working 20 hours 5 days a week and wanted time off from
work. The employment specialist assisted Mary with submit-
ting a request for a day off and arranged with the employer to
schedule one day off a month for Mary.

Outcome Measures

After 21 months on the job, Mary's cumulative wages have been $5,234 and taxes paid have totaled $1,204. Her employment specialist reports that Mary's speech is clearer and that she communicates with others more frequently. In addition, ongoing assessment data indicate that Mary initiates working and keeping busy more than when she was first hired. Supervisor evaluations report that Mary is "doing a fine job" and consistently rate her performance favorably in comparison to the performance of other employees. The rehabilitation counselor closed Mary's case as successfully rehabilitated after 6 months of employment.

CASE #4: JOHN (1985)

Employee Characteristics

John is a 23-year-old man whose primary diagnosis is autism. His psychological test data suggest wide discrepancies in John's abilities. Intelligence test records place him in the moderate range of mental retardation with an IQ of 45. Achievement test results have reported reading skills at the eighth-grade level and math skills at the third-grade level.

John is described as "highly active" and deficient in social and language skills. His movements are very quick and abrupt. His verbalizations are inappropriately loud, one- to three-word staccato phrases. He avoids eye contact, giving very short repeated glances at people when forced to interact with them. He sometimes hums or uses language in a self-stimulatory manner. Other inappropriate behaviors observed of John include walking too fast, pushing people out of his way, perseverating on words and phrases, and flipping objects with his fingers. When upset or frustrated, John has been observed to walk at a fast pace, sometimes in circles, repeating a word or phrase over and over again.

John's school services included a period in a residential program for individuals with autism from age 12 to 18. His vocational training consisted of assembling food packets, shelving books in the library, and filing papers. At age 18, he returned home and was provided school services outside the classroom which consisted on one-to-one instruction provided by a home-bound instructor in the school central office building. His educational program focused on vocational training and applied academic skills. Vocational training involved sorting mail in the central office mail room and shelving books in the professional library. John was described as being difficult to train and extremely dependent on teachers' verbal and physical prompting.

Employment Record

In John's last year in school, he was selected for participation in a supported competitive employment program. Through this program, a supported work employment specialist located a 28-hour-per-week position for John at a local bank operations center as a Proof Operator. The job involved using a specialized computer terminal to enter bank transactions into the main computer system.

After 2½ months of training, it was decided that John would not be able to complete the job duties in the Proof Operator position without ongoing supervision because of the high number of variations and exceptions which occurred in the work that would require judgment decisions to be made by John. John's employer at the bank identified another position at the bank that he felt might be a more appropriate match to John's abilities. After the employment specialist completed a thorough analysis of the position, John was started in the second position.

This position was called a Lockbox Clerk, requiring John to sort and process installment loan payments, which included separating the payment coupons from the clerks, determining if the payment arrived by the due date, and then balancing the amounts paid, using an electronic calculator. He was also responsible for deciding when items needed to be rejected and routed to the loan department. Handwriting was required to mark items or batches of items to indicate the actions to be taken. A sample portion of the task analysis for both the proof operator and lockbox clerk positions can be seen in Table 3.

Table 3. Proof Operator and Lockbox Clerk Jobs in a Bank

Closing a proof machine:
1. *Look* on the journal tape, *find* the last sequence number (on the left side).
2. *Write* this number on your Batch Log Sheet
   (END SEQUENCE NUMBER _____).
3. *Press ND* key, *DN* key, 5 and the _____ key.
4. *Press ADD* key and * key.
5. *Add* up all of the batches from the Batch Log Sheet (hit debit key after each number).
6. *Press* _____ key.
7. The two subtotals should be the same. *Write* numbers on Log Sheet—TOTAL BATCHES.
8. *Press* * key and *release ADD* key.
9. *Press ND* key, *DN* key, 5 and * key.
10. *Press* 1, 9, *PROG* key and _____ key. *Write* two numbers on Log Sheet—ITEM COUNT).
11. *Tear* off top proof journal tape. *Circle* total and *put* your name and the date on it.
12. *Tear* off second proof journal tape. *Fold* it up. *Circle* the total and *put* your name and the date on it. *Put* a rubber band around the tape.
13. *Sign* Batch Log Sheet and *fill* in STOP TIME _____.
14. *Fill* in Time Sheet.
15. *Turn* Time Sheet, Batch Log Sheet, Proof Journal Tapes (both), first practice item and adding machine tapes into *supervisor*.
16. *Turn* the machine off and *cover* the machine. Be sure your work area is clean.

Lockbox clerk task:
1. Compare check with document.
2. Decide action to take with items.
   If check matches, put in "accept" stack.
   If check is slightly larger, put in "accept" stack.
   If check is much larger, put in "reject" stack.
   If check is less, put in "reject" stack.
3. Write correct department on other bank mail.
4. Send items to loan department.
5. Decide when check is a deposit or loan payment with no document.
6. Keep all correspondence.
7. Write AN on front of envelope (If not listed on Corr).
8. Check for date and final payment written on document.
9. Check for bank name and signature on check.
10. If either missing, pass to coworker to stamp.
11. Write correct description on front of envelope (Corr, Ck Reject, Ck/No Doc, Final Payment/Ck Reject).
12. Stop to add up stacks of checks and documents.
13. If adding machine tapes match, rubber-band stacks.
14. If adding machine tapes do NOT match, search for error.
15. Correct error.

Problems Presented and Nature of Intervention

The first position of Proof Operator was determined not to be an appropriate job match due to incomplete job analysis information. Because of the nature of the job, many details were identified after several weeks of doing the job. After deciding the job was not appropriate, the work supervisor together with the employment specialist identified the second position of Lockbox Clerk.

Standard job-site training procedures were used, including an ecological and task analytic approach with behavioral and systematic instructional procedures (Moon, Goodall, Barcus, & Brooke, 1986). The employment specialist provided intensive one-to-one training of all job and social skills, all work-related communication with co-workers and supervisors necessary for the completion of job duties (e.g., asking for more work, notifying a supervisor of equipment malfunction), transportation using the city bus system, ordering lunch in the employee cafeteria, and spending break time appropriately.

In this position, the particular problems presented during training were fading prompts, dealing with exceptions, communication with supervisor and co-workers, and printing legibly and small enough to fit into spaces on forms.

To fade prompts, the employment specialist implemented a question-prompt procedure, that is, "John, what do you do?," followed by a period of withholding any verbal interaction until John finally began to initiate the behaviors independently. Positive reinforcement was given in the form of verbal praise for independent initiating. Care was taken to deliver reinforcement intermittently in order to avoid transferring the dependence to the reinforcer which would inhibit John's initiation of the subsequent behavior required in the task sequence.

To help John respond correctly to the exceptions that occurred in processing the loan installments, the employment specialist developed a checklist of procedures with "if–then" routines for processing irregular items. John's reading skills were utilized to train him to read brief instructional cues placed on his desk blotter that told him what action to take for a given type of exception. Each time an exception would occur, the employment specialist prompted John to refer to the written instructional cues, match the type of exception, and carry out the action as instructed. After many repetitions of this procedure, John was able to handle the exceptions independently. The prompt-fading procedure was also used.

Interactions with co-workers and supervisors were trained by the employment specialist utilizing systematic procedures. As the employment specialist began to fade intervention time, she began prompting John to ask the room supervisor for more work or assistance. She also assisted the supervisor and coworkers in asking John for items, or giving him instructions by modeling the behaviors. Prompt-fading in this instance was achieved by the employment specialist gradually becoming less available for John and co-workers and supervisors. Handwriting problems were solved by modifying some forms to accommodate John's very large printing, and teaching him to use abbreviations.

The total number of intervention hours, as indicated in Figure 4, required for John's ultimate success as a bank employee was very high. Obviously, the majority of the hours

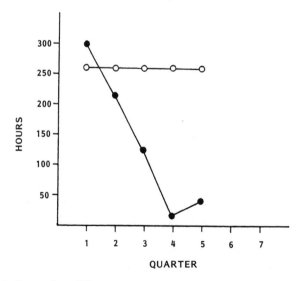

Figure 4. Quarterly staff intervention hours and hours worked: Worker #4—John. Key: ●——● = intervention hours; ●——○ = hours worked.

were required during the first 6 months of John's employment, with the first 3 months involving incompatible job match.

In the second position, John began to perform job duties and other work-related behaviors to preestablished criteria based upon the employer's standards by the sixth month of training. At this point, the employment specialist began to gradually reduce intervention time from the job site. The supervisory role of the employment specialist was transferred to the work-site supervisor during the gradual reduction of time from the job site. After 8 months the employment specialist was able to fade to a level of intervention of less than one hour per week. She continued frequent phone contact with the parents and employer, besides once-a-week visits to the job site.

Two reasons can be offered to explain the high number of intervention hours. First, job development and job analysis in the high technology business world is somewhat more complex than the typical employment settings which have been common for supported employment consumers. Supported employment professionals need more experience in employment settings other than food services and janitorial industries. Far fewer hours might have been possible in a simpler job placement. However, to place John in a position which did not utilize his reading and math skills would be to *underemploy* him *for the sake of programmatic efficiency.* Second, the wide discrepancies evident with John's abilities and inabilities made consumer assessment information difficult to translate for appropriate job match.

Outcome Measures

Beginning the first day of employment in the Lockbox Clerk position, John earned $4.80 per hour working 20 hours per week. His cumulative wages earned at the time of this report was over $8,700 with over $2,000 paid in taxes. His supervisor at the bank has said that John is one of his more accurate workers; "he never makes a mistake." In addition to the primary financial gains, marked improvements in John's adaptive behavior are evident. Figure 5 illustrates pre- and postemployment measures derived from the AAMD Adaptive Behavior Scale of John's skills in areas of independent func-

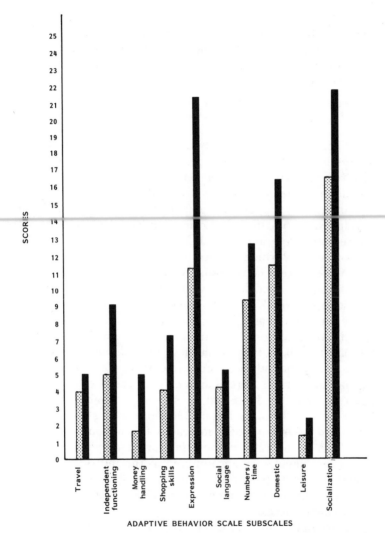

Figure 5. Pre- and postemployment measures on the Adaptive Behavior Scale: Worker #4—John. Key: ⊡ = preemployment score; ■ = 1 year posttest.

tioning, expression, domestic, and socialization (Inge, Parent, & Michaud, 1987). The evaluation was completed by a primary caregiver within one month prior to job placement and then again after John had been employed for 6 months.

By the time John graduated from school he was performing the job at above 95 percent accuracy and his production rate was approaching the standards of the employer. Employer evaluations indicated a high level of satisfaction with John's performance.

DISCUSSION

The preceding case study descriptions document four instances in which individuals previously labeled severely mentally retarded (IQ scores 24–35) or autistic can achieve successful employment outcomes if provided an adequate amount of training and support. The experiences of the four individuals illustrate both the employment potential of persons with severe handicaps and the challenges involved in providing supported employment services to these workers.

While there is considerable variability in employment outcomes and the specific interventions employed with the four individuals, several common elements emerge when the case studies are viewed as a whole. First, all the individuals involved would have traditionally been viewed as unemployable, and in the past it is likely they would have been denied the opportunity to independently work in an integrated community setting. Second, all workers were able to earn at least the federal minimum of $3.35 per hour and, over time, were able to work 20 hours per week (Mary began her job working 16 hours per week and after 6 months increased to 20 hours per week). Third, as is the case in most supported employment placements, problems were encountered as the individual adjusted to and learned to perform the job and the employment specialist used a variety of training and advocacy strategies to ensure employment success.

Also significant is the fact that the individuals involved were able to maintain employment for an extended period of time. All individuals have been employed a minimum of 21 months, and Larry has now been employed over 8 years. One individual (John) recently graduated from school. Although we have not been able to continuously track his employment status through the adult service agency now responsible for providing follow-up support (data reported represent only the first 15 months of employment), a recent follow-up survey indicated that he remains successfully employed.

One area in which substantial differences were found between the four workers concerned the amount of intervention time necessary to train them to perform their jobs and to maintain them in competitive employment. The employment specialists working with the individuals recorded every hour they spent providing intervention to a specific worker. Information regarding the amount of intervention time provided to each worker during 3-month time periods is contained in Table 4, as well as data concerning the number of hours worked during each quarter and program costs associated with each placement.

Direct comparisons of total intervention time provided to the workers may be somewhat misleading, given the fact that the consumers had been employed for varying lengths of time. One useful way of analyzing intervention time is to first look at the total amount of intervention time provided to the workers during their first year of employment, which can then be compared to the average amount of first-year intervention time (161 hours) provided to all consumers in the program (Kregel, Hill, & Banks, 1987). Two of the workers—Mary, who received 113 hours, and Taylor, who received 154 hours—required less intervention time than the average worker in the program. The other two individuals, however, required an extremely large number of intervention hours in the first year, with Larry receiving 328 hours and John receiving 685 hours.

The amount of intervention time provided to each of the workers has significant implications for supported employment

Table 4. Intervention Hours and Program Cost

Worker	Cumulative months employed	First year intervention hours	Cumulative intervention hours	First year program cost	Projected annual program costs after first year
Larry	105	328	1,122	7,544	2,356
Taylor	21	154	174	3,542	613
Mary	22	113	125	2,599	368
John	15	685	720	15,755	3,220

programs. First, the amount of intervention time determines the costs of providing supported employment services to a given individual. Table 4 illustrates the costs of providing services to each of the four workers. For each worker, total program costs were computed by multiplying the total number of intervention hours by $23, which was the hourly unit rate of service for the program during the years covered in the case study.

As is evident in Table 4, the costs associated with the four placements vary dramatically. First-year program costs for Taylor and Mary were $3,542 and $2,599 respectively. These figures are much lower than the $5,000–$6,000 annual costs for day activity programs in each of their respective communities. Coupled with savings associated with potentially reduced Supplemental Security Income payments and the taxes paid by the workers, these placements illustrate that individuals labeled severely mentally retarded can succeed in competitive employment settings and may only require a limited amount of staff intervention that can in fact prove to be very cost-effective.

Table 4 also contains a projection of annual program costs for each worker for all years worked after the first year of employment. This figure was obtained by first calculating the amount of intervention time provided after the first year of employment and multiplying that figure by $23 to obtain a program cost. Projections were then made by dividing this figure by the months employed after the first year and then multiplying by 12 to derive a projected annualized rate. This process resulted in annualized rates that ranged from $368 for Mary to $3,220 for John. These figures should be viewed cautiously, particularly in view of the fact that three of the individuals had been employed less than 24 months, and this process would assume that a relatively stable amount of intervention time would be required by the workers through the remainder of their employment.

Larry and John illustrate cases in which much larger amounts of intervention time, and therefore program costs, were required. Larry has received 1,122 hours of intervention time, but the fact that he has been employed for 105 months has resulted in an annual program cost, after the first year, of

$2,356, substantially less than the average costs for alternative day programs in his area. John's placement, however, resulted in exceedingly high first-year program costs of $15,755. John continues to work and, as indicated in Figure 4, requires less intervention time as his length of time employed increases. Even assuming that John's intervention time would stabilize or decrease and that he would remain employed for a period of several years, many professionals would argue that first-year program costs of $15,755 would be far beyond the fiscal resources of most current supported employment programs.

In one sense, it is quite possible to incorporate workers such as John into a cost-effective supported employment program. Although costs for John are quite high, they are offset somewhat by the costs associated with the other workers. It is because some individuals such as Taylor and Mary are able to succeed in competitive employment with a relatively small financial investment that allows a program to devote a large amount of resources to individual workers such as John. It is important to keep in mind, however, that these figures are generated from the placement of only four workers, all of whom continue to be successfully employed. These results should be viewed only as illustrative, and lack the validity of a large scale benefit cost analysis.

IMPLICATIONS FOR TRAINING

The combined results of the four case studies raise several issues that have direct implications for professionals developing and implementing supported competitive employment programs for individuals with severe mental retardation and autism. First, and perhaps most importantly, some individuals with measured IQ scores of less than 35 can be successfully placed into competitive employment situations. These individuals can earn significant wages, maintain employment for a period of several years, and require an intensity of service no greater than that provided to other supported employment workers.

Second, in most instances, the placement of the individuals

illustrated in the case studies requires employment specialists to use the most advanced state-of-the-art systematic instruction and behavior management strategies that have been developed to date. Even when these strategies are used, effective training and support will require diligence, ingenuity, and creativity on the part of the employment specialists to solve any of the numerous problems that may arise in the course of the individual's employment. In the final analysis, the ability of supported employment programs to effectively serve challenging individuals is entirely dependent on the skill and expertise of the employment specialists providing service.

Third, it must be noted that the four case studies all describe workers who have been successfully employed; that is, they are able to maintain employment for a lengthy period of time after a substantial amount of assistance during the early stages of employment. In our own experience, other workers previously labeled severely mentally retarded have not succeeded in their first competitive placement, even after 200 to 300 hours of intervention. This was also noted in the only slightly better than 50 percent rate of 21 workers with severe retardation presented in an earlier report (Wehman, Hill, Wood, & Parent, 1987). These placements seriously tax the staff and financial resources of a supported employment program. The implication for program managers is that if a program commits its resources to delivering several hundred hours of intervention time to a single individual, it must have a reasonable expectation that this commitment will result in the worker being able to maintain employment for an extended period of time.

SUMMARY

Supported employment programs were initially established to help persons with severe handicaps, but many local programs are serving mildly handicapped persons instead. We must carefully evaluate the intentions of our program efforts in these areas, realizing that if truly severely handicapped persons are not served, then much of the power and impact of supported employment will be lost. At the same time, it is clear to us that most adult service providers do *not* know how to train people with severe and profound mental retardation with the level of competence that is necessary for demonstrated independence in competitive employment. Once again, as in the public school arena, the issue is *not* whether the person with severe retardation has the ability to work; rather, do we as teachers have the ability to train the critical skills to maintain employment? The challenge for improved training is greater than ever. It is on this that success of supported employment programs for people with truly severe handicaps depends.

REFERENCES

Inge, K. J., Parent, W. S., & Michaud, C. (1987). *Quality of life benefits from competitive employment versus sheltered workshop employment.* VCU-RRTC, Richmond, unpublished manuscript.

Kregel, J., Hill, M., & Banks, P. D. (1987). An analysis of employment specialist intervention time in supported competitive employment: 1979–1987. In P. Wehman, J. Kregel, M. Shafer, & M. Hill (Eds.), *Competitive employment for persons with mental retardation: From research to practice,* (pp. 84–111). Richmond: Virginia Commonwealth University.

Mank, D. M., Rhodes, L. E, & Bellamy, G. T. (1986). Four supported employment alternatives. In W. E. Kiernan & J. Stark (Eds.), *Pathways to employment for adults with developmental disabilities,* (pp. 139–153. Baltimore: Paul H. Brookes.

Moon, M. S., Barcus, J., Brooke, V., & Goodall, P. (1985). *A job trainer's manual for supported employment.* Richmond: Virginia Commonwealth University.

Moon, M. S., Goodall, P., Barcus, M., & Brooke, V. (1986). *The supported work model of competitive employment for citizens with severe handicaps: A guide for job trainers.* Richmond: Virginia Commonwealth University.

Rusch, F. R. (1986). *Competitive employment issues and strategies.* Baltimore: Paul H. Brookes.

Snell, M. E. (1987). *Systematic instruction of the moderately and severely handicapped (3rd ed.).* Columbus, OH: Charles E. Merril Publishing Co.

Vogelsberg, R. T. (1985). Competitive employment programs for individuals with mental retardation in rural areas. In S. Moon, P. Goodall, & P. Wehman (Eds.), *Critical Issues Related to Supported Competitive Employment,* (pp. 57–81). Richmond: Virginia Commonwealth University.

Wehman, P. (1986). Competitive employment in Virginia. In F. R. Rusch (Ed.), *Competitive employment issues and strategies,* (pp. 23–34). Baltimore: Paul H. Brookes.

Wehman, P., Hill, J. W., Wood, W., & Parent, W. (1987). A report on competitive employment histories of persons labeled severely mentally retarded. *Journal of the Association for Persons with Severe Handicaps, 12(1)*, 11–17.

Wehman, P., & Kregel, J. (1985). A supported work approach to competitive employment of individuals with moderate and severe handicaps. *Journal of the Association for Persons with Severe Handicaps, 10(1)*, 3–11.

CHAPTER 3

INDUSTRY-BASED SUPPORTED EMPLOYMENT
An Enclave Approach

Larry E. Rhodes and Lee Valenta

Successful employment of people considered severely disabled has been demonstrated repeatedly through the mastery of a wide variety of jobs in multiple work environments (e.g., Gold, 1972; Horner & Bellamy, 1979; Moss, 1979; Rusch & Mithaug, 1980; Wehman, 1981; Wehman *et al.*, 1982). An important implication of these demonstrations is that the prevailing difficulties in attaining access to work can no longer be solely attributed to the presence of a disability. Difficulties must be seen in larger measure as the result of inadequate opportunities or job supports (Bellamy, Rhodes, Bourbeau, & Mank, 1982; DeFazio & Flexer, 1983; Office of Special Education and Rehabilitation Services, 1984).

The well-documented inability of segregated services to provide adequate opportunities and job supports indicates the need for fundamental changes in program development strategies. Individual choice, service needs particular to a commu-

Larry E. Rhodes ● Specialized Training Program, University of Oregon, Eugene, Oregon.   *Lee Valenta* ● Washington Supported Employment Initiative, Seattle, Washington.

nity, available public resources, and differences in local labor market conditions present compelling reasons to create diverse employment opportunities. These opportunities are encouraged within the framework for supported employment emerging in federal regulations (*Federal Register*, 1987). Supported employment is defined as "paid work in a variety of settings, particularly regular work sites, especially designed for handicapped individuals (1) for whom competitive employment at or above the minimum wage is unlikely; and (2) who, because of their disability, need intensive, ongoing support to perform in a work setting" (p. 16984). Many innovative services have been reported which illustrate the variety of approaches that may achieve supported employment.

It is clear that unsupported competitive employmemt involving payment of full wages and benefits in an integrated environment brings the greatest economic benefits to service recipients and the general public. However, time limitations that are frequently placed upon employment supports available to both employer and employee present major difficulties in employing individuals who have lower rates of skill acquisition or less adaptability to job changes. Individuals failing to achieve work rates comparable to other employees frequently face termination at the conclusion of job supports. Speed of performance and quality of work accounted for 47 percent of all terminations of one food service support program with demonstrated success in placing individuals considered moderately and severely handicapped (Food Service Vocational Training Program, 1981; Sowers, Thompson, & Connis, 1979). Greenspan and Shoultz (1981) note that factors such as social behaviors and transportation needs are frequently the reasons for termination. The growing accumulation of data from states implementing supported employment confirm these early reports. In Virginia, for example, over 37 percent of job separations were reported to be associated with factors that could be described as related to support, including quality of work, rate, attitude, aberrant and insubordinate behavior, and attendance (Rehabilitation Research and Training Center, 1988). Too often job placement processes without ongoing and long-term employment support effectively eliminate the participation of individuals anticipated to have such employment problems.

One alternative to segregated programs and to unsupported employment is an *enclave* (Greenleigh Associates, Inc., 1975; Pomerantz & Marholin, 1977). An enclave in its broadest application describes a number of individuals with disabilities who are working with ongoing special training or job supervision within a normal business or industry. Enclaves provide an option that maintains many benefits of integration and the support required to prevent job termination. Examples have been reported through the federally funded Projects with Industry Program, and the Work Stations in Industry (McGee, 1975). These programs frequently have directed their activities toward transitioning workers from time-limited training within an industrial setting to unsupported employment. The focus on transitional training rather than long-term supported employment has limited access for workers considered severely handicapped who are unable to meet standards within the required time limitations.

This paper describes one enclave approach that employs individuals who require substantial, long-term job support, and who are generally excluded from participating in individual supported jobs, competitive placement programs, and other less restrictive programs because of the severity of their disabilities. The demonstration of supported employment that is presented documents the methodology used to employ people within an electronics firm. These results offer consumer groups, industrial managers, and those responsible for vocational policy an example of supported employment within a major industry.

METHOD

In May, 1983, the authors established a working agreement with Physio Control Corporation of Redmond, Washington to create a production line within the company for the purpose of employing up to eight workers labeled severely handicapped. Physio Control manufactures biomedical equipment such as heart defibrillators. It employs approximately 900 people in the Redmond complex, including 250 electronics assemblers. The company was initially approached because its size would facilitate stability and integration and an availability of small parts assembly work. In addition, its positive relationship with its employees, who are referred to as "team members" by Physio, and its commitment to community involvement were demonstrated during all discussions of the feasibility of the program. Physio Control has been recognized nationally for the supportive company culture that makes it a desirable place to work (Levering, Moskowitz, & Katz, 1984, 1985).

Prior to negotiations with Physio Control, two significant events were required: (1) the formation of Trillium Employment Services, a nonprofit organization, and (2) planning with local decision-makers. Trillium, referred to as the "support organization," was to act as the "service provider," have responsibility for overall program quality, individual program planning, and advocacy for program employees within the company. Local planning activities with advocates, funders, and case managers ensured community support for program design and funds for operation. Significant characteristics of the demonstration program at Physio Control include its employees, environmental attributes, and operating procedures.

EMPLOYEES

The first two employees began in early August, 1983, followed by three in September, with additional persons hired gradually over the following months. Each was referred by the state developmental disabilities agency. None had recorded IQ scores that exceeded 47, with the lowest recorded score being 26. Persons were previously employed in work activity centers, unemployed, or transitioning from secondary education. Productivity of those in work activity centers averaged approximately 23 percent, with average monthly wages of $44. Records and discussions with case managers and staff from previous placements indicated that none had major disruptive behaviors, but that all required ongoing support and extensive on-the-job training. None were considered candidates for the several competitive and individual supported employment programs that exist in the Seattle area. Approximately one-third of the employees live in community group homes, one-half reside with parents, and the rest live in supervised apartments. Since their employment at Physio Control, all travel to work by city bus, following travel training by the support organization. All employees are supervised by Physio employees, although legal employment responsibility rests with the support organization until an employee reaches minimum company expectations. Individuals have been hired directly by Physio Control when work rate consistently averages 65 percent of the productivity of other Physio Control employees.

ENVIRONMENTAL ATTRIBUTES

Space

The program was visible and integrated within the normal production flow, rather than operating as an autonomous sheltered unit within the physical plant. The limited initial skills of employees and the need for intensive training and supervision required that a production line be created, rather than dispersing workers to many job stations. This has changed over time as many employees' job skills have approximated those required on other production lines within the company.

Equipment

Tool kits that are normally purchased by Physio Control employees were provided by the support organization. Physio Control provided all other equipment and tooling required for production processes, as well as extra engineering support for creating special fixtures.

Type of Work

Program employees are part of the production line that does preparation for the final assembly of heart defibrillators. The subassemblies completed by the employees include assembling defibrillator components such as chest paddles for electrodes, wire harnesses, and battery support harnesses. To the greatest extent possible, tasks selected are the same type and variety of work as that performed by other workers within the production unit. Initially a few jobs were identified; as worker skills have developed, the number of jobs performed by each person has expanded. Job enlargement constitutes a significant objective: many jobs have to be learned prior to working in independent job stations elsewhere in the Physio plant.

OPERATING PROCEDURES

Manufacturing and Personnel Procedures

The design of an enclave depends greatly upon the expectations of the company. However, several features are necessary from the perspective of the service system and the consumer. Each of these perspectives were considered in developing the most advantageous design for operating procedures within the Physio Control program. As with space, the program has been integrated as fully as possible within the typical manufacturing and personnel processes of the company. Physio Control work orders are received by the production line with drawings for exact specifications and production deadlines. Precise rate and cost data by worker, job, and task are maintained. Program employees work the same 10-hour day and 4-day work week as other employees. Earnings are paid at an hourly rate based upon assessment of productivity following U.S. Department of Labor (1978) standards. As with others employed at Physio Control, program employees are paid biweekly, receive holiday pay, and earn sick leave and vacation.

Training and Supervision

The lead supervisor was employed first with the support organization, and was selected in cooperation with the company on the basis of demonstrated skills in effective training techniques. The supervisor also had prior supervisory experience within an electronics assembly shop employing individuals considered severely disabled. The lead supervisor trained at Physio Control for 6 weeks, becoming acquainted with company systems, personnel, and jobs prior to hiring the first employees. Training and supervision procedures incorporate a behavioral approach characterized by a precise definition of the behavioral requirements of jobs employees are to perform, direct training of the skills required for the task and job completion, and arrangement of social and physical aspects of the work environment to facilitate maintaining and improving work rates. Readers are referred to Bellamy, Horner, and Inman (1979) for a detailed description of the procedures used for training and supervision.

RESULTS

In the first 52 months since the program's inception, 15 individuals have been employed. Four of these employees have either quit or had employment terminated because of a range of behavioral issues. Terminations were made by the company following unsuccessful interventions directed at improving behavior. Four employees have been hired directly by the company, and work elsewhere in the plant. These employees continue to require occasional support on an ongoing basis, but are no longer directly supervised by the enclave supervisor. Others who technically are assigned to the enclave area work partial days elsewhere in the plant.

Absenteeism has not been demonstrated to be greater than with other workers. Illness-related absenteeism is under 1 percent compared with 4 percent typical of the overall Physio work force. There have been no increases in workers' compensation costs to the company as a result of the program.

At the conclusion of the first year of operation, all employees were producing at or above 50 percent of the standard established by the production performance of other Physio Control employees. Figure 1 illustrates the rise in average productivity across months. Productivity figures in Figure 1 only represent persons receiving the specialized supervision of the enclave. Rate data are not collected after individuals are employed by the company.

Total wages earned by all program employees during the first 52 months were $195,596. Employees averaged $430 per

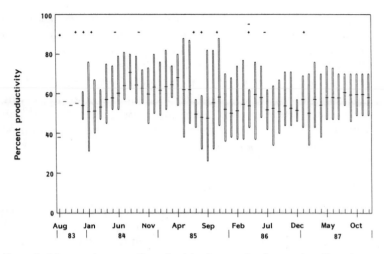

Figure 1. Mean and range of productivity by month of operation. Key: + = new worker(s) added; − = worker hired by company (prod. data not collected after hire).

month of employment at Physio Control. This average represents a tenfold increase in wages from previous employment, and more than 17 times the national average reported by the U.S. Department of Labor (1979) for individuals with mental retardation in work activities centers. Table 1 provides summary data associated with each employee.

Fees for services and grants from the county and state developmental disabilities and vocational rehabilitation agencies provided public support to the program. These public costs totalled $15,945 during this first year of operation, and included staffing, consultation, training, and administration. Public costs to establish the program were $4,682, and included staff salary, administrative support, staff training, and supplies. Figure 2 depicts monthly public costs between the start of the program and the conclusion of the first 52 months. Average monthly costs per person were $112 over this period. These figures demonstrate the variability of costs over time, influenced by such factors as start-up and company hiring staff. A dramatic increase in public costs is also present after approxi-

Table 1. Summary of Individual Employee Data, after 52 Months of Program Operation

Employee number	Age	Previous employment status	Recorded IQ[a]	Months employed Physio	Average monthly wage prior to Physio	Average monthly wage at Physio	Total wages
1	35	Work activity center	45	52	$26	$342	$18,327
2	43	Work activity center	44	0.5	$19	N/A	$130
3	42	Work activity center	43	46	$35	$620	$32,662
4	30	Work activity center	40	4.5	$44	$263	$1,314
5	31	Work activity center	39	50	$110	$367	$18,967
6	35	Work activity center	26	49	$26	$389	$19,694
7	34	Transition from school	33	40	$0	$598	$23,934
8	26	Transition from school	33	14	$0	$284	$3,970
9	26	Transition from school	47	24	$0	$518	$15,817
10	24	Transition from school	37	29	$0	$346	$10,510
11	24	Transition from school	27	29	$0	$374	$11,373
12	24	Transition from school	38	28	$0	$329	$9,704
13	23	Transition from school	43	20	$0	$518	$14,099
14	24	Transition from school	38	20	$0	$414	$8,821
15	23	Transition from school	37	11	$0	$511	$6,274
Mean	29		38	27.9	$44[b]	$430	$195,596 (Total)

[a] Most recent Weschler or Stanford-Binet on record.
[b] Mean computed only for persons with previous work history.

mately 5 years, as Trillium Employment Services increases
direct support in response to individual training and supervision needs.

The ratio between program costs and employee wage benefits constitutes one measure of a program's effectiveness in
converting public costs to service recipient benefits. This Income Benefit:Cost ratio was computed by dividing the total
earnings of program employees by the total public costs. The
ratio was 1.26 or $1.26 earned for every dollar invested dur-
ing the first year of operation. This ratio has risen to 3.93, or
nearly $4 in wages for every public $1 invested. In addition,
employees earned, on an average, $167 per month in benefits,
and paid a cumulative total of nearly $30,000 in federal taxes.

Effective measures of the degree of integration experienced by employees have not been developed (i.e., instances of
social contact between program employees and other Physio
Control employees). Managers and supervisors within the assembly area report frequent daily contact between employees.
These occur within the work environment as well as during

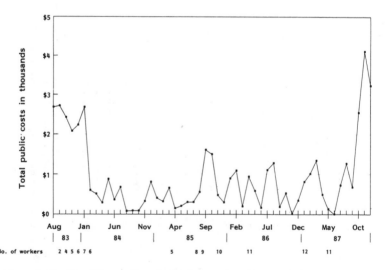

Figure 2. Total public cost by month of operation. Key: − = enc. supervisor
hired by company; + = temp. additional supervisor hired.

breaks and lunch. Contacts are said to be overwhelmingly positive. Social contacts have also occurred through company-sponsored events such as picnics, dinners, and dances, and through privately initiated social events between employees. After 52 months, a production line is still designated for the program, despite the movement of some persons elsewhere in the plant and the addition of team members without disabilities to the enclave line.

DISCUSSION

All too frequently vocational service options exclude individuals who have severe disabilities. The demonstration at Physio Control offers an alternative that combines the desirable outcomes of wages and stable employment with an integrated environment. Initial job success and long-term job stability are likely on as a function of the intensive support provided by a highly skilled supervisor, involved company managers, and external support by a service organization. This approach represents one example of supported employment; many alternatives will be required if the vast majority of individuals with severe disabilities is to become employed.

The experience at Physio Control has contributed to a growing national discussion on employment policies and program developments concerning individuals with severe disabilities. These are discussed from the perspective of employers and of human service professionals.

EMPLOYER CONSIDERATIONS

It may be that the notion of an enclave is of increasing interest to managers, resulting perhaps from a growing sense of corporate social responsibility or federal affirmative action policies (Freedman & Keller, 1981). Yet, employers' perceptions of the risk associated with hiring individuals with handicaps include concerns that insurance rates will increase, profitability will decrease as a result of low productivity of workers with handicaps, and that high absenteeism may occur

(Barnhill-Hayes, Inc., 1979; Steinhauser, 1978; National Governors Association, 1980). Preliminary data from Physio Control do not substantiate these fears, and in fact suggest strong benefits to participating industries.

Workers' Compensation

Companies considering employing persons with severe disabilities may be concerned with increases in industrial accident insurance, fearing that workers labeled severely handicapped may have more accidents. Few data address this issue. A study of 111,000 employees of the DuPont Corporation (Nathanson, 1977) concluded that there were neither increases in compensation costs nor lost-time accidents as a result of employing 1,452 employees with disabilities but not exhibiting severe retardation. In another study reported by Steinhauser (1978), the U.S. Chamber of Commerce indicated that workers with handicaps in general have scored higher than nonhandicapped workers in attendance and safety. While the lack of access to work environments by individuals with severe disabilities precludes direct comparison, the experience to date at Physio Control suggests no effect upon accident or insurance rates.

Work Rate

Many job placement programs have often relied on the good-will of employers for job opportunity and retention (Vandergoot & Worrell, 1979). This approach offers little to attract the investment of a company in an enclave, since employee productivity is a critical factor in determining whether a company will remain in business. It is assumed that an employer would not wish to hire or maintain a group of employees unless these employees make a contribution to the profitability of the company. At Physio Control, lower work rates have not been a financial concern of the company because wages are paid on the basis of work performed. Increasing employee productivity remains an objective, although some employees may not achieve the level of productivity over time that is required of nonhandicapped personnel to maintain employment. Payment for work performed reduces the impact of lower work rates on the cost of labor. It is currently the only method besides time-limited governmental wage subsidies or industrial charity that permits workers with severe disabilities to maintain employment when unable to produce at a competitive minimum level.

Attendance

As with accident rates, absenteeism in industry has not been demonstrated to be any greater in employees having handicaps (Freedman & Keller, 1981). Data from the Physio Control program support this position.

Benefits to Industry

Managers at Physio Control have stated that the contribution the company can make to individuals with disabilities, as well as to state and national policy, are major incentives for their support of the program. Additionally, managers have stated their belief that hiring team members with disabilities has had a positive impact upon the corporate culture of Physio Control. To other companies, replication of the program might be viewed as important in meeting affirmative action obligations (Rehabilitation Act, 1973, 29 U.S.C. 793); taking advantage of tax credits such as the Federal Targeted Jobs Tax Credit Program; and supporting public relations efforts. The sense of contributing to the community, while at the same time improving the company culture through the presence and participation of persons with disabilities, is clearly of interest to many companies. The unity of public and private sectors mutually benefits increasing productivity, giving individuals with severe disabilities access to work, and, in the case of Physio Control, decreasing public costs.

HUMAN SERVICE CONSIDERATIONS

Positive signs of the benefits and costs of the Physio Control enclave are represented in the data revealing employee benefits and earnings now in excess of $615 per month per person. Public costs per person have been less than one-third of other state and regional alternatives. Observations by the lead supervisor, including anecdotal information from other company employees, are also encouraging; desired social contacts are accompanying the physical integration of the employees into the company.

For program developers and industrial managers contemplating this alternative, it will be necessary to insure that employees not become segregated from the rest of the working community (much like the "handicapped wing" of a public school). A balance must be attained in providing the structure to support training interventions, to address low productivity, and to insure adaptability to changing work demands, without sacrificing the advantages of a normal industrial environment.

CONCLUSION

The significance of these implications goes beyond one willing company and its employees, to policymakers and program funders who are seeking alternatives to current employment options. Growing numbers of people moving back to their communities from state institutions and recent and future graduates of high school special education programs are already exerting pressure at the local, state, and federal levels for access to community jobs. The discussion regarding whether people with severe disabilities can perform consequential work is shifting to the support systems required for these individuals to contribute and receive the benefits of work in typical settings.

ACKNOWLEDGMENTS. An earlier version of this chapter appeared in 1985 in the *Journal of the Association for Persons with Severe Handicaps, 10* (1), 12–20, and is updated and reprinted with permission. Preparation of this article was supported in part by Contract No. GOO–8435097 from the Office of Special Education Programs and Contract No. GOO–872012088 from the National Institute on Disability and Rehabilitation Research.

REFERENCES

Barnhill-Hayes, Inc. (1979, May). Handicapped seem least likely to succeed. *Risk Management*, p. 56.

Bellamy, G. T., Horner, R. H ., & Inman, D. (1979). *Vocational habilitation of severely retarded adults: A direct service technology*. Baltimore: University Park Press.

Bellamy, G. T., Rhodes, L. E., Bourbeau, P. E., & Mank, D. M. (1982, March). *Mental retardation services in sheltered workshops and day activity programs: Consumer outcomes and policy alternatives*. Paper presented at the National Working Conference on Vocational Services and Employment Opportunities, sponsored by the President's Committee on Mental Retardation, the President's Committee on Employment of the Handicapped, and the Association for Retarded Citizens, Madison, WI.

DeFazio, N., & Flexer, R. W. (1983). Organizational barriers to productivity, meaningful wages, and normalized work opportunity for mentally retarded persons. *Mental Retardation, 21*(4), 157-163.

Federal Register, May 12, 1987, *53*(92), 16978–16988.

Food Service Vocational Training Program (1981). [Trainee Information Summary, University of Washington]. Unpublished raw data.

Freedman, S., & Keller, R. (1981). The handicapped in the work force. *Academy of Management Review, 6*(3), 449–458.

Gold, M. (1972). Stimulus factors in skill training of the retarded on a complex assembly task: Acquisition, transfer and retention. *American Journal of Mental Deficiency, 76*, 517–526.

Greenleigh Associates, Inc. (1975). *The role of the sheltered workshop in the rehabilitation of the severely handicapped*. Report to the Department of Health, Education and Welfare, Rehabilitation Services Administration, New York.

Greenspan, S., & Shoultz, B. (1981). Why mentally retarded adults lose their jobs: Social competence as a factor in work adjustment. *Applied Research in Mental Retardation, 2*, 23–38.

Horner, R. H., & Bellamy, G. T. (1979). Structured employment: Productivity and productive capacity. In G. T. Bellamy, G. O'Connor, & O. Karan (Eds.), *Vocational rehabilitation of severely handicapped adults: Contemporary service strategies*. Baltimore: University Park Press.

Levering, R., Moskowitz, M., & Katz, M. (1984). *The 100 best companies to work for in America*. Reading: Addison-Wesley Publishing Company.

Levering, R., Moskowitz, M., & Katz, M. (1985). *The 100 best companies to work for in America*, Vol. 2. New York: New American Library.

McGee, J. (1975). *Work stations in industry*. Omaha: University of Nebraska.

Moss, J. W. (1979). *Postsecondary vocational education for mentally retarded adults*. Final report to Division of Developmental Disabilities, Rehabilitation Services Administration, Department of Health, Education, and Welfare, Grant No. 56 P 50281/0.

Nathanson, R. B. (1977). The disabled employee: Separating myth from fact. *Harvard Business Review, 55*, 6–8.

National Governors Association (1980). *Employment and training of handicapped youth.* Washington, DC: Author (draft).

Office of Special Education and Rehabilitation Services (1984). *Supported employment for adults with severe disabilities: An OSERS program initiative.* Unpublished manuscript.

Pomerantz, D. J., & Marholin, D. (1977). Vocational habilitation: A time for change. In E. Sontag (Ed.), *Educational programming for the severely and profoundly handicapped.* Reston, VA: The Council for Exceptional Children.

Rehabilitation Research and Training Center (1988). *Quarterly report: Successful outcomes in supported employment.* Virginia Commonwealth University, Richmond, VA.

Rusch, F., & Mithaug, D. (1980). *Vocational training for mentally retarded adults: A behavior analytic approach.* Champaign, IL: Research Press.

Sowers, J., Thompson, L., & Connis, R. (1979). The food service vocational training program. In G. T. Bellamy, G. O'Connor, & O. Karan (Eds.), *Vocational rehabilitation of severely handicapped persons: Contemporary service strategies.* Baltimore: University Park Press.

Steinhauser, C. (1978, September). Rehabilitation of the handicapped: A boon to employers. *Risk Management* (pp. 34–38).

U. S. Department of Labor (1978). *Cost estimating procedures for sheltered workshops,* (Vol. 2), Washington, DC: U. S. Department of Labor.

U. S. Department of Labor (1979). *Study of handicapped clients in sheltered workshops,* (Vol. 2), Washington, DC: U. S. Department of Labor.

Vandergoot, D., & Worrell, J. (1979). *Placement in rehabilitation: A career development perspective.* Baltimore: University Park Press.

Wehman, P. (1981). *Competitive employment: New horizons for severely disabled individuals.* Baltimore: Paul H. Brookes.

Wehman, P., Hill, M., Goodall, P., Cleveland, P., Brooke, V., & Pentecost, J. H., Jr. (1982). Job placement and follow-up of moderately and severely handicapped individuals after three years. *Journal of the Association for the Severely Handicapped, 7*(2), 5–16.

CHAPTER 4

THE SMALL-BUSINESS SUPPORTED-EMPLOYMENT OPTION FOR PERSONS WITH SEVERE HANDICAPS

Anne O'Bryan

The small business model as described within the supported employment literature emerged from research and development at the University of Oregon between 1973 and 1982. During the course of this research, the Specialized Training Program (STP) benchwork model was defined and replicated in 17 communities in North America and Australia. Continuing development of the model has occurred through collaborative efforts of managers of replication sites. With ongoing support from the University of Oregon, managers have dealt with challenges of a changing economy and a supported employment definition which decreased program size and increased expectations of wage and integration success. Benchwork managers have also developed collaborative relationships with other organizations that have attempted to use similar business strategies. While this paper addresses the broader issue of small business models in supported employment, its focus is shaped by the author's involvement over the last 10

Anne O'Bryan ● EAS, 123 North Pitt Street, Suite A-210, Alexandria, Virginia 22314.

years in efforts to implement and adapt the STP benchwork model.

Over this long period of development, the benchwork program focus has moved from research and development to emphasis on service delivery and a reflection of community goals as well as business success. This paper is written from the perspective of what distinguishes the benchwork or small business model from other supported employment models as well as awareness that the best qualities of true supported employment—individuals making friends, choosing options, and experiencing success and the respect of others—are not related to organizational models but to successful individual adaptation. Some strategies work. Some do not. No model works all the time. The small business model contains many risks for service administrators as well as program managers. Still, its many contributions make this model well worth both discussion and reflection on its future, now that it has been complemented by other supported employment models.

PROGRAM PHILOSOPHY

The research conducted at the Specialized Training Program has clearly resulted in the knowledge that personal competence is both desirable and possible for persons with the most severe intellectual disabilities (Boles, Bellamy, Horner, & Mank, 1984). The systems used in all benchwork sites reflect this belief and are aimed at resulting in specific, measurable program outcomes. Probably the most measurable indicator of program and individual success is worker wages. Twelve communities across the United States and Australia are presently using the benchwork model. Recent data indicate that across all of these companies, worker wages average twice the national average for individuals in work activity centers. Companies which have used this model for at least 5 years are reporting wages which average more than $125 in an individual monthly wage, which is more than four times the national average of persons in activity centers (Mank, Rhodes, & Bellamy, 1985). Although this income does not represent a living wage it has frequently led to an increase in the wage earner's options and opportunities to make individual choices. Often changes related to earning money have contributed to the wage earner being viewed as a competent person able to work, able to move about in his or her community, and able to live in that community.

In addition to wages, benchwork replications are organized to achieve several other goals aimed at providing employees with a high-quality place to work. Since individuals receiving service in these companies have extreme difficulty in learning and generalizing skills, as well as behaviors that significantly get in the way of their functioning as independent adults, the model aims at providing its employees with a permanent job rather than a time-limited training program. Thus, employment in a company using this model should only be considered if it is the least restrictive alternative available to that individual.

Additional program goals relate to the quality of working life that an individual employed by a company using the benchwork model can expect. Work and wage accomplishments include increasing the number and complexity of worker skills through intensive training and supervision, thus providing the employee with interesting and challenging work and the support to accomplish it successfully. Employees also receive training and support in their participation in the community surrounding the workplace. This involvement might include using public transit to commute to work or going out to lunch. Some companies which have been using the benchwork model for several years report an average of more than one integrated community activity per person per day (Mank *et al.*, 1985). Almost all of these activities are performed individually rather than in the company of other persons with disabilities.

Sites employing the benchwork model are also committed to providing public data related to the cost/benefit ratio of this employment option. Planning and start-up costs require additional funding to hire and train managers, to acquire basic equipment, and to begin operations. However, if viewed as a long-term community investment, replications of the benchwork model cost the taxpayer about the same as work activity or developmental centers serving individuals with similar disabilities (Mank *et al.*, 1985). Most sites reduce their public cost over time as they experience an increase in commercial revenue and fiscal stability.

MODEL COMPONENTS

Systems developed by the Specialized Training Program to provide long-term supported employment include: commercial operations, habilitation and training, and management and finance. Since successful employment depends solely upon the employer's ability to provide an adequate supply of work, the commercial operations component of the benchwork model is of utmost importance and has had to become increasingly sophisticated in order to overcome numerous employment barriers. Benchwork sites have had to invest in technical expertise and equipment, build exemplary records for quality assurance and on-time delivery, and develop competitive pricing procedures. The commercial operations component provides policies and procedures for marketing and sales, job design, production operations, and production control. Each of these model elements reflects the unique characteristics of the employees with disabilities and the organization's effort to maximize individual wages. Specializing in the defined business area of benchwork usually related to electronics assembly has increased the likelihood that sites will become successful private enterprises since management efforts can be focused on that area.

The structure of the small business model also facilitates intensive training and ongoing support to employees with severe intellectual disabilities through the habilitation and training component. The individual program planning process is used in each company to develop annual and semiannual objectives for each employee receiving service. Emphasis is placed on sharing places with nondisabled individuals, expanding choices, increasing skills (and wages), and support for making friends and gaining respect (Lyle & O'Brien, 1986). Ongoing support provided to individuals in settings which use the benchwork model include: individual training on electronic subassemblies, retraining when customer specifications change or errors occur, individual training in community integration activities near the workplace, support for integration within the workplace, and continuous supervision and behavioral support to maintain and increase wages to assist the employee to develop and maintain successful employment. The intensity of the habilitation component of the benchwork model underscores the model's unsuitability for individuals whose support needs are less severe.

Management and finance components are found in all successful organizations. The benchwork model includes well-defined procedures for planning, organizing, staffing, directing, and controlling. Each small not-for-profit corporation is overseen by a board of directors which guides company policy and monitors progress toward objectives. Standardized policies and procedures have helped each site increase its chance of cost-effective success while retaining its own flexibility and local adaptation.

STAFFING

Like other supported employment models, the small business model seeks to provide high-quality ongoing employment through the use of intensive training and support to individuals who have previously been considered unemployable. Unlike supported jobs, crews, or enclaves, this option requires the start-up of a separate small, one-site business. Historically, businesses using this model have employed 15 to 20 persons with severe disabilities. However, new benchwork replications are limited to no more than eight persons in order to follow recently adopted federal guidelines (*Federal Register*, August 14, 1987). Because of its single-purpose nature, benchwork sites have been successful in effectively reaching people whose challenging behaviors or disabilities prevent access to other supported employment options. This emphasis on persons who have sometimes learned rather desperate ways to attempt to control their lives, often during lengthy stays at institutions, also distinguishes the small business model from sheltered workshops. No applicant is turned down due to lack of skill or because of a behavioral history. Indeed, sites choose not to employ individuals whose skill repertoire appears to be too great to benefit from participation in this option. In addition, replications of this model are willing to assist other service providers with training and behavioral support in order to ensure that employees continue coming to work. This may take the form of training or behavioral support coming to or leaving work, assisting families in getting support services or wheelchairs, or learning how to provide medical or physical assistance at work, during lunch, or in the restroom.

An emphasis on one-to-one training and intensive ongoing supervision allows employees to succeed even when they have repeatedly failed in other environments.

Management typically includes a general manager, a personnel manager, and a production manager, *each with direct service as well as management responsibilities.* This ensures that the all-important training and behavioral intervention occur frequently and appropriately within the context of a working day and that trainers and supervisors have the expertise required. In addition, since managers are required to accomplish a variety of complex outcomes, manager training and development continue to be an important emphasis of each company, particularly in its first few years.

The third type of employee found in companies replicating the benchwork model is the assembler without disabilities. New firms which have not fully used their production capacity employ additional assemblers only on an as-needed, part-time basis. However, as commercial success increases it has become feasible in some sites to offer full-time employment to assemblers without disabilities. As the benchwork model continues to develop and change, it is likely that more and more persons without disabilities will be employed in successful sites as assemblers. Company policies and procedures, aimed at providing a high-quality place to work for all employees, must be sure to include these assemblers' interests as well.

All assemblers with disabilities receive wages based on piece-rate which is established from the prevailing wage in similar local firms. This wage is typically higher than minimum wage throughout the electronics industry. However, few individuals employed by companies using the benchwork model have been provided with full-time remunerative employment. Workers' wages are in part related to the degree of commercial success achieved by the company and in part due to the number of tasks each worker knows how to perform successfully. Initially, management salaries are usually approved by the local funding agency in conjunction with the board of directors. As commercial success is achieved, sites may allocate additional monies to augment annual increases. However, it is typically the policy of companies using the benchwork model to share the profits among all employees through salary increases, bonuses, improved benefits, and/or profit sharing. A major constraint of this model, however, is that job security, benefits, and workfloor integration depend on the organization's commercial success.

All sites see changes in their employees over the years (Mank, 1985). These changes are related to earning money, gaining buying power, and learning to live as people without disabilities live. These changes are the product of committed advocates, resolute parents, creative foster families, and skilled group home managers, as well as supported employment environments which make wages and livelihoods possible.

An assumption from STP research emphasized that program goals for employees receiving service would have to be age-appropriate, socially equitable, and reflect the surrounding community's value system. As previously mentioned, the benchwork model shares many features and constraints with traditional sheltered workshops although it is designed for persons with significantly greater disabilities. Opportunities for employee integration are limited within the workplace since the employment of nondisabled assemblers is contingent upon a surplus of assembly work available after all assemblers with disabilities have been scheduled on their best-paying task(s). However, managers using this benchwork model believe strongly in the value of regular interaction with nondisabled peers, as well as the right for each individual to experience the regular daily, weekly, and monthly rhythms of the local community. Therefore an active emphasis on community integration is an important feature of the successful small business option. This policy is put into practice in both program design and implementation. The smallness of the program size and the carefully chosen locations close to stores, restaurants, and other community amenities provide the opportunity for regular participation in the surrounding community as appropriate to the working day. Benchwork model replications do *not* provide training in skills that do not relate to a typical working day. Of course, people who need assistance with eating or using the restroom during the workday are provided with the training they need within the appropriate context and time frame. The major focus of such training remains, however, on providing people with the skills to use their community in a competent, dignified, and natural way.

Although the benchwork model has an excellent track record in employee success, it has not managed to ensure the longevity of its replications. Seventeen sites have dwindled to 12 in the last few years. Therefore, it is important to consider the features which make the small business option work. Corporate values and commitment head the list of requirements.

Expertise in business is another essential feature of the small business model. For supported employment to be offered at all, the business *must* be successful. Otherwise none of the wage or integration outcomes can be achieved and the result is a work activity center. Therefore, managers must often comply with tight contract performance deadlines with stringent quality-assurance standards while implementing highly individualized training and supervision. Managers must be technically skilled in systematic training and production supervision. If not, it is likely that the wrong people will be selected as employees or that the remunerative work will never get to them. Two new features have joined the list since the federal definition of supported employment. The first is the effort of financially successful benchwork sites to reduce employees with disabilities to no more than eight per site. Although these efforts predate the federal definition, it is hoped that they can be accelerated with community and state support. Sites that continue to employ larger numbers of persons with severe disabilities will find it more and more difficult to provide the individualized supports and achieve the individual quality of life outcomes experienced by participants in other supported employment options. The financially successful sites are also discovering the need to develop as good employers for nondisabled people. As assemblers without disabilities are integrated into the work environment, it becomes important to ensure they find the company a satisfying place to work. As with company managers, job enlargement and advancement opportunities are necessary as well as support in interactions with disabled coworkers.

Finally, a commitment to data collection and analysis is an important feature of the successful benchwork replication. Only through careful attention to task analysis and behavioral data can successful learning be ensured. Similarly, progress toward individual and company objectives must be tracked and the resulting information used if success is to be achieved. Each of those model features presents its own achievement challenges. However, small businesses which have been successfully making this model work over some years have been able to see remarkable differences in individual employee accomplishments.

THE SMALL BUSINESS MODEL: ONE PERSON'S STORY

Karl is 52 years old. Thirty-five of those years were spent in large state institutions. His measured intelligence (IQ) is 25. At the age of 28, he was said to be "unable to carry out any work assignment; he is a limited, concrete type of person." When Karl came to his present job at an STP benchwork site in 1976, his head was shaved and his clothes were dirty. He was missing most of his teeth and usually smelled bad. He had had an infection in his gum and jaw which had necessitated surgery to remove part of his jawbone. As a result, his head and skull are noticeably misshapen. Karl has a history of inappropriate behavior. For example, he has been and continues to be fascinated with watches and frequently grabs the watches on people passing near him. He works slowly and often builds bizarre behaviors into the performance of his work. These behaviors continue to require significant staff intervention.

On his job Karl works slowly yet often initiates returning

to his job of circuit board or volume control device assembly after breaks and lunch by heading for his workstation. His productivity varies from 25 to 35 percent. In 1978 he earned about $15 a month; in 1983 he earned as much as $104 a month. Karl's earnings are not a living wage nor is his productivity competitive with the industry standard. However, he has come to be viewed as a person with competence, able to work, able to get around and use his community by himself, able to live, with support, in an apartment with one other person. Being viewed as a competent working adult has made a difference in how he is viewed in other settings. Now he is considered "able" to learn a wider variety of tasks. In the company where he works, managers insisted on a focus on work despite claims that he needed first to learn other types of behaviors. As a result of their advocacy, Karl moved into a supported apartment program where he has demonstrated competence in a wide variety of personal management areas while he has the opportunity to work.

Today, Karl independently prepares his own breakfast and lunch. He receives assistance in preparing dinner. Earnings and opportunity allow him to have a stylish haircut, to buy and wear flattering clothes, to have a healthy diet and an exercise bicycle which he uses regularly, to take skiing lessons, and to go on vacation with nondisabled friends. Karl has a variety of activities he enjoys when the personal management tasks of a working adult are completed. He often walks to a nearby restaurant in the evenings for a cup of coffee. He enjoys baseball games, bowling, and going to the library. Such opportunities are available to him even though he is not completely independent. For example, going to the library and getting home again requires close attention to time and bus schedules. Karl cannot tell time nor read bus schedules. Before he leaves, a support person sets his digital watch for the time at which he must leave the library and go to the bus stop to catch the bus he needs. When it beeps, he leaves for the bus stop. It is not totally independent participation, yet it is functional. Karl has the money to go out to dinner some evenings and the money to buy cameras, watches, and radios. He saved the money to take a vacation going by air rather than car because he made it clear that he would like to go "up."

Karl's life is remarkably different from his life in years past. With support, with stern advocates requiring a change in services, with the opportunity to participate, and with earnings, he joins the work force and assumes the life-style of an employed American adult (Mank, 1985).

IMPLICATIONS OF THE SMALL BUSINESS MODEL: FUTURE DIRECTIONS

Karl's story is a typical one and the small business model has changed many peoples' lives in similar ways. However, many questions must be asked about its future. Where does it go from here? Where does it fit in an array of supported employment options? Does it have a future? Perhaps this model is an intermediate step in the evolution of employment programs. As our technical skill develops with our imagination and creativity, will we be able to serve the same people in different employment contexts? That depends on many variables—job availability, funding commitments, employer flexibility, and, perhaps, pay adaptations. The benchwork structure has certainly been an excellent proving ground for testing the effectiveness of environmental supports, nonintrusive interventions, and coworker integration. If we can all use the knowledge acquired in this setting to support individuals and small groups in successful competitive employment, we may no longer need the more structured yet riskier undertaking of developing a specially focused small business.

Second, how appropriate is it to include this option with the other supported employment models? Clearly, as originally designed to serve 15 individuals with severe disabilities, the benchwork model does not meet the requirements of the federal definition of supported employment. Efforts to reduce its size to 8 persons technically result in complying with the definition. However, if there is widespread demonstration that other supported employment models can accommodate people with greater challenges within the current program funding limits, then the small business model will have much less of a place in the array of viable options.

Thirdly, what has been the contribution of the benchwork

model? Primarily, it has been the procedural technology development which now underlies all other options. Perhaps also it has been the policy of commitment to employees with severe disabilities and willingness to take responsibility for ensuring individual success rather than to allow failure while blaming individual weaknesses.

A fourth question to be asked concerns this model as a necessary step between long-term institutionalization and employment options. Such a step is probably not needed unless service administrators insist on group deinstitutionalization, resulting in large numbers of persons needing intensive support all at once.

Fifth, can a small business option look more like an integrated community business rather than the way the benchwork model was developed? Is it possible to develop the business first, bringing in employees with disabilities singly into an already operational business with at least as many nondisabled employees?

A final question that should be asked is whether this option could and should be used in communities where there are far more people requiring services than there are available jobs. Since this model allows the importing of work from outside the immediate area, it could be used in areas that are finding it difficult to support crews where there are no developed service sectors or enclaves which require large businesses.

The risks of this model must also be acknowledged and weighed against its merits. The greatest risk is in finding and hiring the highly skilled personnel needed to replicate this model well. Managers must be entrepreneurs who can successfully start and operate a small, highly technical business. They must be skilled and well-organized trainers able to train individuals who may never have learned how to learn, and to schedule up to 9 months of daily training per person per task among a myriad of other job demands. They must deal with organizational stress as the company develops and changes, as well as with the personal stress resulting from supporting up to 15 people who have learned rather frightening ways of communicating pain or distress. This makes it particularly important that each manager's value base is strong enough to support his or her continuing efforts to develop options and choices for each employee with disabilities both inside the company and in the surrounding community. Unfortunately, this service need is often such that a program using this model can endure without providing individuals with ever-increasing wages and opportunities for integration. Therefore, managers must often take on additional advocacy and self-evaluation roles to ensure that employees are benefiting from their participation.

This dependency on the skills and values of each member of the management team leads to major disruptions in service quality whenever turnover occurs. Thus much time and energy has to go into personnel development and support. Good management techniques are essential to provide each manager with the support needed for job satisfaction and enlargement. However, even with a firm commitment to treating personnel well, employees with many sought-after skills are bound to move on to other job opportunities, leaving the training and development process to begin all over again. When a general manager leaves, the board of directors must be especially vigilant in hiring and defining the role of the new general manager.

A reputation for personnel with fine training expertise as well as experience in successful nonaversive intervention brings about yet another risk. In many communities there is pressure from service administrators to accept more people with challenging needs than there is work available. Without work this model differs very little from the developmental centers it is attempting to replace. Thus for the small business option to be viable, communities must make a long-term commitment to support and reward quality rather than quantity.

The field has challenged its leaders to develop employment options for persons considered unemployable. Supported jobs, enclaves, and crews have done much to increase job options for many people. So far, however, the benchwork model is unique in providing employment opportunities for persons with the greatest difficulty in learning and adapting to the employment setting. As the field develops better and better community service options, the use of the benchwork model should decline; but until we are more successful in accommodating persons with severe disabilities within other supported employment options, it is logical to expect state and local program managers to continue to press for the development of this small business option.

REFERENCES

Boles, S., Bellamy, G. T., Horner, R. H., & Mank, D. (1984). Specialized training program: The structured employment model. In S. C. Paine, G. T. Bellamy, & B. Wilcox (Eds.), *Human services that work: From innovation to standard practice.* Baltimore: Paul H. Brookes.

Federal Register, August 14, 1987, *52*(15), 30546–30552. Washington, DC: U.S. Government Printing Office.

Lyle, C., & O'Brien, J. (1986). *Framework for accomplishments: A workshop on building cooperating communities.* Atlanta: Responsive Systems Associates.

Mank, D. (1985). Work and quality of life: Personal description from the Specialized Training Program. Unpublished manuscript.

Mank, D., Rhodes, L., & Bellamy, G. T. (1985). Four supported employment alternatives. In W. Kiernan & J. Stark, *Pathways to employment for developmentally disabled adults.* Baltimore: Paul H. Brookes.

CHAPTER 5

MOBILE WORK CREWS
An Approach to Achieve Long-Term Supported Employment

Philip E. Bourbeau

Since the late 1970s great strides have been made in providing more appropriate vocational services for individuals who experience moderate or severe mental retardation. Results of nationwide studies conducted in the middle 1970s (U.S. Department of Labor, 1977, 1979) showed the relative ineffectiveness of time-limited rehabilitation programs in both effecting independent competitive placements or generating significant productivity and wages for consumers with developmental disabilities (Bellamy, Rhodes, Bourbeau, & Mank, 1985). Concurrently, however, researchers in the field were successfully documenting the vocational potential of these individuals (Gold, 1972; Bellamy, Peterson, & Close, 1975). This discrepancy in outcomes, coupled with the strongly emerging ideology of normalization (Wolfensberger, 1972) fueled a concerted effort by researchers and practitioners to assist persons with severe handicaps in entering the work force.

Philip E. Bourbeau ● Supported Employment Resource Project, Oregon Health Sciences University—UAP, Portland, Oregon.

In many sites across the nation, programs were developed which successfully trained many individuals with severe handicaps and placed them into competitive jobs in their communities (Sowers, Thompson, & Connis, 1979; Wehman, 1981) by providing the structure and support needed to achieve and retain such goals. Despite the laudable success of these efforts, large numbers of people with more severe handicaps remained in programs which either limited or denied them opportunities to access meaningful work and wages (Bellamy, Sheehan, Horner, & Boles, 1980). For individuals with severe disabilities, some authors advocate for additional forms of supported employment (Horner & Bellamy, 1979) in which adult vocational service agencies would operate simultaneously as a habilitation program and a small business. Using this approach to supported work, the employees of the business (workers with severe handicaps) would be trained on the job and would then continue to function productively in that environment while receiving the support necessary to do so. The objectives of such programs would be to facilitate production and wage earning for employees, rather than prepare individuals to move on to other employment. In this manner the service providers could attend to developing solid business practices and a firm market for its goods or services.

Long-term supported employment may occur in many forms. The purpose of this chapter is to describe one such form—mobile work crews—and to delineate some of the major considerations related to establishing and operating a supported employment program of this type.

DEFINITION AND BASIC CONCEPTS

A mobile work crew offers community-based supported employment and training opportunities for four to six persons who are developmentally disabled. The crew utilizes this work force plus the organizational and managerial skills of a crew supervisor to accomplish service work objectives at various job sites in the community. The approach is not new. Its successful use as an habilitation approach has been documented in the mental health and mental retardation literature (Fairweather, 1969; Jacobs, 1974). Employing this method to provide long-term supported work for adults with severe developmental disabilities, however, is rather unique and requires a heavy emphasis on particular variables which might be safely ignored in other applications.

BENEFITS TO BE DERIVED FROM USING A WORK CREW APPROACH

Utilizing a crew approach as part of a vocational services system has many potential advantages, foremost of which is flexibility in program design. For example, in a rural area the program may be operated as a single crew serving four to six individuals. In more populous zones, the program may consist of multiple crews performing many different kinds of jobs and serving up to 24–28 people. Workers may remain on one specific crew indefinitely, or rotate among crews to experience a variety of working and supervisory conditions. Likewise, a work crew program can easily be structured to fit the labor needs of the surrounding community. In urban areas, janitorial work is usually in demand; in suburban settings, domestic labor such as grounds maintenance and housecleaning may provide the most job opportunities. Similarly, farm work in rural regions and motel room cleaning in tourist areas are frequently successful marketing approaches.

Consumers derive great benefits when served in a program which employs a crew approach. The skills needed to perform most crew-type tasks are, typically, not intricate and therefore are quickly mastered, allowing a worker to function productively after only minimal training (Cuvo, Leaf, & Borokove, 1978). Wages earned by workers in crew programs are usually higher than those earned by piece-rate workers in sheltered workshops. In addition, the fact that the work is performed at job sites in the community provides workers with a constant variety of settings and events, as well as occasions to interact with nonhandicapped people while on the job. Travel about the community also offers workers numerous opportunities to take breaks and lunches at coffee shops, restaurants, and other highly visible locations while receiving training in skills appropriate to those sites. Finally, the workers often receive a "thank you" or "well done" directly from satisfied customers. That is a reinforcer that is hard to beat.

There are also benefits for the community in which a crew is operated. The overhead costs of a crew program, which requires only minimal building space to store equipment and supplies, are lower than that for traditional workshop facilities. Also, commercial revenue generated by the program can frequently cover a substantial portion of operating expenses after wages are paid. More importantly, however, the community benefits by opportunities to observe people with developmental disabilities functioning competently and productively in its midst. Such "community education" is sorely needed as our field continues to progress toward full integration.

PREIMPLEMENTATION CONSIDERATIONS

There are certain administrative concerns which must be resolved when initiating any vocational service programs. Such matters as procuring funding, safeguarding same, obtaining Department of Labor certification to pay wages, developing mission statements, annual plans, data systems, and the like are generic to all vocational programming endeavors. Implementing a work crew program, however, presents additional issues which require attention prior to commencing business operations.

MARKET

As indicated previously, a work crew program has the inherent flexibility to fit the labor needs of various communities. These labor needs must be ascertained before other start-up steps, such as the purchase of equipment and supplies, can be accomplished. A market analysis is particularly important for programs expecting to offer janitorial and/or landscaping services, as these jobs are frequently competed for by both legitimate business operations as well as "moonlighters" who work quite inexpensively. Furthermore, successful operation of a crew focusing on the provision of janitorial work will most likely require workers to be on the job during evenings or weekends, hours not typically included in most day programs. On the positive side, buildings used to house state or federal offices are frequently "set aside" for bids by human service programs. These possibilities should be thoroughly researched.

EQUIPMENT AND SUPPLIES

Results of the market analysis should indicate the type(s) of work on which the crew will focus. The extent to which this work can be competitively bid and accomplished will depend greatly on the equipment available to be used, as is always the case with labor intensive work. There are vast numbers of machines and supplies which can be purchased, leased, or rented for various purposes. It is usually advisable to seek the recommendation of experts in the area before making final decisions. Factors to consider in deciding whether to procure specific equipment or supplies include cost, expected return on investment, complexity of operation regarding training workers to use and maintain the equipment, and likelihood of the equipment being easily transported and its potential durability. Table 1 lists the minimum needed by a single crew to accomplish basic janitorial and groundskeeping tasks.

Table 1. Minimum Equipment Needed by a Crew of Five to Perform Janitorial and Groundskeeping Work

Janitorial	
1 24″ push broom	2 24-oz. mops
2 corn brooms	1 21″ floor buffer with attachments
2 upright vacuum cleaners	2 5-gal. buckets
1 mop bucket on wheels with wringer	2 squeegees
Cleaning chemicals	1 50-ft. extension cord
Buffer pads	Rubber gloves
Rags	Assorted sponges

Groundskeeping	
1 sidewalk broom	2 hand pruners
2 weeding hoes	3 soft rakes
2 flat shovels	1 garden rake
1 spade	2 swing blades
2 21″ commercial rotary mowers	1 edger
2 grass clippers	1 toolbox
Plastic bags	

TRANSPORTATION

Safe and reliable transportation is the backbone of mobile work crews. The vehicle utilized must be capable of carrying a crew of six workers plus equipment and supplies for an entire day's work (which may entail four or five different jobs). Some form of restraint to prevent equipment from sliding around in transit is necessary and, ideally, the equipment should be protected from the elements and safely locked. The most appropriate vehicles for this task include six-passenger crew cab pickup trucks and large vans. The option of towing a small utility trailer is also frequently appreciated by crew supervisors. Although the initial expense of procuring such a vehicle will be high, the investment will prove its value time and again in the course of daily operations.

INSURANCE

Although adequate insurance coverage is required for all human service programs, the specific type of coverage required for work crews must cover additional areas such as damage to customers' property and theft. Bonding is the mechanism which usually protects against these possibilities. Frequently insurance companies and bonding agencies are confused concerning how to classify and cover work crew programs. Therefore, it is wise to anticipate a fairly complicated series of meetings when seeking coverage.

STAFF

The job of crew supervisor is absolutely crucial to successful operation of a work crew. This individual must simultaneously fulfill many varied and complex roles related to training, production supervision, public relations, and administration. In larger businesses comprised of multiple crews there will probably be a program manager whose responsibilities include the majority of administrative functions, as well as many of the commercial operations duties related to job procurement, bidding, contracting, inventory, billing, and worker payroll. In smaller businesses, these duties, as well as the daily production and training obligations, fall on the crew supervisor. Typical duties performed by the crew supervisor in a small work crew are listed below:

1. Provide vocational training and job supervision for five workers:
   —Develop and implement individual program plans.
   —Collect and summarize daily behavioral and performance data.
2. Provide training in community skills for all workers on the crew.
3. Locate potential jobs, analyze for suitability, submit bids, and contract for work to be done.
4. Purchase required equipment and supplies, manage inventory, and maintain equipment in good working order.
5. Conduct time studies as required by regulations.
6. Compute payroll for workers.
7. Collect and summarize data, maintain records, and compile reports.
8. Assure the quality of work performed by the crew and maintain excellent community relations.
9. Transport workers to and from job sites.

The preceding list strongly suggests the range of skills which must comprise the repertoire of a crew supervisor. An individual functioning in this role must combine a strong organizational capacity with specific expertise in behavioral training techniques as well as extensive knowledge of business practices related to the areas of work performed by his/her crew.

Even crew supervisors who are organized and well skilled often encounter situations in which they are unable to allocate their time in a desired manner. Heavy work demands or broken equipment may require the supervisor to accomplish some portion of the work alone. Meetings with customers likewise may interrupt the supervisors' regular functions and decrease the crews' overall efficiency. One method of controlling for these unpredictable events is to hire a nonhandicapped person as a crew member. This individual would be paid from commercial revenues and would have no habilitation responsibilities. His/her functions would be to increase overall crew productivity, handle out of the ordinary or highly complicated operations and serve as a role model for other workers on the crew. If a nonhandicapped person is to be used in this capacity, however, it is imperative that the crew supervisor be particularly mindful of the need to prioritize work allocation and wage earning in line with the needs of crew members with impairments, as one major function of the program is to maximize opportunities and wages for workers with handicaps.

DAILY PROGRAM OPERATIONS

The supervisor's duties listed in the previous section suggest the range of activities that must occur on a daily basis in order to provide training and habilitation for the crew's workers, as well as conduct the very important commercial aspects of the program. In and of themselves, neither of these two sets of activities is particularly complex or unique to work crews programs. A large number of books on behavioral training techniques or small business practices are available to provide guidance in these areas for the interested reader. What is unique to work crews employing workers with severe handicaps, however, is the need to match workers and tasks at a variety of different job sites in order to effect maximum individual productivity and wage earning while simultaneously maintaining overall crew efficiency and assuring that quality services are delivered to customers. The remainder of this chapter will describe a strategy which has been developed to interrelate the network of factors involved in attaining the following objectives: (1) work must be accomplished to produce professional results, (2) all crew members should function productively while at the job site, and (3) work should be assigned to produce maximum wages for each worker.

JOB ANALYSIS

Job analysis is the initial step taken by the crew supervisor upon encountering a new job site. A thorough job analysis permits the supervisor to: (1) select appropriate job sites; (2) bid the work accurately; (3) structure the job in terms of tasks, time, equipment, and supplies; and (4) assign tasks to crew members. An example of a completed job analysis is presented in Figure 1. The form used provides the supervisor with information concerning the major components of the job, the specific tasks within each major component, the equipment required to accomplish the work, and any other significant considerations which may effect task performance or supervision.

WORK ASSIGNMENT

On any given crew there will be some workers who can perform many tasks and some who can only perform a few. In addition, individual workers will differ with regard to their rates of performance and needs for assistance. Using the job analysis sheet and personal knowledge of crew members' skills, the supervisor can assign tasks to workers in a manner that keeps everyone busy, allows each worker to have access to the equipment that he or she will need, and permits the supervisor to provide assistance and insure quality control where needed. As workers demonstrate increasing competence on assigned tasks, larger units of work may be assigned. For example, a worker who is involved in cleaning a restroom may initially need to have each task assigned and checked separately by the supervisor. Eventually, however, the chain of behavior may be expanded to the point at which the cue "clean the men's restroom" will be all that is required for that worker to assemble all the necessary supplies and then proceed to clean toilets, sinks, mirrors, and floors unassisted, thus allowing the supervisor to work more intensively with other crew members.

For both payroll purposes and program management needs, it is essential that a system be employed to document (1) which tasks workers have been assigned, (2) how much time was required to complete them, and (3) the extent to which assistance was needed. Such data comprise vital information for both the commercial and habilitative aspects of the program.

JOB NAME:	Peddler's Village		CONTACT PERSON:	John Prince
ADDRESS:	Rt. Manasquan		WHEN DONE:	Wed./weekly, 10-2
PHONE:	722-5300		PRICE:	$40

Major component	Tasks	Frequency	#/Amt.
Bathrooms (6)	Toilets	Wkly.	4 ea.
	Sinks	Wkly.	2 ea.
	Mirrors	Wkly.	2 ea.
	Mop floors	Wkly.	
	Walls	Whenever	
Hall floor	Spray buff hall floor in west wing of store (approx. 2500 sq. ft.)	Wkly.	1-2500 sq. ft. narrow
Trash	R/R plastic liners from trash cans; put in dumpster	Wkly.	30-in. hallways throughout store
Windows	Wash windows outside of drug store in west wing	Wkly.	

Figure 1. Sample job analysis.

TRAINING

Much of the specific skill training that crew members receive will occur at job sites while actually performing the day's work. Supervisors can structure the opportunity to conduct one-to-one training by seeing that all workers are assigned tasks requiring only minimal supervision. While the crew is thus occupied, the supervisor can train one worker for 10 to 15 uninterrupted minutes. If it is not possible to assign independent tasks in this way, the alternative is to *create* tasks, such as scraping corners or washing chairs, which do not require a high level of skill or quality assurance in their accomplishment. The entire crew can be put to work on these tasks while the supervisor works one-to-one on a rotating basis with different crew members. These "busywork" tasks are also a valuable means of insuring that all crew members remain productive after completing their major work assignments at any job site. These efforts also seldom go unnoticed by customers.

DIRECTIONS: RT. 33 east to north on 79 to Brielie; PV is on the circle	
TRAVEL TIME: 20 minutes	
ACCESS: Back door by dumpster	
Equipment needed	**Other considerations**
Caddy with Comet, Windex end bag, sponge, paper towels, rubber gloves Mop: bucket, wringer, mop, hose	
21" buffer with spray attachment, white pad, 2 cans of spray buff, putty knife, adapter	Poor lighting, very dark Floor is deep brown No distractors, good for training
Liners and ties, gloves	Difficult to supervise
Use their big cart	
Squeegee, bucket and soap brush, extension stick, rag	Bucket to be filled in janitor's closet, not bathroom Use only 1/2 cup of soap

Figure 1 (*Continued*)

SUMMARY

Mobile work crews have been used as a long-term supported work model in many locations with great success. In the mid-1970s the New Jersey Division of Mental Retardation began utilizing the approach as an alternative to sheltered workshop referral for many clients who had been enrolled in adult day programs. Program developers in the state of Washington, which specifices the provision of long-term supported work in its adult services guidelines, also have used work crew programs successfully in various sites. Opportunities for productivity, wage earning, and community integration, coupled with the cost-effectiveness and extreme flexibility of the approach in adapting to a variety of setting conditions, provide strong support for widespread application as one method of employing individuals with severe handicaps.

REFERENCES

Bellamy, G. T., Rhodes, L., Bourbeau, P., & Mank, D. (1985). Mental retardation services in sheltered workshops and day activity programs: Consumer benefits and policy alternatives. In F. R. Rusch (Ed.), *Competitive employment: Service delivery models, methods and issues.* Baltimore: Paul H. Brookes.

Bellamy, G. T. Sheehan, M. R., Horner, R. H., & Boles, S. M. (1980). Community programs for severely handicapped adults: An analysis of vocational opportunities. *Journal of the Association for the Severely Handicapped, 5*(4), 307–324.

Bellamy, T., Peterson, L., & Close, D. (1975). Habilitation of the severely and profoundly retarded: Illustrations of competence. *Education and Training of the Mentally Retarded, 10,* 174–186.

Cuvo, A. J., Leaf, R. B., & Borakove, L. S. (1978). Teaching janitorial skills to the mentally retarded: Acquisition, generalization and maintenance. *Journal of Applied Behavior Analysis, 11,* 345–356.

Fairweather, G. W. (1969). *Community life for the mentally ill: An alternative to institutional care.* Chicago: Aldine.

Gold, M. (1972). Stimulus factors in skill training of the retarded on a complex assembly task. *American Journal of Mental Deficiency, 76,* 517–526.

Horner, R. H., & Bellamy, G. T. (1979). Long-term structure employment: Productivity and productive capacity. In G. T. Bellamy, G. O'Connor, & O. C. Karan (Eds.), *Vocational habilitation for developmentally disabled persons: Contemporary service strategies.* Baltimore: University Park Press.

Jacobs, J. W. (1974). Retarded persons as gleaners. *Mental Retardation, 14*(6), 42–43.

Sowers, J., Thompson, L., & Connis, R. (1979). The food service vocational training program. In G. T. Bellamy, G. O. O'Connor, & O. C. Karan (Eds.), *Vocational rehabilitation of severely handicapped persons: Contemporary service strategies.* Baltimore: University Park Press.

U. S. Department of Labor. (1977) *Sheltered Workshop Study: Volume II.* Washington, D. C.

U. S. Department of Labor. (1979 March). *Sheltered Workshop Study: Volume II.* Washington, D. C.

Wehman, P. (1981). *Competitive employment: New horizons for severely disabled persons.* Baltimore: Paul H. Brookes.

Wolfensberger, W. (Ed.). (1972). *The principle of normalization in human services.* Toronto: National Institute on Mental Retardation.

PART II

SUPPORTED EMPLOYMENT
Research Analysis and Policy

CHAPTER 6

COMPETITIVE EMPLOYMENT FOR PERSONS WITH MENTAL RETARDATION
A Decade Later

Paul Wehman, John Kregel,
and P. David Banks

Remarkable progress has been made within the past decade in demonstrating the competitive employment potential of persons with mental retardation. The standard of vocational excellence is no longer participation in a sheltered workshop, but good pay in a real job, working alongside predominantly non-disabled peers. Since the late 1970s there has been a steady movement away from single-case, isolated demonstrations (e.g., Wehman, Hill, & Koehler, 1979) and toward descriptions of how larger groups of persons with mental retardation fare in competitive employment (Bates, 1986; Brown *et al.*, 1987; Thornton, 1985; Wehman, Hill, Hill, Brooke, Pendleton, & Britt, 1985). While virtually none of these larger group demonstrations has had the experimental control associated with

---

Paul Wehman, John Kregel, and P. David Banks ● Rehabilitation Research and Training Center, Virginia Commonwealth University, Richmond, Virginia.

more rigorous scientific research, results from these efforts have amply served the purpose of seriously raising questions about the present adult service system for persons with mental disabilities. The longest demonstration to date reported in the literature is the Wehman *et al.* (1985) study which spanned a period of approximately 6 years.

With the improved prospect of employability and job retention for many persons with mental retardation, the adult service system, which is dominated by workshops and day activity centers, must resolve the dilemma of how to accommodate what research tells us is possible. Adult service programs are in fact now wrestling with exactly this problem, as supported employment implementation activities have accelerated (Bellamy, Rhodes, Mank, & Albin, 1988). As Chapter 1 by Shafer has indicated, supported employment is a key intervention strategy which has made paid, real work a better likelihood for persons with severe disabilities than ever before. Local and state agencies are presently in the difficult process of modifying and, in some cases, fully converting their existing segregated center structure to a smaller, more dispersed mode of service delivery. For example, if the majority of mentally retarded persons in a local program can work competitively, as research seems to support currently, then there is not very much need for them to go to a large center every day. While this is a somewhat oversimplified example due to job turnover, failure, and attrition, there are still other less restrictive work alternatives such as work crews and enclaves (described in previous chapters) which can be developed, and which do not necessitate the presence of a large center.

In order to further understand the long-term outcomes associated with competitive employment programming, we undertook another analysis of data generated by our university-based demonstration program. Our group began a supported work model of competitive employment in 1978 and there have been two published updates at 3-year (Wehman *et al.*, 1982) and 6-year junctures (Wehman *et al.*, 1985), as well as one benefit–cost analysis done by Hill and Wehman in 1983, and a more recent one reprinted in this text (Hill *et al.*, 1987). Therefore, the purpose of this report is to describe selected dimensions of the competitive employment program we have operated since 1978. This analysis is limited to persons labeled mentally retarded. It should also be noted that most of the workers initially placed, trained, and followed are now the responsibilities of local programs. These programs have developed the philosophical commitment and capacity to do this work.

METHOD

PROGRAM PARTICIPANTS

The population of consumers used in this analysis is made up of 255 individuals whose primary disability has been diagnosed as mental retardation. Referrals to the demonstration programs since the late 1970s have come from a variety of sources, and have changed over the years as our demonstration activities have varied in focus. From 1978 to 1984, referrals were accepted from adult day programs, parents, case managers, special education programs, and rehabilitation counselors. Efforts during these years were focused on demonstrating the employment potential of individuals labeled moderately or severely mentally retarded.

In July 1984 the Rehabilitation Research and Training Center (RRTC) became vendored through the Virginia Department of Rehabilitation Services to provide supported employment services to individuals referred by local rehabilitation counselors. Many of the individuals referred by the counselors were individuals labeled mildly mentally retarded who had not been able to be successfully employed through other rehabilitation services.

Also in 1984, placement efforts began to focus more extensively upon individuals 18 to 21 years of age in response to an OSERS-funded project to demonstrate the efficacy of supported employment services to transition-aged individuals. Since 1986, placement efforts have again changed slightly in focus as a particular effort has been made to place individuals with measured IQs under 35 into competitive employment. In all instances, we have attempted to serve individuals who have

Table 1. Age Categories of Consumers at First
Placement

Age categories	Percentage of consumers
18 to 25	36.1
26 to 35	43.0
36 to 45	16.0
46 to 55	2.5
56 to 65	2.4

been traditionally excluded from employment services or who
have been unsuccessful in other employment programs.

Nearly two-thirds (65.5 percent) of the individuals in the
study population were male. Their average age was 30, with a
range 18 to 69. Table 1 specifies age categories for consumers
at the time of first placement, indicating that the vast majority
(79.1 percent) were between 18 and 35 at the time of their
initial placement. The mean IQ of all consumers was 51, with a
range from 18 to 79. As indicated in Table 2, slightly over half
of all consumers had been classified as moderately mentally
retarded, and another third had been labeled mildly mentally
retarded.

Almost half (47.5 percent) of all consumers were reported
to have a secondary disability in addition to mental retardation.
Frequently cited secondary disabilities included cerebral palsy,
convulsive disorders, learning disabilities, long-term mental illness, and hearing, language, and visual impairments. Table 3
provides detailed information regarding the percentage of in-

Table 2. Previously Diagnosed Functioning Level of
Consumers ($N = 255$)

Functioning level	Percentage of consumers
Profound	0.4
Severe	6.5
Moderate	52.4
Mild	33.0
Borderline	7.7

Table 3. Type of Additional Disabilities for Placed Consumers[a]

Additional disabilities	Cumulative totals	
	Number	Percentage
Cerebral palsy	18	7.1
Convulsive disorder	22	8.6
Long-term mental illness	7	2.7
Hearing impairment	6	2.4
Learning disability	14	5.5
Language impairment	65	25.5
Spinal cord injury	1	0.4
Visual impairment	19	7.5

[a] 122 individuals were reported to possess one or more disabilities in addition to mental retardation.

dividuals in the population possessing specific secondary disabilities.

Almost all (92.4 percent) of the consumers were Supplemental Security Income (SSI) recipients at the time of referral, with 73.3 percent also receiving Medicaid benefits. Relatively few individuals (5.8 percent) were receiving SSDI benefits prior to referral. Twenty-two percent of the consumers had previously resided in state institutions for persons labeled mentally retarded, and 19 individuals had formerly been institutionalized for more than 10 years.

EMPLOYMENT SPECIALISTS

The employment specialists, also known as job coaches, who provided supported employment services during this 10-year period usually had bachelor's or sometimes master's degrees in psychology, rehabilitation, special education, or social work. They spent their time doing job development, job placement, job-site training, and substantial amounts of work with parents, employers, and referring counselors and teachers. The employment specialist is *the* key person in implementing supported employment programs.

Data Collection and Management System

The Supported Employment Management Information System operated by the Rehabilitation Research and Training Center (RRTC) at Virginia Commonwealth University was established to track the longitudinal outcomes of demonstration supported employment programs that were first begun in 1978 (Wehman *et al.*, 1982). While first developed to monitor the employment outcomes achieved by over 200 individuals placed into competitive employment by university-based research and demonstration programs, the system was ultimately expanded to track the progress of a large number of community-based programs begun between 1985–1987 as a result of federal and state supported employment initiatives. Over 1,500 consumers participating in supported employment programs operated by over 70 local agencies in eight states are tracked through the system.

The complete management information system is designed to monitor the outcomes of individuals with a variety of primary disabilities in an array of different supported employment models and has been described in detail elsewhere (RRTC, 1987). Extensive data are collected on *each* consumer, as opposed to alternative systems that rely on aggregated employment outcomes. Data collection occurs continuously, rather than, for example, in a once-a-year "snapshot" fashion. This allows the system to monitor an individual's status throughout the course of employment. The result is a powerful research tool that allows the examination of individual consumer variability and repeated measures analysis over time.

The system consists of over 200 data elements which provide detailed information regarding key demographic and functional characteristics of individual consumers, comprehensive data concerning the specific job held by the consumer, supervisors' evaluations of the consumer's job performance, and complete information regarding job retention and reasons for job separation.

Program Model of Placement and Intervention

We have successfully used a supported work model of employment services (e.g, Wehman & Kregel, 1985). With this model, professional staff provide individualized and intensive assistance to the client in: (1) making the placement, (2) providing job-site training and assessment, and (3) engaging in long-term follow-along support as needed. Below are described the principle components of this model. Readers interested in more detail regarding this approach are referred to Wehman and Moon (1988).

Job Placement

Placement into a job appropriate to the individual's ability is the first major component to the supported work model. A great deal has been written about job placement. However, we believe that the process of job placement involves more than simply finding a job for a client. Major aspects of the job placement process include:

1. Facilitating an employer interview and interaction,
2. Facilitating parent or caretaker communications,
3. Establishing travel arrangements or providing travel training, and
4. Analyzing the job environment to verify all potential obstacles which may arise.

There are several key points to highlight about job placement within the supported work model. First, effective placement is predicated on an accurate analysis of work environment requirements. This process has been variously referred to as ecological analysis, top-down curriculum, or job analysis. It is critical that adequate detail be provided in terms of job requirements, characteristics of the work environment, and other features that may influence job retention. This detail will then facilitate the job match, that is, pairing job requirements with client abilities.

The second key point is that job placement can take place with individuals who do not possess all the necessary work or social-skill competencies for immediate job success. The strength of a supported work model approach is that whoever is making the placement knows that job-site help will be available once the placement formally occurs. This is a significant departure from traditional placement approaches, which require the client to be "job-ready" at the time of placement, and has been crucial to making our track record successful with clients traditionally excluded from services.

A third important element is that travel, social security, job interview, and other non-work-related factors are actively handled in the job placement process. Within a more traditional placement framework, it is often accepted that the client or caretaker will handle most of these concerns. However, with many persons who are mentally retarded, job placement cannot occur without a specialist to help.

Job-Site Training

On-the-job training is certainly not a new concept. However, traditionally there has not been active involvement after the placement is made from a trained professional staff person. Employers usually take responsibility for the training and receive wage reimbursement for the clients. All too often, no specific training is provided, but instead, brief and infrequent follow-up checks or visits are made by the rehabilitation counselor after the placement. In short, a major step—skill training and/or generalization and adjustment to the work environment—is omitted. Most of the people described in the earlier section of this paper who are still working would not be without this type of assistance. Our experiences in placement, as well as communication with others using a supported work model, strongly indicate that job-site training and advocacy are essential features of the supported work model. Two major processes are involved: (1) behavioral training of skills, and (2) advocacy on behalf of the client. Training is the application of systematic instruction techniques at the job site; and advocacy is the promotion of the client to employers or coworkers in relation to job retention.

Ongoing Assessment

There is a need to immediately assess the employer's perceptions of the performance of the worker with mental retardation once a placement is made. There will usually be two major indicators of performance: supervisor's evaluations and client progress data. Without these sources of data, we would not have been in a position to determine the performance level of the clients with whom we are working. Program decisions are made and presented to employers based upon *data*, not intuition. The amount of assessment data collected is clearly related to variables, such as the ability level of the client, amount of staff available for data collection, and, above all, the specific need for data to evaluate a certain problem.

Job Retention and Follow-Along

Follow-along is an activity or service which is consistently referred to in the rehabilitation system; yet it is unclear how much follow-along in terms of frequency of employer contact, communication with clients, and replacement into an alternative job is actually provided. It is these variables which influence the quality of placement and maintenance. All the clients reported in this paper have received, and continue to receive, follow-along services as needed.

RESULTS

EMPLOYMENT OUTCOME MEASURES

The 255 consumers have been placed into a total of 398 jobs, resulting in an average of 1.6 jobs per individual. The types of jobs held by the consumers remain predominantly food service (51.8 percent) and janitorial/custodial (33.4 percent) in nature. A complete listing of the types of jobs held by the consumers is provided in Table 4. Almost three-fourths of all jobs were found in the private sector. Only 27 percent of all jobs were obtained through private nonprofit or local, state, or federal government agencies.

The average number of hours worked per week by all consumers in the demonstration program was 26. Twenty-four percent of the positions held by the consumers provided less than 20 hours per week of employment. This figure should be

Table 4. Type of Job (N = 398 Positions)

Type of job	Cumulative totals	
	Number	Percentage
Food service	206	51.8
Janitorial/custodial	133	33.4
Unskilled labor	7	1.8
Bench work/assembly	17	4.3
Laundry	14	3.5
Stock clerk/warehouse	14	3.5
Transportation	2	0.5
Clerical/office work	2	0.5
Groundskeeping	3	0.8
Total	398	100.0

interpreted cautiously, however, because a number of individuals held two or more part-time jobs simultaneously that in combination totaled more than 20 hours per week. It should also be kept in mind that the data presented reflect a large number of placements made in the late 1970s and early 1980s. Since the initiation of the OSERS systems-change projects in 1985, no individual has been placed in a position providing less than 20 hours per week of employment. Table 5 provides a categorical breakdown of the hours worked per week across the 398 positions.

The average hourly wage for individuals employed across all 398 positions is $3.56. This average must also be interpreted

Table 5. Number of Hours per Week in Position (N = 398)

Hours worked per week	Cumulative totals	
	Number	Percentage
Less than 20 hours	96	24.1
20 to 29 hours	135	33.9
30 to 40 hours	166	41.7
More than 40 hours	1	0.3
Total	398	100.0

Table 6. Government Benefits Received by
Consumers at Referral

Government benefits	Percentage of consumers
SSI	92.4%
SSDI	5.8%
Medicaid	73.3%
Food stamps	0.6%
Other aid	4.7%

across time. Many early placements were made when the statutory federal minimum wage was $2.65. *All* individuals participating in the demonstration projects have in every instance been placed into positions paying at least the federal minimum wage. The cumulative total of all wages earned by all participating individuals is $2,659,121, meaning that the average individual has earned $10,428. The use of an average figure in this instance may be somewhat misleading, however, since some individuals may have been employed for one week or less. For example, one of the consumers in the program has earned $61,750 to date. Our most recent benefit/cost analysis indicates that the 255 individuals have paid a total of $611,598 in local, state, and federal taxes.

Data regarding the fringe benefits received by consumers are available on 342 of the 398 positions. Almost half (47.1 percent) provided no fringe benefits. This may be reflective of the large number of individuals employed in part-time positions. About a third of all positions provide sick leave and paid vacations; but medical insurance was provided in only 28.4 percent of the positions. A summary of all fringe benefits received across the positions is provided in Table 6.

EMPLOYMENT RETENTION AND REASONS FOR SEPARATION

Employment retention may be analyzed in a number of different ways. The number of individuals remaining in employment for a minimum of 6 months has remained remarkably constant over several years, fluctuating between 65 and 72 percent of the consumers placed. Currently, 68 percent of consumers work a minimum of 6 months. The average individual has been employed 104.6 weeks, approximately 2 years. At least two factors should be kept in mind when interpreting this information. First, approximately 35 individuals have been placed very recently and those individuals have not yet had an opportunity to work an extended period of time. Second, many individuals have been employed in two or more different jobs. The number of weeks employed *by position* is 67, with a range of from less than one week to 454 weeks.

Throughout the course of the demonstration projects a large number of individuals have been separated from their jobs for a variety of reasons. A total of 299 separations have occurred to date, resulting in 99 of the 255 individuals still working in jobs obtained for them by the RRTC demonstration projects. A large number of separated individuals have subsequently been placed into employment by local supported employment programs after being separated from their initial jobs. Although 299 separations have occurred, less than half (43.8 percent) of those have resulted from terminations or firings. Separations have also included a large number of individuals who have either resigned or been laid off from their positions. Table 7 provides a categorical breakdown of the type of separation across all consumers.

The data management system also allows for the tracking of the specific reasons for separation, based upon information

Table 7. Type of Separation from Employment

Separation type	Cumulative totals	
	Number	Percentage
Resigned	107	35.8
Laid off	53	17.7
Terminated	131	43.8
Leave of absence	7	2.3
Deceased	1	0.3
Total	299	100.0

Table 8. Reason for Separation from Employment (N = 299)

Separation reason	Cumulative totals	
	Number	Percentage
Transportation problem	8	2.7
Moved away	3	1.0
Does not want to work	48	16.1
Parent/guardian initiated	19	6.4
Economic situation	41	13.7
Slow work	15	5.0
Low-quality work	14	4.7
Poor appearance	1	0.3
Poor social skills	2	0.7
Poor attendance/tardiness	21	7.0
Insubordinate behavior	10	3.3
Aberrant behavior	8	2.7
Parent interference	2	0.7
Poor work attitude	13	4.3
Employer uncomfortable	19	6.4
Financial support interference	1	0.3
Continual prompting	9	3.0
Medical/health problem	5	1.7
Poor job match	5	1.7
Seasonal layoff	12	4.0
Took better job	27	9.0
Criminal behavior	10	3.3
Deceased	1	0.3
Other reason	5	1.7
Total	299	100.0

obtained from both the employment specialist and the employer. The three most frequently cited reasons for separations have included: (1) the individual did not choose to work any longer; (2) the individual was laid off as the result of an economic situation with the specific employment; and (3) the individual resigned to take a better job. It is important to note that only 19 of the 299 separations were initiated by the individual's parent or guardian, and only two were reported to be the result of parental interference. A complete listing of reasons for all 299 separations is contained in Table 8.

SUMMARY

The employment outcomes of consumers' participating in the demonstration programs operated by Virginia Commonwealth University since 1978 are unique in several ways. A major strength of these programs, the results of which this chapter has described, is that they have been operating continuously for a period of over a decade, far longer than most of the supported employment programs in operation today. As such, they provide a valuable resource for professionals studying the long-term feasibility and efficacy of supported employment for individuals with disabilities.

However, the extended length of time the program has been in operation makes difficult the direct comparison of consumer outcomes to those achieved by newly-created supported employment programs. Many placements occurred during a time when the federal minimum wage was less than the current $3.35 per hour. The program has endured a variety of economic conditions, including the recession of the early 1980s. The vast majority of the placements represented in the data occurred prior to the development of the Title VI-C regulations in 1986. Finally, the nature of the consumer population served has varied considerably over the course of the ten years in response to the unique purposes of the several specific demonstration projects. These factors in combination make it extremely difficult to directly compare measures such as hourly wage, functioning level of consumers served, and job separations to programs in operation for a shorter period of time.

The results described above are also unique in that they were achieved through a series of university-based projects, as opposed to a locally funded and operated supported employment program. This has had a major influence upon the individuals selected for participation in the program, many of whom were chosen to participate based upon a need to demonstrate the effectiveness of supported employment services with specific types of individuals, as opposed to mirroring the selection processess in effect in local employment programs. Since the mid-1980s, as local programs have developed the capacity to provide supported employment services, many consumers originally placed through the demonstration programs have been discharged to local providers. A number of these individuals are no longer tracked through the RRTC data management system, although they continue to work with support from local programs, a situation that to a degree has artificially deflated the number of consumers still working as reflected in the data described above.

Another unique feature of the demonstration programs is their philosophical commitment to rely exclusively upon the individual placement model to place individuals into positions that pay at least the federal minimum wage. Alternative supported employment service delivery models, subminimum wage agreements, and volunteer work have been avoided throughout the course of the demonstration projects. The only subsidies that have been utilized are the Targeted Jobs Tax Credit (when in effect) and the ongoing support provided to employers and consumers by project staff. In a number of instances, individuals unable to succeed in the individual placement model utilized by the projects have subsequently been able to successfully participate in group employment situations operated by local providers.

Several trends have emerged across the array of consumer employment outcomes discussed above that are worthy of additional comment. One of the most interesting trends pertains to the number of individuals who have held more than one job throughout the course of their employment. This factor is documented by a number of different measures, including the average of 1.6 different jobs held by consumers, the large number of individuals who resigned their positions as opposed to being terminated, and the 27 individuals whose reason for separation was to take a better job.

The fact that the individuals participating in the program change jobs frequently should not be surprising. This finding is consistent with data available regarding job turnover among nondisabled individuals in entry-level service occupations (National Hotel and Restaurant Association, 1983). The frequency with which consumers change jobs has significant implications for local supported employment providers. Local programs should anticipate that consumer movement will be a regular occurrence which must be considered when providing follow-along services to consumers. Many individuals will express a desire to change jobs because of a preference for higher wages, improved working conditions, more convenient working hours, or because of a dissatisfaction with their present employment situation.

A final factor to be emphasized are the results presented that address the role of parents or guardians in the supported employment process. Although parents have been occasionally viewed as having a detrimental effect upon the supported employment participation of their son or daughter, the results of this longitudinal analysis do not support this view. Of the 299 separations from jobs reported, only two were identified as being due to parental interference with the placement, and only 19 were initiated by parents and guardians. Rather than being impediments to successful supported employment, it appears that when parents are involved as active, informed participants in the supported employment process, they can have an extremely positive effect upon the supported employment outcomes achieved by their sons and daughters.

REFERENCES

Bates, P. (1986). Competitive employment in Southern Illinois: A transitional service delivery model for enhancing competitive employment outcomes for public school students. In F. R. Rusch (Ed.), *Competitive employment issues and strategies*, pp. 51–64. Baltimore: Paul H. Brookes.

Bellamy, G. T., Rhodes, L. E., Mank, D. M., & Albin, J. M. (1988). *Supported employment: A community implementation*. Baltimore: Paul H. Brookes.

Brown, L., Shiraga, B., Ford, A., VanDeventer, P., Nisbet, J., Loomis, R., & Sweet, M. (1987). Teaching severely handicapped students to perform meaningful work in nonsheltered vocational environments. In R. Morris & B. Blatt (Eds.), *Perspectives in special education: State of the art*. Glenview, IL: Scott Foresman.

Hill, M., Banks, P. D., Handrich, R., Wehman, P., Hill, J., & Shafer, M. (1987). Benefit-cost analysis of supported competitive employment for persons with mental retardation. *Research in Developmental Disabilities, 8*(1), 71–89.

Hill, M., & Wehman, P. (1983). Cost benefit analysis of placing moderately and severely handicapped individuals into competitive employment. *The Journal of the Association for Persons with Severe Handicaps, 8*(1), 30–39.

Nelan, P. (1983). *National Hotel and Restaurant Association*. Washington, DC: Personal communication.

Thornton, C. (1985). Benefit-cost analysis of social programs: Deinstitutionalization and education programs. In R. H. Bruininks & K. C. Lakin (Eds.), *Living and learning in the least restrictive environment*, pp. 225–244. Baltimore: Paul H. Brookes.

Wehman, P., Hill, J., & Koehler, F. (1979). Placement of developmentally disabled individuals into competitive employment: Three case studies. *Education and Training of the Mentally Retarded, 14*(4), 269–276.

Wehman, P., Hill, M., Goodall, P., Cleveland, P., Brooke, V., & Pentecost, J. (1982). Job placement and follow-up of moderately and severely handicapped individuals after three years. *Journal of the Association for the Severely Handicapped, 7*(2), 5–16.

Wehman, P., Hill, M., Hill, J., Brooke, V., Pendleton, P., & Britt, C. (1985). Competitive employment for persons with mental retardation: A follow-up six years later. *Mental Retardation, 23*(6), 274–281.

Wehman, P., & Kregel, J. (1985). A supported work approach to competitive employment of individuals with moderate and severe handicaps. *Journal of the Association for Persons with Severe Handicaps, 10*(1), 3–11.

Wehman, P., & Moon, M. S. (1988). *Vocational rehabilitation and supported employment*. Baltimore: Paul H. Brookes.

CHAPTER 7

AN ANALYSIS OF SERVICES PROVIDED BY EMPLOYMENT SPECIALISTS IN THE INDIVIDUAL PLACEMENT MODEL OF SUPPORTED EMPLOYMENT

John Kregel

As described in previous chapters, supported employment embodies a nationwide attempt to use newly developed service technologies to assist persons with developmental and other severe disabilities previously excluded from community-based employment opportunities. Supported employment represents a significant departure from traditional rehabilitation services for individuals with disabilities, which were characterized by (1) a requirement that individuals demonstrate a documented potential for employability prior to receiving services; (2) an emphasis on preemployment "readiness" training prior to competitive employment placement; and (3) a limit to the amount of time an individual could receive rehabilitation services (Wehman & Kregel, 1988).

In contrast, supported employment programs focus their services upon individuals for whom competitive employment

John Kregel ● Rehabilitation Research and Training Center, Virginia Commonwealth University, Richmond, Virginia.

has not traditionally occurred (Will, 1984). As a result large numbers of individuals are now able to obtain and maintain employment for the first time. New service technologies have been developed which emphasize a "place and train" philosophy (Rusch, 1986) in which the vast majority of training and support services are provided in the community while the individual is gainfully employed. In addition, supported employment services are provided on an ongoing basis as long as the individual is employed. This feature of supported employment is a major change from the time-limited support traditionally provided in rehabilitation programs such as transitional employment, where support services may only be provided for a few months. As a result, many individuals with substantial handicaps are able to earn significant wages in integrated, community-based job sites while receiving training, supervision, and support throughout the course of their employment.

A variety of different supported employment service models have begun to gain widespread acceptance (Bellamy, Rhodes, Mank, & Albin, 1988). Several of these models involve placing groups of individuals with disabilities in work environments where continuous training and supervision is provided by professional staff. These models have been described in detail in previous chapters—the enclave in industry model described by Rhodes and Valenta in Chapter 3, the work crew model outlined by Bourbeau in Chapter 5, and the small business model described by O'Bryan in Chapter 4. Another major supported employment model focuses on the placement of one individual in a real job in a work environment with predominantly nonhandicapped workers. This individual placement model has been variously termed the supported work model (Wehman & Kregel, 1985), supported jobs (Mank, Rhodes, & Bellamy, 1986), the job coach model (Wehman & Melia, 1985) and supported competitive employment (Wehman, 1986).

The individual placement model has been thoroughly described by Moon and her colleagues (Moon, Goodall, Barcus, & Brooke, 1986). The key feature of the model is the identification of an employment specialist who develops a one-to-one relationship with a single consumer in need of individual services. The employment specialist is generally responsible for all aspects of the consumer's service program, including special assistance in locating an appropriate job, intensive job-site training until the consumer is able to perform the job to industry standards, and permanent, ongoing follow-along services to enable the individual to maintain the job for an extended period of time. Moon *et al.* (1986) have identified five major duties of employment specialists, encompassing job development, consumer assessment, job placement, job-site training, and ongoing assessment and follow-along.

The role of the employment specialist in supported employment is a challenging one. Employment specialists are faced with the task of delivering an array of nontraditional employment services to, in essence, a nontraditional population of consumers, the vast majority of whom have never before participated in community-based employment services. While both pre-service (Kregel & Sale, 1988) and in-service (Inge, Barcus, & Everson, 1988) training programs are rapidly expanding, only limited information (e.g., Winking, DeStefano, & Rusch, 1988) is available that has attempted to examine key issues, such as the activities engaged in by employment specialists on a day-to-day basis, the number of consumers an employment specialist can successfully maintain on his/her caseload at one time, or the major problems encountered by employment specialists as they attempt to deliver effective services.

This lack of empirical information regarding the day-to-day activities of employment specialists also creates problems for supported employment program administrators. Without accurate data, program managers will have a difficult time supervising and monitoring the activities of employment specialists. For example, managers will have difficulty determining if an employment specialist is spending too little or too much time with individual consumers. It will also be very difficult to determine the number of employment specialists required to serve a group of consumers with a particular type of disability, estimate the number of placements that should be made by a newly established program, or project the short-term and long-term costs of services. Little factual information exists at the present to assist program managers in making these decisions (Schalock & Hill, 1986).

Perhaps the most effective way to develop an understanding of the day-to-day activities of employment specialists in individual placement models is to thoroughly analyze the amount and type of *intervention time* provided to individual consumers throughout the employment process. Intervention time as defined in previous chapters may be viewed as all training, support, and advocacy services provided by an employment specialist to enable an individual consumer to obtain, learn, perform, and maintain a job (Kregel, Hill, & Banks, 1987). An analysis of the *types* of intervention provided will help empirically to define the major duties and activities of employment specialists in the individual placement model. An analysis of the *amount* of intervention time provided in a sense represents the *intensity* of service, and in programs funded on a fee-for-service basis directly determines the costs of serving an individual consumer.

The remainder of this chapter will describe the results of a detailed analysis of the type and amount of intervention provided to over 900 individuals with developmental and other severe disabilities currently tracked through the Supported Employment Management Information System maintained by the Rehabilitation Research and Training Center at Virginia Commonwealth University. Information will be presented that illustrates the relative amount of time employment specialists spend in eight distinct types of activities to clarify the day-to-day activities of employment specialists. Data regarding the total amount of intervention time provided to individual consumers will then be presented to illuminate the intensity of training and support services required to maintain individuals in competitive employment. Finally, differences in the type and amount of intervention provided to consumers identified as possessing various types of primary disabilities will be examined to identify the unique types of services required by individuals with specific primary disabilities.

METHODS OF ANALYZING THE TYPE
AND AMOUNT OF INTERVENTION TIME

The Virginia Commonwealth University Supported Employment Management Information System was described in

Chapter 6. A key feature of the information system is its ability to continuously track the amount of time employment specialists spend providing various types of services to individual consumers. The instrument used to collect this data is the RRTC Consumer-Specific Intervention Time Recording Sheet. Employment specialists participating in the system are asked to account for and record every hour of intervention provided for each consumer they serve. Within 70 participating programs, intervention time is recorded daily for each consumer and is then forwarded to the RRTC for data entry and analysis. When intervention is submitted, a data management specialist reviews it for completeness and consistency with previous data, obtains missing data, and clarifies any inconsistencies prior to entering the data for computer analysis. At the end of each calendar quarter a summary of the intervention data submitted is returned to the participating programs for review and verification. This process is designed to maximize the accuracy and reliability of the data.

The Consumer-Specific Intervention Time Recording Sheet identifies eight different categories of employment specialist activity. Two categories are directly related to job-site training activities (Time Active and Time Inactive) and six categories of activities indirectly related to job skill training (Travel/Transport Time, Consumer Training Time, Consumer Program Development, Direct Employment Advocacy, Indirect Employment Advocacy, and Consumer Screening/Evaluation). These categories have evolved over a 10-year period and represent an effort to capture the scope of employment specialist training and support activities. Each of the categories will be briefly described below, expanding upon definitions contained in the RRTC Data Management System Operations Manual (RRTC, 1987).

Time Active

Time active intervention refers to all time spent by an employment specialist working directly with the consumer at the job site. Intervention in this category is directly related to the acquisition and performance of required job skills as well as the social skills necessary for the consumer to be socially integrated in the job site. Examples of activities included in this category are providing verbal or hands-on instruction for the consumer, assisting the consumer in completing the job, actively observing the consumer performing the job to assess his or her level of proficiency, or teaching the consumer to properly clock in and out of the workplace, take breaks at the appropriate time and in the appropriate location, seek assistance from the supervisor when necessary, and so forth.

TIME INACTIVE

Time inactive refers to *all* time spent on the job site by the employment specialist between periods of *active* intervention. This type of activity generally occurs when the employment specialist feels that the initial training of the consumer is nearing completion and begins to fade his or her presence from the job site. The employment specialist may choose to remove him- or herself from the consumer's immediate work area to determine if the consumer is able to independently complete the task. In a food service environment, for example, the employment specialist may want to allow the consumer to perform the job independently for an extended period of time, but yet remain on the job site to assist the consumer should the need arise during a particularly heavy rush period, or if the consumer experiences excessive difficulty in completing an assigned task. Time-inactive is distinguished from time-active intervention in that during *time inactive* the employment specialist is totally removed from active involvement with and/or active observation of the consumer.

TRAVEL/TRANSPORT TIME

Travel/transport time denotes all time spent by an employment specialist traveling to and from the job site, to a meeting with the consumer and/or the consumer's family in their home, or to a meeting concerning the consumer with representatives of other agencies. Travel/transport time also refers to all time spent transporting the client to any location such as the job site, a medical appointment, the social security office, and so on.

Travel/transport time is particularly important in supported employment programs serving a predominantly rural or large geographic area. In this instance travel/transport time will represent a significant cost to the program.

CONSUMER TRAINING TIME

Consumer training time refers to all activities engaged in by an employment specialist that involve training the consumer in areas other than the consumer's specific job duties and tasks. Consumer training activities in this category will always take place away from the job site. When working with consumers with moderate or severe mental retardation, for example, the employment specialist may provide training in the use of public transportation to get to and from work, establishing a bank account and using banking services for deposits or withdrawals, or the development of appropriate grooming or dressing skills. Counseling activities that may be necessary for individuals with long-term mental illness, for example, would also be included in this category. The key features of intervention in this category are that the employment specialist is actively involved in training or counseling and that this activity take place away from the job site.

CONSUMER PROGRAM DEVELOPMENT

Counsumer program development includes all time spent by an employment specialist in the design and development of instructional plans or programs to assist a specific client. Examples of this type of activity would include developing task analysis or instructional programs for later use in training the consumer at the job site, or developing behavior management programs to deal with a specific inappropriate behavior or a specific work performance problem exhibited by the consumer. Time spent designing adaptive devices or job modifications for a consumer with cerebral palsy would be included in this category, although teaching the consumer to use the device or negotiating a job modification with the employer would not be included. Also, consumer-specific job development activities are *not* included in this category.

Direct Employment Advocacy

Direct employment advocacy refers to all time spent by an employment specialist advocating on behalf of the consumer with individuals at the job site for purposes directly related to employment. Consumer-specific job development activities are included in this category. Also included would be any interactions between the employment specialist and employers, supervisors, coworkers, and customers. For example, the employment specialist may engage in activities designed to encourage the acceptance and support of the consumer by coworkers, to promote the individual's social integration at the job site. Or the employment specialist may attempt to negotiate a change in job duties with the consumer's immediate supervisor to identify duties and tasks that the consumer will be able to perform while exchanging job duties that may be difficult for the consumer to independently perform for extended periods of time. Direct employment advocacy must involve advocacy activities with individuals present in the consumer's work environment.

Indirect Employment Advocacy

Indirect employment advocacy refers to all activities engaged in by the employment specialist while advocating on behalf of the consumer with individuals not directly present at the work site. Examples of these activities would include advocacy efforts directed towards bus drivers for individuals using public transportation to get to and from the work site, working with school personnel for consumers still enrolled in public school programs, meeting with caregivers and family members regarding concerns they may have about the consumer participating in the supported employment program, assisting the consumer in dealing with problems that may arise regarding his or her Supplemental Security Income or Social Security Disability Insurance status, or helping the consumer deal with landlords, bank personnel, or other individuals. Key features of activities in this area are that the individuals involved are not directly present at the job site and that the activity involves advocating for or assisting the consumer rather than training the consumer to perform a specific task.

CONSUMER SCREENING/EVALUATION

Consumer screening/evaluation refers to any time spent by an employment specialist while collecting or analyzing any information relevant to a consumer's employment potential or any time devoted to recording and communicating the consumer's progress while participating in supported employment. Activities related to evaluating eligible consumers might include such things as screening consumer referrals to determine eligibility for services, reviewing consumer records, observing the consumer in simulated work settings or at the consumer's day program prior to admission to the program, or interviewing the consumer to determine the consumer's work attitudes and employment preferences. Activities relating to communicating the consumer's progress might include recording information for inclusion in the information system, developing written reports regarding the consumer, or communicating the results of these reports to family members, caregivers, or other agencies.

The description of these eight categories of intervention illustrates the scope and variety of activities regularly engaged in by employment specialists. It is important to note that intervention as defined in the information system refers only to activities engaged in on behalf of a *specific* consumer. Activities of a general nature (community job screenings, staff development activities, program staff meetings, etc.) would not be considered consumer-specific intervention time. Excluding community survey and general job development activities from consumer-specific intervention time is not meant in any way to minimize their importance. These activities are essential elements of any successful supported employment program and may take up a substantial amount of employment specialists' time. In most instances, however, local programs are only able to request reimbursement from agencies funding initial placement and training for job development activities conducted on behalf of a specific consumer. General community awareness and survey activities are viewed as program operating expenses. Within the RRTC Supported Employment Management Information System, therefore, emphasis has been placed on job development activities that focus on finding a suitable job for an individual consumer.

It is also important to recognize that in almost all instances intervention may only be provided by the employment specialist actively involved in job development, job-site training, or ongoing support activities. Activities of supported employment program supervisors or administrators, which in a few instances may be focused on behalf of a specific consumer, are generally felt to be designed to assist or support the employment specialist, and therefore would not be viewed as consumer-specific intervention.

EMERGING TRENDS IN THE AMOUNT OF SERVICES PROVIDED TO CONSUMERS

To investigate the specific types of activities engaged in most frequently by employment specialists, a comprehensive analysis was completed that examined all reported intervention time provided to consumers tracked through the Supported Employment Management Information System. A total of 980 consumers with a variety of diagnosed primary disabilities are represented in the current analysis. The 980 individuals received a total of 139,220 hours of reported intervention over 10 years. The large amount of intervention time reported reflects patterns of services provided by literally hundreds of employment specialists over that period and permits an analysis of the amount and types of services required by diverse groups of individuals with developmental and other disabilities.

By far the largest group of individuals contained in the sample of 980 consumers were persons previously diagnosed as mentally retarded. Persons with moderate or severe mental retardation made up 38.5 percent of the total, while individuals with mild or borderline mental retardation accounted for another 49.6 percent of the entire group. Other groups represented in the data base in relatively large numbers included persons with traumatic brain injury (1.6 percent) and individuals with long-term mental illness (4.9 percent). Fifty-three individuals with other identified primary disabilities such as autism, cerebral palsy and other physical disabilities, and sensory impairments, were also represented. However, total numbers in these categories were relatively small, and individuals with these primary disabilities were not included in subsequent analyses. Table 1 describes the number of individuals served and the number of intervention hours provided across all consumers represented in the data base.

To fully understand the type and amount of services provided to consumers, it is important to first consider some of the key employment outcomes achieved by the individuals represented in the system. Factors such as the number of different jobs held, the total number of weeks employed, and the number of hours worked per week will have a significant effect upon the amount of intervention provided to consumers. Table 2 summarizes these key employment outcomes for the consumers in the data base. Almost half (49.4 percent) of the consumers represented were reported to have more than one identified disability. To investigate the possibility that individuals with multiple disabilities may require more intensive, unique services, these individuals have been included in all subsequent analyses.

The consumers held an average of 1.27 jobs per person, ranging from a low of 1.13 jobs for individuals with traumatic brain injuries to a high of 1.34 jobs for persons with moderate or severe mental retardation. To a large degree the number of jobs can be interpreted as an indicator of a person's stability on the job. Those groups with a lower average number of jobs held generally had a higher rate of employment retention. Remarkable consistency was found when the average number of hours worked by consumers per week was analyzed. All means in this area fell between 25 and 28 hours per week.

The total number of weeks employed was also computed for each of the groups of consumers. The mean for all consumers was 48 weeks, indicating that the average individual had worked approximately one year. Table 2 indicates two significant exceptions to this average. Individuals with traumatic brain injuries were employed an average of 29 weeks and persons with long-term mental illness averaged 26 weeks of employment. The primary reason that these two groups have

Table 1. Number of Individuals Served and Number of Intervention Hours Provided by Primary Disability

	Number of consumers placed	Percentage of consumers placed	Number of intervention hours provided	Percentage total intervention hours provided
Traumatic brain injury	16	1.6	4,109	3.0
Long-term mental illness	48	4.9	4,722	3.4
Moderate/severe mental retardation	377	38.5	57,927	41.6
Mild/borderline mental retardation	486	49.6	65,218	46.8
Other primary disabilities	53	5.4	7,244	5.2
All consumers	980	100.0	139,220	100.0

Table 2. Key Employment Outcomes for Individuals with Various Primary Disabilities

	All consumers	More than one reported disability	Traumatic brain injury	Long-term mental illness	Moderate/severe mental retardation	Mild/borderline mental retardation
Total number of consumers placed	980	484	16	48	377	486
Average number of jobs per consumer	1.27	1.28	1.13	1.25	1.34	1.24
Average number of hours worked per week	26	25	26	28	25	26
Average number of weeks employed	48	50	29	25	56	47
Average number of intervention hours per consumer placed	142	158	256	98.4	153	134
Average number of intervention hours adjusted to a hypothethical job of 40 hours per week and 52 weeks	187	205	630	234	170	184

worked a shorter time is that the programs represented in the data base that focus on placing these individuals have been in existence for only a short time, and consumers from these disability groups have not yet had the opportunity to work for extended periods. It would be erroneous to interpret these averages to mean that individuals with traumatic brain injury or long-term mental illness are unable to hold a job for an extended time in supported employment programs. The only justifiable conclusion to be drawn from this data is that individuals with primary disabilities other than mental retardation have only recently begun to be incorporated into supported employment programs.

Table 2 also contains information on the average number of hours of intervention provided to individual consumers. In fee-for-service supported employment programs, in which local programs charge a funding agency for each hour of service delivered, the number of intervention hours each person receives directly determines the costs of serving individual consumers (Kregel, Hill, & Banks, 1987). To account for differences among the groups in the average hours worked per week and the total number of weeks worked, intervention figures were adjusted to a hypothetical job of 40 hours per week in which the consumer had been employed 52 weeks.

The adjusted figures reveal that a relatively consistent amount of intervention is provided to individuals in the various groups. Several significant trends emerge from a close examination of these data. First, as might be anticipated, individuals with more than one reported disability required slightly more intervention time than individuals diagnosed as mentally retarded. Second, it is also important to point out that individuals with moderate or severe mental retardation required the lowest amount of adjusted intervention time. This is a particularly significant finding in light of the fact that some rehabilitation professionals have expressed concerns that it may prove too costly to serve individuals with the most severe handicaps in supported employment programs (Shafer, 1988). Finally, the higher figures for persons with traumatic brain injury and long-term mental illness, as discussed previously, result from newly established supported employment programs (Wehman *et al.*, 1988) and are based on such a relatively small number of individuals that definitive conclusions are simply not possible at this time.

TYPES OF SERVICES PROVIDED BY EMPLOYMENT SPECIALISTS

In order to investigate the amount of time employment specialists were engaged in different activities, relative percentages of intervention time reported for each of the eight categories on the Consumer-Specific Intervention Time Recording Form were computed. In this section, the results of this analysis will first be discussed based upon combined data from all 980 consumers. Relative percentages for each of the previously identified groups will then be presented in an attempt to determine whether consumers with various primary disabilities require different types of employment specialist services.

Table 3 displays the relative percentage of intervention time reported in each of the eight categories for all consumers. Several interesting findings emerge from a close examination of these data. Over half of all intervention time (55.4 percent) was devoted to active time on the job site directly training the consumer. Another 12.4 percent of employment specialists' time was spent in inactive time on the job site, indicating that employment specialists spent at least two-thirds of their reported time directly on the job site. In contrast, a very small percentage of time (3.1 percent) was devoted to consumer screening and evaluation. This illustrates that supported employment programs emphasize the delivery of intensive services to the consumer *after* the individual is placed on the job rather than extensive preemployment evaluation and testing services.

Another major component of the individual placement model as defined by Moon *et al.* (1986) is its commitment to advocacy services on behalf of the consumer throughout the employment process. This commitment is documented in the data contained in Table 3. A combined total of 10.7 percent of the employment specialists' time was spent in either direct or indirect employment advocacy. An equivalent amount of time

Table 3. Percentage of Consumer-Specific Intervention Devoted to
Specific Activities ($N = 980$)

Category	Percentage of intervention time reported
Active time on job site	55.4
Inactive time on job site	12.4
Travel and transport time	11.0
Consumer training time	3.4
Consumer program development	4.1
Direct employment advocacy	6.8
Indirect employment advocacy	3.9
Consumer screening and evaluation	3.1

(11.0 percent) was spent in travel and transport activities, while consumer training and consumer program development activities accounted for 3.1 percent and 4.2 percent of employment specialist's time respectively.

It is very important to point out that not all activities engaged in by employment specialists are directed toward serving an individual consumer. Therefore, time spent in activities included in the Consumer-Specific Intervention Time Recording Form do not represent the entirety of an employment specialist's weekly or monthly activities. Employment specialists routinely spend a significant amount of time in activities such as surveying the community for potential jobs and engaging in general (not consumer-specific) job development, attending staff meetings, receiving in-service training, meeting with representatives of other agencies, and a variety of other functions. Thus, the data contained in Table 3 should not be interpreted as percentages of a 40-hour employment specialist work week.

The percentages contained in Table 3 should be interpreted in the context of the total amount of time the employment specialist has available for consumer-specific intervention. It has been estimated that approximately 65 percent of an employment specialist's time is devoted to consumer-specific intervention throughout the course of a year (RRTC, 1988). An employment specialist who works a typical 40-hour work week, for example, would have approximately 26 hours available for consumer specific intervention. The 55.4 percent of the time devoted to active time on the job site should be viewed as a percentage of the 26 available hours, indicating in this instance that an *average* of about 14 hours per week will be spent by this employment specialist in active training time on the job site. It must also be remembered that these percentages represent averages across a year or more of time. During some time periods, such as initial consumer training, the employment specialist in fact may spend 100 percent of the time for several weeks in active time on the job site.

Percentages of intervention time across the identified groups of individuals are provided in Table 4. While the data across groups are quite consistent, several trends appear that may be used to justify hypotheses for future testing. For example, when serving individuals with traumatic brain injury, employment specialists tended to spend a little less of their time in active training on the job site and a larger portion of their time in direct and indirect employment advocacy. This finding may reflect the fact that in most communities an active case management system is not in place to meet the needs of persons with traumatic brain injury, and employment specialists may be required to devote an extra amount of time advocating on behalf of the consumer with insurance companies, the Social Security Administration, and other agencies. The fact that many of these individuals may possess some degree of physical impairment may require employment specialists to spend time discussing job modifications with employers and co-workers. While it is not possible to confirm these hypotheses from the existing data, they do·generate issues that should be the subject of future investigations.

IMPLICATIONS OF THE FINDINGS ON THE EMERGING ROLE OF THE EMPLOYMENT SPECIALIST

As discussed earlier, the employment specialist is a personnel role that has newly emerged in rehabilitation services for individuals with developmental and other severe disabilities. When compared to placement specialists in transitional em-

Table 4. Intervention Category Percentage by Primary Disability of Individuals Served

	More than one reported disability	Traumatic brain injury	Long-term mental illness	Moderate/severe mental retardation	Mild/borderline mental retardation
Active time on job site	56.8	49.4	54.3	55.1	57.6
Inactive time on job site	12.2	12.9	7.0	11.7	13.4
Travel and transport time	10.5	12.3	12.2	11.8	10.3
Consumer training time	3.1	1.5	7.0	3.3	3.3
Consumer program development	4.2	5.1	2.4	4.1	4.2
Direct employment advocacy	6.4	8.7	6.7	6.9	5.7
Indirect employment advocacy	3.7	5.2	4.1	3.7	3.1
Consumer screening and evaluation	3.1	5.0	6.3	2.6	2.6

ployment programs, for example, employment specialists obviously provide more intensive services on the job site for a much greater period of time. To this point little has been known about the day-to-day activities of these individuals. The present analysis—given the fact that it documents the activities of over 200 employment specialists who have served almost 1,000 diverse consumers—begins to shed light on the major duties and responsibilities of this new role.

It is clear that employment specialists engage in a wide variety of activities requiring an array of sophisticated skills. Individuals filling this role must be proficient at marketing the supported employment service, able to develop job analyses and design job modifications, and be highly skilled in direct training methodologies. At the same time, employment specialists must have the communication skills to coordinate their efforts with family members and personnel in other agencies, as well as the ability to effectively advocate with a variety of individuals on behalf of the consumers they serve. This diversity in job duties makes the role of employment specialist a challenging occupation.

It is also readily apparent from this analysis that employment specialists spend a vast amount of their time performing activities away from the facility in which they may be based. In addition to the time spent directly on the job site training the consumer, which makes up the bulk of their activities, all of the time spent in travel and transport activities and much of the time spent in consumer training, employment advocacy, and consumer screening and evaluation functions take place in the community. This means that employment specialists will often spend long periods of time isolated from other individuals performing the same duties, which makes it difficult for them to provide support and assistance to their colleagues.

That fact that employment specialists spend so much time away from their home facility also presents a challenge for their supervisors. It frequently becomes very difficult for supervisors to observe the employment specialists while they perform their major job duties, in order to provide feedback and evaluation. Additionally, significant logistical problems may arise when attempting to schedule in-service activities, or simply to schedule a staff meeting. Managers of supported employment programs obviously need to possess a great deal of flexibility when supervising personnel with whom they may not have a great deal of contact for extended periods of time. Perhaps one of the most surprising findings of this analysis was the significant consistency that existed in the amount and types of services provided to individuals with different primary disabilities. It is frequently suggested that the unique characteristics and needs of various groups of individuals may require different types and amounts of services to enable them to hold jobs successfully through supported employment services. It should be reemphasized that the data presented in this regard are based upon a relative small number of consumers and should be viewed as preliminary in nature. Supported employment program models were first developed almost exclusively to serve individuals with mental retardation, and persons with mental retardation still represent the vast majority of consumers receiving supported employment services through the individual placement model. It is hoped that this analysis will serve as a benchmark against which to compare future efforts designed to provide quality employment outcomes to individuals with a wide array of disabilities for whom competitive employment in integrated work settings has not previously occurred.

REFERENCES

Bellamy, G. T., Rhodes, L., Mank, D. M., & Albin, J. E. (1988). *Supported employment: A community implementation guide.* Baltimore, MD: Paul H. Brookes.

Inge, K., Barcus, M., & Everson, J. M. (1988). Developing inservice training programs for supported employment personnel. In P. Wehman & M. S. Moon (Eds.), *Vocational Rehabilitation and Supported Employment*, (pp. 145–161). Baltimore: Paul H. Brookes Publishing Co.

Kregel, J., Hill, M., & Banks, P. D. (1987). An analysis of employment specialist intervention time in supported competitive employment: 1979–1987. In P. Wehman, J. Kregel, M. Shafer & M. Hill (Eds.), *Competitive employment for persons with mental retardation: From research to practice*, (pp. 84–111). Richmond: Virginia Commonwealth University.

Kregel, J., & Sale, P. (1988). Pre-service personnel preparation of supported employment specialists. In P. Wehman & M. S. Moon (Eds.), *Supported Employment and Vocational Rehabilitation*, (pp. 129–143). Baltimore: Paul H. Brookes.

Mank, D. M., Rhodes, L. E., & Bellamy, G. T. (1986). Four supported employment alternatives. In W. E. Kiernan & J. A. Stark (Eds.), *Pathways to employment for adults with developmental disabilities*, (pp. 139–154). Baltimore: Paul H. Brookes.

Moon, M. S., Goodall, P., Barcus, M., & Brooke, V. (1986). *The supported work model of competitive employment for citizens with severe handicaps: A guide for job trainers*. Richmond: Virginia Commonwealth University.

RRTC (1987). *Data management system operations manual (second edition)*. Richmond: Author.

RRTC (1988). *Interagency vendorization: Expanding supported employment services*. Richmond, VA: Virginia Commonwealth University.

Rusch, F. R. (1986). *Competitive employment issues and strategies*. Baltimore: Paul H. Brookes.

Schalock, R. L., & Hill, M. (1986). Evaluating employment services. In W. E. Kiernan & J. A. Stark (Eds.), *Pathways to employment for adults with developmental disabilities*, (pp. 285–304). Baltimore: Paul H. Brookes.

Shafer, M. (1988). *A national survey of state agency rehabilitation counselors: An assessment of knowledge, attitudes & training needs regarding supported employment*. Virginia Commonwealth University, Unpublished dissertation.

Wehman, P. (1986). Competitive employment in Virginia. In F. R. Rusch (Ed.), *Competitive employment issues and strategies*, (pp. 23–34). Baltimore: Paul H. Brookes.

Wehman, P., & Kregel, J. (1985). A supported work approach to competitive employment of individuals with moderate and severe handicaps. *Journal of the Association for Persons with Severe Handicaps, 10*(1), 3–11.

Wehman, P., & Kregel, J. (1988). Adult Employment Programs. In Gaylord-Ross, R. (Ed.), *Vocational Education for Persons with Handicaps*, (pp. 205–223). Mountain View, CA: Mayfield Publishing Company.

Wehman, P., Kreutzer, J., Stonnington, H. H., Wood, W., Sherron, P., Diambra, J., Fry, R., & Groah, C. (1988). Supported Employment for Persons with Traumatic Brain Injury: A Preliminary Report. *Journal of Head Trauma Rehabilitation, 3*(4), pp. 82–92.

Wehman, P., & Melia, R. (1985). The job coach: Function in transitional and supported employment. *American Rehabilitation, 11*(2), 4–7.

Will, M. (1984). Let us pause and reflect—but not too long. *Exceptional Children, 51*, 11–16.

Winking, D. L., DeStefano, L., & Rusch, F. R. (1988). *Supported Employment in Illinois*: Urbana-Champaign: The Secondary Transition Intervention Effectiveness Institute, University of Illinois.

CHAPTER 8

INTEGRATION IN THE WORKPLACE
Perceptions and Experiences of Employees without Disabilities

Michael S. Shafer, Martha Larus Rice, and Helen M. D. Metzler

For individuals who are severely handicapped, supported employment provides the opportunity for more meaningful and rewarding employment alongside peers who are not handicapped. This opportunity to work in environments that are integrated simultaneously represents the most significant promise of supported employment as well as the most serious challenge facing supported employment (Bellamy *et al.*, 1984; Brown *et al.*, 1984).

The promise of integration lies in the opportunity for workers with severe handicaps to make new acquaintances, to be fully exposed to the nondisabled culture of this country, and to engage in the type of work that is valued and performed by the mainstream of our society. This promise is realized as workers with handicaps become part of the car pool at their

Michael S. Shafer, Martha Larus Rice, and Helen M. D. Metzler ● Rehabilitation Research and Training Center, Virginia Commonwealth University, Richmond, Virginia.

job, or join the company softball team, or attend the company's New Year's Eve party. Unfortunately, this promise is often compromised as workers with handicaps are employed in positions that offer minimal opportunities to interact with others who are not handicapped.

Clearly, one of the challenges facing supported employment is the ability to provide and sustain employment opportunities that afford workers true and valued integration and not simply physical presence within an integrated setting. As demonstrated by research on mainstreaming and educational integration, physical presence or contact is not sufficient to assure interaction (Gaylord-Ross, Haring, Breen, & Pitts-Conway, 1984). Rather, focused and often intensive efforts may be needed to get nondisabled and disabled people to interact (Gaylord-Ross, Stremel-Campbell, & Storey, 1986; Shafer, Egel, & Neef, 1984; Strain, Kerr, & Ragland, 1979).

As supported employment has been implemented by social planners and policy makers (Developmental Disabilities Act, 1987; Vocational Rehabilitation Act Amendments of 1986; Will, 1984), the importance of developing a technology of workplace integration has been enhanced. This young technology thus far includes the identification and assessment of social competency factors related to employment retention (Chadsey-Rusch, 1986; Cheney & Foss, 1984; Foss & Peterson, 1981; Greenspan & Scholtz, 1981; Hill, Hill, Wehman, & Goodall, 1986; Kochany & Keller, 1981; Schalock & Harper, 1978), sociometric strategies for measuring integration (Horner, 1987; Nisbett & Vincent, 1986), and a host of clinical techniques for improving workers' social behavior (Chadsey-Rusch, Karlan, Riva, & Rusch, 1984; Rusch & Menchetti, 1981; Rusch, Weithers, Menchetti, & Schutz, 1980; Shafer, Brooke, & Wehman, 1986; Stanford & Wehman, 1980). While each of these endeavors represent promising and essential aspects for a technology of workplace integration, a more basic element of workplace integration has yet to be defined. Specifically, the values and perceptions assigned to severely disabled workers by nondisabled individuals and the effect that supported employment services has upon these perceptions and values have not been determined.

Previous research has attempted to evaluate these percep-
tions within educational and residential contexts and to identify
variables responsible for their development (see review by
Siperstein & Bak, 1985a). For example, physical appearance
(Siperstein, Budoff, & Bak, 1980), academic performance
(Budoff & Siperstein, 1978), and social behavior (Siperstein &
Bak, 1985b) have all been correlated with specific attitudes and
perceptions about individuals with disabilities.

The impact which *physical* integration in educational or
residential environments has upon these perceptions has also
been studied. Consistently, this research has demonstrated that
physical presence may enhance perceptions while not necessar-
ily affecting interactions or other overt forms of social integration (Brinker & Thorpe, 1986; Voeltz, 1980). Nonetheless,
positive perceptions and values are an essential ingredient for
the occurrence of desired interaction patterns. As discussed by
Fortini (1987), the attitudes that nondisabled individuals have
toward their disabled peers plays a significant role in determining whether social interactions and approaches will occur.

Supported employment would appear to provide the potential for improving the perceptions that nondisabled individuals have toward persons who are handicapped. Sociologists
have studied at length the central position which the performance of productive labor has in the classification of individuals and groups as valued members of society (Savall, 1981;
Wirth, 1983; Stanley, 1978). A reasonable assumption would be
that supported employment consumers are more highly valued
and perceived more positively by nondisabled peers because
they perform productive work that is valued and observed by
these peers. However, a paucity of research is available that
explores the perceptual and attitudinal factors related to vocational integration.

In this chapter, we describe the process of studying vocational integration by surveying nonhandicapped coworkers
of supported employment consumers. In studying vocational
integration we concentrated upon three components that we
considered to be essential for quality social integration to occur.
First, the level of comfort or willingness that nondisabled workers express about working with coworkers who are mentally

retarded was evaluated. Second, the perceptions that these nondisabled workers held regarding the vocational and social competence (Rusch, 1979) of workers with mental retardation was assessed. Finally, we were concerned about the level of contact and interaction that nondisabled workers report they have with coworkers who are mentally retarded.

METHOD

SUBJECTS

Employing Businesses

We surveyed 226 employees of 31 businesses located in two states. Businesses in which employees were surveyed had to meet two criteria. First, all businesses employed a worker with mental retardation who was receiving supported competitive employment services (Wehman & Kregel, 1985) at the time of the survey. Second, the employers or supervisors of each business agreed to allow his other employees to be surveyed.

Only one supported employment consumer was employed at each participating business. The businesses represent a wide array of commercial enterprises, including restaurants, libraries, schools, health care facilities, service providers, and other commercial businesses. Sixty-five percent of these businesses are private for profit, 17 percent are private nonprofit, and another 18 percent are part of the state and local government system.

Surveyed Employees

The 226 surveyed employees were all employed in companies that also employed workers with mental retardation. As indicated by Table 1, these individuals held a variety of positions within their companies, including principal, teacher, waitress, hostess, cashier, chef, kitchen manager, administrator, janitor, bartender, and veterinarian. Over 61 percent of those surveyed were female, 66 percent being 30 years of age or younger. Forty-three percent of those surveyed were currently

Table 1. Employee Characteristics ($N = 226$)

	n	Percentage
Positions held by surveyed co-workers		
Administrative/secretarial/clerical	7	3
Administrative/managerial/supervisory	28	12
Cashiers	8	4
Food service	130	58
Janitorial/custodial/housekeeping	16	7
Shipping/receiving	5	2
Educator	3	1
Miscellaneous	29	13
Age		
20 or younger	54	24
21 to 30	95	42
31 to 40	31	14
41 to 50	28	12
51 and older	18	8
Education		
Less than high school	45	20
High school graduate	83	37
Some college	66	29
College graduate	32	14
Gender		
Male	89	39
Female	137	61

attending or had attended college while another 20 percent had not graduated from high school.

A varying number of employees were surveyed at each site. This variability was due to the different sizes of the businesses, the effort of the employers at each site to distribute and pick up the surveys from the employees, and the willingness of employees to complete the survey. Five employees or less were surveyed at 33 percent of the participating businesses while 6 to 10 employees were surveyed at 48 percent of the businesses. More than 10 employees at any one business represented 18.5 percent of the participating business.

Supported Employment Consumers

The 31 employees with mental retardation who were employed at these businesses were all receiving supported competitive employment services at the time of the survey. These workers had held a total of 46 positions. The employees sampled in this study, and the population of workers with mental retardation for whom the RRTC maintains active files, are demographically comparable in relation to age, sex, functioning level, and job type (see Wehman *et al.*, 1985). Specifically, 79 percent of the workers in this sample were male, with an average age of 30 (range 21 to 66). These workers were functioning predominately in the moderate (61 percent) and mild (23 percent) ranges of mental retardation with smaller samples of workers functioning in the borderline (23 percent), severe (10 percent), and profound (3 percent) ranges.

INSTRUMENTATION

A 33-item questionnaire was designed to be completed by nonhandicapped individuals. This instrument consisted primarily of 21 statements describing various stereotypes or descriptions of individuals with mental retardation. Approximately one-half of these statements described characteristics of social skill competence including such domains as compliance, humor, anger, and appearance. An equally represented number of statements described characteristics of vocational skill competence and included such domains as productivity, quality, ability to acquire novel tasks, and work independence. A smaller set of statements described the employees' willingness to work with a coworker who is mentally retarded.

For each statement, the employee was provided with a five-point Likert scale ranging from Strongly Disagree (1) to Not Sure (3) to Strongly Agree (5) with Agree and Disagree serving as intermediate points. Instructions were provided that directed the employees to circle the statement that most closely described their reaction to each of the statements. The coworkers were instructed to circle one number only.

In addition to the 21 statements, a series of multiple-choice and fill-in questions were provided as well. Five questions were

Table 2. Supported Employment Consumer Characteristics (N = 31)

	Mean	Range
Age	30	21 years to 66 years
Hourly wage	$3.86	$2.90 to $5.64
Hours worked per week	26	6 hours to 40 hours
Total weeks employed[a]	125	3 weeks to 480 weeks
IQ	46	24 to 72

	Percentage
Level of functioning	
Profound	3
Severe	10
Moderate	61
Mild	23
Borderline	3
Type of work	
Food service	63
Janitorial/custodial	29
Unskilled labor	4
Stock clerk warehouse	2
Transportation	2

[a] Consumers may not be employed in their original job; consumers average about 1.4 jobs per person.

included to determine demographic information about the employees. Specific information that was requested included the employees' sex, age, educational level, current position, and job satisfaction. Additionally, questions were presented to assess employees' past experience with individuals who are mentally retarded. Finally, six questions were presented to evaluate employees' current experience in working with coworkers who are mentally retarded. The questionnaire and instructions accompanying the questionnaire can be obtained from the authors. (See Table 2.)

Instrument Development

After the questionnaire was developed and reviewed internally, a group of 9 individuals recognized as leading experts in the areas of supported employment and survey research were asked to review the content of the questionnaire, the wording of the statements and questions, and the array of responses provided. Additionally, the reviewers were asked to identify the items that assessed social competence or vocational competence. Based upon the feedback provided by 8 of these experts, modifications were made to the questionnaire (a copy of the expert panel's comments and reviews may be obtained from the authors). Finally, the questionnaire was evaluated by a reading specialist to ensure that the reading level required to comprehend the questionnaire did not exceed that of the third grade. The questionnaire was then typeset and printed on blue stock as a four-panel fold-out flier.

PROCEDURE

We distributed the questionnaire to 226 employees who were working at 31 different businesses in 2 states. As indicated previously, the selected businesses had to employ a worker with mental retardation at the time of the survey and the employer had to consent to allow his employees to be surveyed. This consent was generally requested when a research team member would contact the employer by telephone and explain the purpose of the survey and the requirements if the survey was to be conducted. The employers were informed that their approval was entirely voluntary and a variety of options were offered to complete the survey. If the employer denied access for the survey to be conducted, the research team member replied that he understood, and thanked the employer for his time.

Employers who agreed to allow their employees to be surveyed were offered three methods for conducting the survey. First, a member of the research team could approach the employees directly, distribute the survey, and wait at the business site until the employees had completed and returned the survey. This was the method that we had preferred; unfortunately, less than 6 percent of the completed questionnaires were collected in this way. Three of the employees who completed the survey in this fashion had the questionnaire read to

them by the research team member because they could not
read. The second approach for completing the survey that was
proposed to the employers was for the research team member
to approach the employees directly, distribute the questionnaires, and return to the business a few days later to collect
them. This method of collection was used for 38 percent of the
completed surveys. The final method of collection relied upon
the employers to distribute and collect the questionnaires. This
approach was utilized for 56 percent of the completed questionnaires.

RESULTS

EMPLOYEES' CONTACT AND EXPERIENCE WITH WORKERS WHO ARE MENTALLY RETARDED

A series of questions were provided to assess employees
past and current experience or contact with individuals who
are mentally retarded. As indicated by the accompanying
figure, less than 17 percent of all surveyed employees indicated
that they had no experience with someone who was mentally
retarded. The specific types of experiences indicated by these
employees varied a great deal. Most frequently, 62 percent of
those responding indicated that they knew someone who was
mentally retarded, while 41 percent of those responding

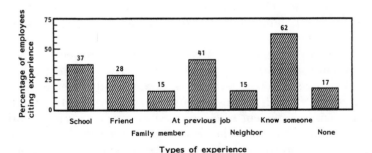

Figure 1. Types of prior experience employees report they have had with
people who are mentally retarded.

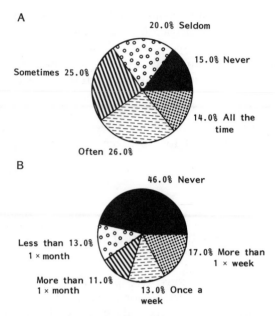

Figure 2. Frequency and type of contact. (A) Frequency with which co-workers depend upon the work of a co-worker with mental retardation. (B) Frequency with which co-workers take breaks or eat lunch with a co-worker who has mental retardation. (C) Frequency with which co-workers have contact at work with co-workers who are mentally retarded. (D) Frequency with which co-workers have social contact after work with a co-worker who has mental retardation.

indicated they had worked with a mentally retarded person in a previous job. Most promising, slightly more than 28 percent of those responding indicated they had a friend who was mentally retarded.

Slightly more than 83 percent of those surveyed indicated they currently worked with someone who was mentally retarded. These individuals will be subsequently referred to as "co-workers" to distinguish them from "non-co-workers"—the remaining 17 percent who indicated that they do *not* currently work with someone who is mentally retarded. Thirty-two percent of the coworkers had worked 6 months or less with a fellow employee who is mentally retarded. Co-workers reporting 6 and 12 months' experience comprised 21 percent of

C

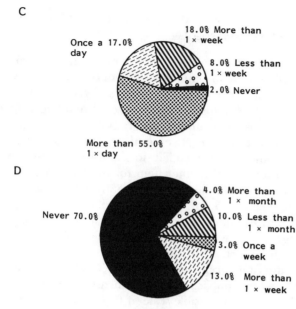

18.0% More than
1 × week

Once a 17.0%
day

8.0% Less than
1 × week

2.0% Never

More than 55.0%
1 × day

D

4.0% More than
1 × month

Never 70.0%

10.0% Less than
1 × month

3.0% Once a
week

13.0% More than
1 × week

Figure 2 (Continued)

those surveyed. Twenty-five percent of the identified co-workers responded that they had worked with a mentally retarded
co-worker for more than 2 years in their current position.

The frequency and type of contact with employees who
are mentally retarded is summarized in the following four pie
charts. As the first pie chart indicates, over 65 percent of those
surveyed indicated that they depended upon a co-worker with
mental retardation to complete their jobs. In contrast, 35
percent of the co-workers indicated that they depend upon a
mentally retarded worker seldomly (20 percent) or never (15
percent).

Over 72 percent of those responding indicated they had
contact at least daily with a co-worker who was mentally retarded. However, the context of this contact appears to be
primarily work-related, as over 46 percent of the co-workers
indicated they never take a break or have lunch, while another
70 percent of the co-workers responded they never saw their
mentally retarded co-worker after work.

Employees' Willingness to Work with a Co-worker Who Is Mentally Retarded

Three statements on the questionnaire assessed the comfort and willingness of employees in working with individuals who are mentally retarded. The responses were combined and normed across the items for each survey containing responses to all three items to create a Comfort Index. Since two of the statements expressed negative comfort, response patterns to these statements were recoded to conform to the positive response patterns of the other item for the score on the Comfort Index. For example, the 1 for "Strongly Disagree" was recoded to become 5 for "Strongly Agree" and so on. The normed Comfort Index scores ranged from 3, indicating complete disagreement with the three statements, to 15, indicating complete agreement.

The interitem reliability for the Comfort Index was computed using Cronbach's alpha (Bohrnstedt & Knoke, 1982) and yielded .80 on a possible scale of 0.00 to 1.00. Coefficients in excess of .70 are commonly considered to be acceptable (Bohrnstedt & Knoke, 1982). Means and standard deviations for the individual and summed scores comprising the Comfort Index are contained in the accompanying table.

As these data indicate, co-workers of persons with mental retardation express slightly more comfort than non-co-workers. These differences were statistically significant for only the third statement in Table 3, "I would be willing to work with someone who has mental retardation," $F(1,222) = 10.33$, $p < .001$. Additionally, analyses of variance conducted to assess relationships between employees' expressed comfort and their demographic characteristics yielded one statistically significant finding. Employees with less education provided Comfort Index scores that were statistically significantly lower than scores provided by employees with more education; $F(3,218) = 6.74$, $p < .005$.

Post hoc analyses using Student-Newman Keuls Test revealed that employees who indicated they had not graduated from high school yielded significantly lower Comfort Index scores ($\overline{X} = 11.13$) than the other three categories: employees

Table 3. Employee Sample: Comfort Index

	Co-worker			Non-co-worker		
	n	Mean	SD	n	Mean	SD
Comfort Index[a]	188	12.48	2.38	36	11.75	2.37
Individual items[b]						
If I had my choice, I would *not* want to work with a person who has MR.	186	1.79	0.94	36	1.97	0.97
I feel uncomfortable working around someone who has mental retardation.	187	1.89	1.04	36	2.06	1.04
I would be willing to work with someone who has mental retardation.	188	4.23	0.74	36	3.78	0.83

[a] The possible range on this index is from 3 to 15.
[b] 1 = strongly disagree; 2 = disagree; 3 = not sure; 4 = agree; 5 = strongly agree.

with some college experience ($\overline{X} = 13.10$), high school graduates ($\overline{X} = 12.34$), or college graduates ($\overline{X} = 12.81$).

EMPLOYEES' PERCEPTIONS OF THE VOCATIONAL COMPETENCE OF CO-WORKERS

Seven items from the questionnaire were designed to evaluate the perceptions the nondisabled employees held of the vocational competence (Rusch, 1979) of the workers with mental retardation. Cronbach alpha tests indicate an inter-item reliability between these items at .72.

These items were summed for each complete survey, producing a *Vocational Index*. Three of the statements comprising this index expressed negative stereotypes regarding vocational competence. Consequently, responses to these items were reversed when summing for the index; response patterns to these statements were recoded to conform to the positive response patterns of the other items for the score on the Vocational Index. For example, the 1 for "Strongly Disagree" was recoded to become 5 for "Strongly Agree," and so on. The normed Vocational Index scores ranged from 7, indicating complete disagreement with the statements, to 35, indicating complete agreement. The nonreversed means and standard deviations for the individual items and the summed Vocational Index of both the employee samples (co-workers and non-co-workers) are presented in Table 4.

Analysis of variance failed to identify any statistically significant differences in the response patterns of employees

Table 4. Employee Sample: Vocational Index

	Co-worker			Non-co-worker		
	n	Mean	SD	*n*	Mean	SD
Vocational Index[a]	188	20.98	4.21	36	21.00	4.49
Individual items[b]						
People with MR usually do their share of the work.	185	3.83	0.91	35	3.86	0.73
People with MR are more likely to get hurt on the job than other people.	188	2.49	0.93	35	2.66	1.03
People with MR are best at doing simple jobs where they do the same thing over and over again.	185	3.59	1.07	36	3.36	1.07
People with MR take just as long as other workers to learn a new job.	188	2.99	1.05	36	2.86	1.15
People with MR can do their jobs just as fast as those without mental retardation.	185	2.96	1.07	35	2.94	0.91
Individual items[b]						
People who have MR can meet the same work standards as other people.	187	3.20	1.06	36	3.47	0.88
People with MR need more direction than other workers.	184	3.71	1.00	36	3.83	0.74

[a] The possible range on this index is from 7 to 35.
[b] 1 = strongly disagree; 2 = disagree; 3 = not sure; 4 = agree; 5 = strongly agree.

identified as co-workers and non-co-workers. As the data in Table 4 suggest, employees from both samples expressed comparable perceptions about the vocational competence of persons with mental retardation.

EMPLOYEES' PERCEPTIONS OF THE SOCIAL COMPETENCE OF CO-WORKERS

Nine items from the questionnaire were considered to address issues regarding the social competence (Rusch, 1979) of the workers with mental retardation. Cronbach alpha tests (Bohrnstedt & Knoke, 1982) indicate an interitem reliability for these nine items was .53. Because of the low correlation of items 3 and 4 with the other variables included in the index, these items were eliminated from the index. After the elimination of items 3 and 4, the interitem reliability test produced an alpha of .57. The remaining 7 items will be referrred to as the *Social Index*. One of the statements comprising this index expressed a negative stereotype regarding social competence. Consequently, response patterns to this statement were recoded to conform to the positive response patterns of the other items for the score on the Social Index. The normed Social Index scores ranged from 7, indicating complete disagreement with the statements, to 35, indicating complete agreeement. The nonreversed means and standard deviations for the individual items and the summed Social Index of both the employee samples (co-workers and non-co-workers) are presented in Table 5.

As these data indicate, employees from both samples (co-workers and non-co-workers) expressed comparable perceptions regarding the social competence of persons with mental retardation. Analyses of variance identified one significant relationship as coworkers more consistently agreed with the first statement in Table 5 (People with mental retardation make friends easily at work) than non-co-workers, $F (1,218) = 4.09$, $p < .05$. No other relationships were noted between the individual or summed items assessing social competence and employee sample (co-worker versus non-co-worker) or employees' personal demographics.

Table 5. Employee Sample: Social Index

	Co-worker			Non-co-worker		
	n	Mean	SD	n	Mean	SD
Social Index[a]	188	24.11	3.75	36	23.61	3.80
Individual items[b]						
People who have MR make friends easily at work.	184	3.90	0.84	36	3.58	0.91
People with MR don't get mad any easier than people without MR.	186	3.32	1.07	36	3.03	1.08
People with MR look neat and clean at work.	186	3.68	0.90	36	3.67	0.79
People with MR don't always do what they are told to at work.	188	2.76	1.14	35	2.94	1.08
People with MR are more patient on the job than most people.	186	3.02	1.05	35	3.09	0.78
People with MR are just like anyone else.	187	3.44	1.17	36	3.69	0.95
People with MR can have a normal social life.	188	3.72	0.93	35	3.77	0.81

[a] The possible range on this index is from 7 to 35.
[b] 1 = strongly disagree; 2 = disagree; 3 = not sure; 4 = agree; 5 = strongly agree.

DISCUSSION

Supported competitive employment provides the opportunity for integration to occur. As employment specialists gradually reduce their amount of intervention and assistance at the job site (Kregel, Hill, & Banks, 1987), supported employment consumers and their nondisabled coworkers are left to initiate their own interactions, develop their own friendships, and settle their own arguments without the assistance (or hindrance) of employment specialists.

The results obtained in this survey of coworkers indicate that vocational integration of nondisabled workers and workers who are mentally retarded is primarily concentrated upon issues surrounding the performance of work. Sixty-five percent of those surveyed were at least sometimes dependent upon a mentally retarded co-worker to complete their own tasks. Clearly, the majority of individuals with mental retardation who are represented in this survey appear to be well integrated with regard to the performance of vocational activity. These individuals are performing tasks that are essential to the operation of their job sites and valued by their fellow employees or employers (Shafer, Hill, Seyfarth, & Wehman, 1987).

In spite of the integration or interdependence of tasks performed by the supported employment consumers, these individuals do not appear to be well integrated within the social fabric or network of their co-workers. Although 72 percent of the responding co-workers have daily contact with a mentally retarded employee, 46 percent indicate that they *never* take a break or lunch with the employee. These results are not surprising and in fact support related research regarding the generalized effects of planned interventions (Gersten, Crowell, & Bellamy, 1986; Halpern, Nave, Close, & Nelson, 1986; Stokes & Baer, 1977).

Consistently, the impact of interventions has been shown to generalize or spread to only those areas in which the intervention was applied (Halpern *et al.*, 1986). As noted by Stokes and Baer (1977), generalization occurs only when it is planned. As such, the infrequency with which nondisabled co-workers report to interact with mentally retarded co-workers during break or after work is reflective of the intervention(s) (or lack thereof) by employment specialists. Simply put, integration at break and lunch may not be occurring because employment specialists do not focus sufficient intervention efforts on these activities.

Although social skill development is certainly identified to be an important aspect of job-site training (Moon *et al.*, 1986; Shafer, 1986; Wehman & Kregel, 1985), the primary emphasis of skill training provided by employment specialists is vocational task performance. Concentrated efforts to enhance the social skills or social integration of supported employment consumers has been reported in only a handful of reports

(Rusch *et al.*, 1980; Shafer *et al.*, 1986; Stanford & Wehman, 1980). Similarly, training manuals and textbooks developed for employment specialists have typically provided limited attention to the issues of social interaction and peer relationships (cf. Moon *et al.*, 1986; Rusch, 1986). Clearly, increased emphasis must be placed upon the development of strategies that foster social contact between disabled and nondisabled employees.

A significant finding of this study was the relative comfort and willingness expressed by co-workers about working with someone who is mentally retarded. As previously noted, significantly more co-workers than non-co-workers expressed a willingness to work with people who are mentally retarded. Two hypotheses may be developed to explain this finding. First, co-workers may express more comfort in order to conform their feelings and values about persons who are mentally retarded with their actual experience of working with such individuals. In short, these co-workers may be attempting to minimize the amount of cognitive dissonance they experience.

An alternative hypothesis is that physical integration in the workplace enhances the acceptance of individuals with mental retardation by their nondisabled peers. This hypothesis does appear to be partly supported as a statistically significantly higher level of agreement was noted by coworkers regarding the statement, "Persons with mental retardation make friends easily at work." Specifically, 80 percent of the co-workers agreed or strongly agreed with this statement, in contrast to only 41 percent of the non-co-workers.

A disappointing and as yet unexplained finding was the nonsignificant differences in the perceptions expressed by employees of both samples about the social and vocational competence of persons who are identified as mentally retarded. We had hypothesized that employees identified as co-workers of individuals who are mentally retarded would express more positive perceptions than employees identified as non-co-workers. Furthermore, we had expected employees' perceptions to be more positive about social competence as opposed to vocational competence (Shafer *et al.*, 1987). Our results fail to suggest that experience in the workplace has any positive (or for that matter negative) effect upon the way nondisabled employees perceive the competence of individuals with mental retardation. Furthermore, these results do not suggest that employees perceive persons with mental retardation to be more socially competent rather than vocationally competent. In fact, these results suggest fairly comparable perceptions for both domains.

A close inspection of the individual item scores for the social and vocational indices suggest that employees, regardless of their sample designation, express slightly more positive perceptions about the social competence of workers with mental retardation in comparison to the vocational competence of these workers. While these differences were statistically insignificant, they do provide tentative support to similar findings obtained from employers (Shafer *et al.*, 1987; Shafer, Kregel, Banks, & Hill, in press).

A number of methodological considerations can be identified that adversely affect the validity of these findings. First, the nondisabled employees surveyed in this study represent a nonrandom sample from two metropolitan areas. It is reasonable to assume that replication efforts conducted in other states or geographical regions (e.g., rural) might produce different findings. Second, the designation of coworkers and non-coworkers that we applied were entirely reliant upon responses provided by the surveyed employees. While all businesses sampled in this study were known to employ workers with mental retardation, it is safe to assume that many of the employees of these businesses were not aware of the mentally retarded worker. Third, the relatively low inter-item reliability of the Social Index weakens the results of these findings and suggests the need for additional instrumentation efforts. Fourth, all of the supported employment consumers represented in this survey were identified to be mentally retarded.

Future research assessing the social integration and perceptions of other supported employment consumers (e.g., chronically mentally ill, traumatically brain injured, physically handicapped) is needed. Finally, the supported employment consumers represented by this survey are all recipients of one form of supported employment, supported competitive employment. It is reasonable to assume that nondisabled employees who are exposed to workers with mental retardation employed under different arrangements (enclaves, entrepreneurial models) would report different perceptions and levels of integration.

IMPLICATIONS FOR INTEGRATION IN THE WORKPLACE

The results of this study present a number of implications regarding the delivery of supported employment and the social integration of workers who are disabled. First, employment specialists need to provide services to ensure that their consumers experience maximal social integration in the workplace. In particular, implementing strategies to enhance social contact during breaks or lunch (Rusch *et al.*, 1980) would appear to be warranted. Second, employment specialists need to actively program for social integration to occur after work with nondisabled peers. Efforts to involve co-workers to provide after-work integration or the development of nonwork-related social integration services may represent areas for future research and development. Third, employment specialists should continue to enhance and improve the vocational competence of their consumers. While these consumers may be viewed as more socially competent, vocational incompetence generally results in getting fired (Hill *et al.*, 1986). Finally, employment specialists should recognize and market the competencies that are frequently valued by employers and employees alike: qualities such as friendliness, loyalty, and satisfactory job performance.

ACKNOWLEDGMENTS. Development of this chapter was supported in part by Grants G008635235 and G008301124 from the National Institute on Disability and Rehabilitation Research, U. S. Department of Education. The opinions expressed in this chapter are solely those of the authors and no endorsement from the Department is to be assumed. The authors gratefully acknowledge the assistance of Carole Jesiolowski, Randy Keen, Michael Haring, Trudie Hughes, and Susan Killam for data collection and entry; and the guidance and consultation of John Kregel, P. David Banks, and John Seyfarth.

REFERENCES

Bellamy, G. T., Rhodes, L. E., Wilcox, B., Albin, J. M., Mank, D. M., Boles, S. M., Horner, R. H., Collins, M., & Turner, J. (1984). Quality and equality in employment services for adults with severe disabilities. *The Journal of the Association for Persons with Severe Handicaps, 9,* 270–277.

Bohrnstedt, G. W., & Knoke, D. (1982). *Statistics for social data analysis.* Illinois: F. E. Peacock Publishers Inc.

Brown, L., Shiraga, B., York, J., Kessler, K., Strohm, B., Rogan, P., Sweet, M., Zanella, K., VanDeventer, P., & Loomis, R. (1984). Integrated work opportunities for adults with severe handicaps: The extended training option. *The Journal of the Association for Persons with Severe Handicaps, 9,* 262–269.

Budoff, M., & Siperstein, G. N. (1978). Low income children's attitudes toward the mentally retarded: Effects of labeling and academic behavior. *American Journal of Mental Deficiency, 82,* 474–478.

Chadsey-Rusch, J. (1986). Identifying and teaching valued social behaviors. In F. R. Rusch (Ed.), *Competitive employment issues and strategies* (pp. 273–288). Baltimore: Paul H. Brookes.

Chadsey-Rusch, J., Karlan, G. R., Riva, M. T., & Rusch, F. R. (1984). Competitive employment: Teaching conversational skills to adults who are mentally retarded. *Mental Retardation, 22*(5), 218–225.

Cheney, D., & Foss, G. (1984). An examination of the social behavior of mentally retarded workers. *Education and Training of the Mentally Retarded, 19,* 216–221.

Fortini, M. E. (1987). Attitudes and behavior toward students with handicaps by their nonhandicapped peers. *American Journal of Mental Deficiency, 92,* 78–84.

Foss, G., & Peterson, S. L. (1981). Social-interpersonal skills relevant to job tenure for mentally retarded adults. *Mental Retardation, 19*(3), 103–106.

Gaylord-Ross, R., Haring, N., Breen, C., & Pitts-Conway, V. (1984). The training and generalization of social interaction skills with autistic youth. *Journal of Applied Behavior Analysis, 17,* 198–199.

Gersten, R., Crowell, F., & Bellamy, G. T. (1986). Spillover effects: Impact of vocational training on the lives of severely mentally retarded clients. *American Journal on Mental Deficiency, 90*(5), 501–506.

Greenspan, S., & Sholtz, B. (1981). Why mentally retarded adults lose their jobs: Social competence as a factor in work adjustment. *Applied Research in Mental Retardation, 2,* 23–38.

Halpern, A. S., Nave, G., Close, D. W., & Nelson, D. J. (1986). *An empirical analysis of the dimensions of community adjustment for adults with mental retardation.* University of Oregon, Eugene, unpublished manuscript.

Hill, J., Hill, M., Wehman, P., & Goodall, P. (1986). Differential reasons for job separation of previously employed mentally retarded persons across measured intelligence levels. *Mental Retardation, 24*(6), 347–351.

Kochany, L., & Keller, J. (1981). An analysis and evaluation of the failures of severly disabled individuals in competitive employment. In P. Wehman

(Ed.), *Competitive employment: New horizons for severely disabled individuals.* Baltimore: Paul H. Brookes.

Kregel, J., Hill, M., & Banks, P. D. (1987). An analysis of employment specialist intervention time in supported competitive employment: 1979–1987. In P. Wehman, J. Kregel, M. Shafer, & M. Hill (Eds.), *Competitive employment for persons with mental retardation: From research to practice,* (pp. 84–111). Richmond: Virginia Commonwealth University, Rehabilitation Research and Training Center.

Moon, S., Goodall, P., Barcus, M., & Brooke, V. (Eds.). (1986). *The supported work model of competitive employment for citizens with severe handicaps: A guide for job trainers.* Richmond, VA: Virginia Commonwealth University, Rehabilitation Research and Training Center.

Nisbet, J., & Vincent, L. (1986). The differences in inappropriate behavior and instructional interactions in sheltered and nonsheltered work environments. *The Journal of the Association for Persons with Severe Handicaps, 11*(1), 19–27.

Rusch, F. R. (1979). Toward the validation of social/vocational survival skills. *Mental Retardation, 17*(3), 143–145.

Rusch, F. R. (in press). *Competitive employment: Service delivery models, methods, and issues.* Baltimore: Paul H. Brookes.

Rusch, F. R. (in press). Competitive employment for mentally retarded persons. *Mental Retardation.*

Rusch, F. R., & Menchetti, B. M. (1981). Increasing compliant work behaviors in a non-sheltered work setting. *Mental Retardation, 19*(3), 107–112.

Rusch, F. R., Weithers, J., Menchetti, B., & Schutz, R. (1980). Social validation of a program to reduce topic repetition in a non-sheltered setting. *Education and Treatment of the Mentally Retarded, 15,* 208–215.

Savall, H. (1981). Work and people: An economic evaluation of job enrichment. In A. G. Wirth (Ed.), *Productive work—In industry and schools: Becoming persons again.* New York: University Press of America.

Schalock, R. L., & Harper, R. S., 1978. Placement from community-based mental retardation programs: How well do clients do? *American Journal of Mental Deficiency, 83*(3), 240–247.

Shafer, M. (1986). Utilizing co-workers as change agents. In F. R. Rusch (Ed.), *Competitive employment issues and strategies,* (pp. 215–224). Baltimore: Paul H. Brookes.

Shafer, M., Brooke, V., & Wehman, P. (1986). Developing appropriate social-interpersonal skills in a mentally retarded worker. *Vocational Evaluation and Work Adjustment Bulletin, 18*(2), 76–81.

Shafer, M., Egel, A. L., & Neff, N. A. (1984). Training mildly handicapped peers to facilitate changes in the social interaction skills of autistic children. *Journal of Applied Behavior Analysis, 17,* 461–476.

Shafer, M. S., Hill, J. W., Seyfarth, J., & Wehman, P. (1987). Competitive employment and workers with mental retardation: An analysis of employers' perceptions and experiences. *American Journal of Mental Retardation, 92*(3), 304–311.

Siperstein, G. N., & Bak, J. J. (1985a). Attitudinal responses of the nonretarded to their mentally retarded peers. In C. J. Meisel (Ed.), *Mainstreaming handicapped children: Outcomes, controversies, and new discoveries.* Hillsdale, NJ: Erlbaum.

Siperstein, G. N., & Bak, J. J. (1985b). Social behavior: How it affects children's attitudes toward mildly and moderately retarded peers. *American Journal of Mental Deficiency, 90,* 319–327.

Siperstein, G. N., Budoff, M., & Bak, J. J. (1980). Effects of the labels "mentally retarded" and "retard" on the social acceptability of mentally retarded children. *American Journal of Mental Deficiency, 84,* 596–601.

Stanford, K., & Wehman, P. (1980). Improving the social interactions between moderately retarded and nonretarded coworkers: A pilot study. In P. Wehman & M. Hill (Eds.), *Vocational training and placement of severely disabled persons (Vol. 3),* (pp. 141–159). Richmond: Virginia Commonwealth University, Rehabilitation Research and Training Center.

Stanley, M. (1978). The technological conscience: Survival and dignity in an age of expertise. In A. G. Wirth (Ed.), *Productive work—In industry and schools: Becoming persons again.* New York: University Press of America.

Stokes, T. F., & Baer, D. (1977). An implicit technology of generalization. *Journal of Applied Behavior Analysis, 10,* 349–367.

Strain, P. S., Kerr, M. M., & Ragland, E. V. (1981). The use of peer social initiations in the treatment of social withdrawal. In P. S. Strain (Ed.), *The utilization of classroom peers as behavior change agents.* New York: Plenum Press.

Voeltz, L. M. (1988). Children's attitudes toward handicapped peers. *American Journal of Mental Deficiency, 84,* 455–464.

Wehman, P., Hill, J., Wood, W., & Parent, W. (1987). A report on competitive employment histories of persons labeled severely mentally retarded. *Journal of the Association for Persons with Severe Handicaps, 10*(1), 11–17.

Wehman, P., Hill, M., Hill, J., Brooke, V., Pendleton, P., & Britt, C. (1985). Competitive employment for persons with mental retardation: A follow-up six years later. *Mental Retardation, 23*(6), 274–281.

Wehman, P., & Kregel, J. (1985). A supported work approach to competitive employment of individuals with moderate and severe handicaps. *Journal of the Association for Persons with Severe Handicaps, 10*(1), 3–11.

Will, M. (1984). *Supported employment: An OSERS position paper.* Washington, D.C.: U. S. Department of Education.

Wirth, A. G. (1983). *Productive work—In industry and schools: Becoming persons again.* New York: University Press of America.

PART III

SUPPORTED EMPLOYMENT
Local and State Implementation

CHAPTER 9

COMMUNITY-BASED EMPLOYMENT FOR PERSONS WITH AUTISM

Patricia D. Juhrs and Marcia Datlow Smith

Relatively few published efforts are available describing supported employment for persons with severe autism. Individuals who are labeled autistic, or who are "autistic-like" in behavior present unique and complex challenges for job placement into integrated paid employment. Traditionally these persons have been placed into residential facilities, institutions, and other nonwork-related day programs. The expectation is that people with such severe communication, social, and behavioral difficulties would not be able to work in any real job.

With many of the significant advances in behavior-training technology that have occurred since the late 1970s, however, it is clear that persons with autism have greater vocational potential than once thought. It is also clear that traditional approaches to vocational rehabilitation and job placement will not work for this group of people. A more comprehensive and long-term approach to structured placement and on-site training is imperative. A commitment to job maintenance programming must be demonstrated as well.

Patricia D. Juhrs and Marcia Datlow Smith ● CSAAC Training Institute, Community Services for Autistic Adults and Children, Rockville, Maryland.

Our group at Community Services for Autistic Adults and Children (CSAAC) is based in Rockville, Maryland and has been involved in developing nonsheltered vocational programs since 1980. The target group upon which these efforts have been focused comprises individuals with severe communication and social problems who have autism. This chapter presents data from our vocational program and describes the successes as well as the problems which we have encountered.

CHARACTERISTICS OF THE TRAINING PROGRAM

Individuals are admitted to the CSAAC nonsheltered training program on the basis of need for services to avoid institutionalization and the necessity for specialized programs and services designed to meet the unique behavioral and educational training needs of those severely disabled by autism.

When a person enters CSAAC, an interdisciplinary team meets to discuss prioritized goals for the client for the coming year. This meeting results in an Individual Program Plan (IPP), which specifies goals and objectives to be met through training. These goals and objectives are specific to the needs of the client and the work site.

Instructors are assigned to clients on the basis of need as indicated by the IPP. An employee of CSAAC provides "external supervision" of trainees in the nonsheltered worksite, supervising, training, and implementing programs with the clients. These instructors are referred to as job coaches or vocational program counselors. Instructors are paraprofessionals who are hired, trained, and supervised by CSAAC to implement the individual program plans. Consultants such as speech and language therapists, psychologists, occupational therapists, and other related service specialists provide consultation as indicated on the client's IPP to the clients and their instructors to the greatest degree possible in the actual work and other training environments.

Instructional, social, and behavioral goals related to job performance are all trained on the job by the job coaches. The job coaches are provided with formal written training plans for all instructional, behavioral, and social skills which are targeted on the IPP. The job coach implements these programs at the work site.

Among the skills taught by the job coach before and after workday hours are: transportation skills, such as the use of public transportation to get to and from work; money skills, including banking money, budgeting, and purchasing needed or desired items from stores; and after-work social skills—for example, participating in company outings or eating out after work with coworkers.

Each client is assessed by criterion-referenced data prior to determining worksite placement. Individual occupational preferences are determined by giving the client the opportunity to experience different types of work in nonsheltered environments. This method also provides data relating to the potential success of the client in the occupation or particular environment.

CSAAC clients are supervised on the job throughout the workday by CSAAC job coaches at a ratio of one coach to two clients. Several clients have achieved independence and are visited several times a week by a job coach or administrator. Currently, CSAAC employs a total of 26 job coaches who supervise 52 clients. These job coaches are supervised by three Vocational Program Coordinators, who in turn are supervised by a Vocational Program Director.

Training is typically ongoing at the work site, since clients will always have goals targeted by their IPP, related to their work and social skills. Behavioral assessments done by the job coach, as specified on the instructional or behavioral programs, are done at the job site. The job coach remains with the client at work, implements instructional and behavioral programs, and provides the necessary supervision and instruction for a successful job placement.

Numerous social skills are targeted for instruction, depending on the client's needs and the demands of the work site. A sample list is as follows: greeting coworkers, greeting supervisors, sharing the work area, asking for assistance, initiating conversations, terminating conversations, accepting criticism, revealing problems to the job coach as necessary, and social amenities. In those cases where supervision by the job coach can be faded, drop-in supervision is conducted on a schedule which is acceptable to both the interdisciplinary team and the employer.

Placement decisions are made initially by a team consisting of the client, the job placement specialist, the vocational director, the case manager, and the psychologist. The placement decision is then brought to the client's interdisciplinary team for approval. County service coordinators, family, and advocates as well as CSAAC staff are members of this team, and all participate in approving the decision. If a job becomes available and must be filled quickly, team members may be polled by telephone.

STAFF TRAINING

A key feature of the program is the systematic training of all program staff. CSAAC has developed a Basic Training Schedule. This is a standardized training procedure in which all newly hired staff must participate. Basic Training consists of the following:

1. All new employees spend a specified amount of time observing trained counselors working with clients before beginning work.

2. All new employees view the following in-service training videotapes (developed by CSAAC trainers): Policies and Procedures, Behavior Modification, Normalization, Individual Program Plan, Non-Aversive Physical Intervention, Medication Administration, First Aid Basics, and Defensive Driving.

3. All new employees meet with the CSAAC Behavioral Specialist (Assistant to the Psychologist) to review client behavior programs before beginning full-time employment, or as soon as possible.

4. All new employees review the client's record, including instructional programs, for their assigned clients.

Staff are given tests that cover the basics of each course given in basic training. In order to maintain employment with the agency, staff must achieve a certain level of performance on each test.

After going through Basic Training, staff receive individualized instruction at the work site or in the group home on implementation of instructional and behavioral strategies. This training follows a prescribed format which includes: program description and explanation; modelling by the trainer; observation by the trainer as the counselor first implements the procedures; feedback by the trainer; and, if necessary, additional modeling and explanation.

Observation of staff implementation of training procedures indicated that compliance with procedures ranged from approximately 50 percent to 100 percent. Toward the end of refining the model, the following procedures were put into place:

1. Staff were provided with on-site training until they achieved a minimum of 90 percent compliance with procedures.

2. A system of ongoing follow-up and evaluation was developed. Direct supervisors of staff observe, provide necessary training, and do formal evaluations on a systematic basis with a predesignated minimum number of contacts.

3. A study was designed and carried out which explores the use of videotaped feedback in training counselors. Counselors were observed and videotaped while implementing behavioral treatment plans. The use of verbal feedback was compared with the use of videotape feedback in achieving counselor compliance with instructional strategies. The results indicated that use of videotape is superior to the use of instructional feedback alone in teaching counselors to implement behavior management plans.

4. CSAAC staff receive videotaped training in behavioral management procedures and instructional procedures.

The program has devised a system of providing systematic follow-up and monitoring of the residential program and vocational program counselors. This system allows for self-evaluation by staff and also evaluation by supervisors. Data are kept on all follow-up training and evaluation visits to counselors by trainers. These data are used in determining the need for retraining or administrative or personnel actions.

Counselor turnover and failure of some counselors to give adequate notice when leaving were discovered to present difficulties in providing services to persons with autism. A number of measures have been implemented in an attempt to provide support for the counselors with the aim of reducing turnover and increasing the length of notice given by departing staff, including merit raises, staff management by objectives, incentives to give adequate notice, survey of staff characteristics, random reinforcement of staff, and differential support and rating, which would depend on severity of problems faced by staff. These and other tactics have been implemented to support staff who are working with clients with severe disabilities.

CHARACTERISTICS OF POPULATION AND ENVIRONMENT

CLIENT DEMOGRAPHIC DATA

Clients served by the CSAAC program are all diagnosed as having autism. Autism is a disorder which is associated with a number of deficits, disabilities, and behavior problems. Table 1 gives breakdowns of the number of clients showing various deficits related to their primary diagnosis of autism. The project has served 55 youth and adults through July 1987, ranging in age from 15 to 45. It should be noted that many of these individuals have severe behavior problems; that is, 44 have a history of property destruction, and 43 are self-injurious. This is an extraordinarily difficult population to place into integrated employment.

ENVIRONMENTAL CONDITIONS

CSAAC is located in suburban Washington, D.C. All training was done on nonsheltered job sites, both private and nonprofit, located in the Washington, D.C. metropolitan area. The community is spread out over a very large area and at times transportation problems arose and limited the types and locations of jobs which could be accepted.

Table 1. Behavioral Characteristics of Population

Characteristics	No. of clients
Language	
No verbal language	18
Uses words and phrases without meaning	3
Uses words and phrases with meaning	5
Fluent speech but often inappropriate	23
Fluent speech	6
Level of intelligence (IQ)	
Below 30	14
30–49	8
50–70	16
Above 70	17
Behavior problems (Note that some clients have more than one problem.)	
Withdrawn/isolated	53
Aggressive	44
Self-injurious	43
Destroys property	44
Sleep disturbances	8
Ritualistic motor behavior	11
Ritualistic verbal behavior	14
Prior institutionalization	46

EMPLOYMENT PLACEMENT CATEGORIES/DEMOGRAPHICS

Since this program began in September 1980, 55 clients who are severely disabled by autism have held a total of 176 placements through September 1987. These clients range in age from 15 to 45 years. Clients have all been placed in supported employment. The tables that follow show the number of hours per week clients worked at their most recent job and the hourly wage of all clients. (See Tables 2 and 3.)

SUPPORTED EMPLOYMENT MODEL AND OUTCOMES

The CSAAC model has placed 55 persons with severe autism into competitive supported employment in the community. CSAAC clients now work in a diverse range of jobs, at placements which include printing companies, libraries, man-

Table 2. Hours Worked per Client

Hours worked per week	No. of clients
8	1
10	2
12	1
15	2
20	4
21	2
24	2
25	8
30	19
32	2
33	1
35	9
40	2

ufacturing firms, retail clothing and housewares, toys, laundries, restaurants, and government. More detailed job data are presented in Tables 4, 5, and 6.

A process was developed for fading counselor support from work sites in which clients were ready to function more independently. As a result, five clients achieved drop-in supervision status, instituted according to the needs of the clients. In some cases, drop-in is daily, in others it is on a weekly basis. For those clients who continue to need a job coach on site, where possible, plans have been implemented that involve gradual fading from the clients.

Employment data were collected on each project participant. For each participant, the following data were collected: level of IQ, types of behavior problems, number of jobs held, type of job, salary, length of employment at each job, and benefits. A data sheet was designed specifically for the purpose of collecting this information.

Data on client performance were collected by observational behavioral measures by the job coaches in the target settings. Instruments included antecedent-behavior-consequence forms, time block data sheets, social skills data sheets, tally forms, forms for computing productivity, and forms for computing tasks mastery.

Employment data results are summarized in the three

Table 3. Range of Hourly Wages

Hourly wage[a]	No. of clients
0.00	2
1.68	2
1.75	3
2.05	2
2.35	1
2.50	2
3.35	2
3.50	3
3.58	2
3.60	1
3.65	1
3.75	3
3.80	2
3.85	1
4.00	7
4.06	2
4.10	1
4.25	3
4.35	2
4.40	2
4.80	1
4.85	2
5.00	2
5.50	4
6.25	1
6.60	1

[a] The mean hourly wage is $3.85.

tables that follow. Employment data have been displayed to demonstrate the results of supported employment with persons with various disabilities associated with autism, including communication deficits, self-injury, aggression, and property destruction.

In each table, the numbers in the cells represent clients. In cells in which there is a number and a percentage, the percentage indicates the percent of clients included in that cell. (See Tables 4, 5, and 6.)

These tables reveal that persons with severe behavior problems, including aggression, property destruction, and self-injury, have been able to maintain employment.

Table 4. Percentage of Time in CSAAC Employed with and without Self-Injury

	Self-injury	
	Without	With
9% to 25%		6 14.0%
26% to 50%		6 14.0%
51% to 75%	3 25.0%	6 14.0%
76% to 100%	9 75.0%	25 58.1%

Table 5. Percentage of Time in CSAAC Employed with and without Aggression

	Without	With
9% to 25%		6 14.0%
26% to 50%		6 14.0%
51% to 75%	1 8.3%	8 18.6%
76% to 100%	11 91.7%	23 53.5%

Table 6. Percentage of Time in CSAAC Employed with and without Property Destruction

	Without	With
9% to 25%		6 14.6%
26% to 50%	1 7.1%	5 12.2%
51% to 75%	1 7.1%	8 19.5%
76% to 100%	12 85.7%	22 53.7%

EMPLOYMENT RETENTION

The length of employment is shown as a function of time in program, since clients served entered the program at different times. The table below shows percent of time employed by time in the CSAAC program for all clients served. It is apparent from the table that approximately 75 percent of the CSAAC clients who have been in the program 3 years or longer, all of whom are considered to be severely handicapped, have been employed from 91 to 100 percent of the time that they have been in the CSAAC program. As length of time in CSAAC increases, so does the percentage of time employed. (See Table 7.)

The employment process for persons with severe handicaps often involves the client trying several jobs before finding one which suits his interests and skills. Table 8 shows the number of jobs held by time in the CSAAC program. As one might expect, the clients who have had the greater number of jobs have been in the program the longest.

Unsuccessful Job Placements

Table 9 shows the length of employment for unsuccessful placements over the past 6 years.

Table 7. Percentage of Time Employed in Program

Percentage time employed	Time in program		
	Up to 1 year	1 to 3 years	More than 3 years
9% to 25%		5 23.8%	1 3.2%
26% to 50%	1 33.3%	2 9.5%	3 9.7%
51% to 90%	1 33.3%	4 19.0%	4 12.9%
91% to 100%	1 33.3%	10 47.6%	23 74.2%

Table 8. Number of Jobs Held by Time in Program

Time in program	Number of jobs				
	1	2	3	4	5 or more
Up to 1 year	3				
1 to 3 years	5	5	8	1	2
More than 3 years	2	1	10	4	14

Jobs have been lost for a variety of reasons including:

> employees laid off due to lack of work;
> employees fired due to low productivity;
> employees fired due to behavior problems at work;
> company goes out of business;
> company moves from area;
> work site not adequately prepared prior to start-up;
> poor match between client and job;
> client not interested in particular job;
> client has opportunity for higher paying, better job at another company, so resigns.

The main reason for job loss has been clients laid off due to lack of work.

Table 9. Range of Employment Duration

Length of employment	Number of jobs
Less than 3 months	43
3 to 6 months	42
7 to 12 months	28
1 to 2 years	18
2 to 3 years	3
More than 3 years	6

SUMMARY

The data presented in this brief chapter provide an incisive look at the vocational outcomes of the CSAAC program over a number of years. Our program does not focus significantly on pre-placement preparatory activities, but instead directs staff energies at the job site while the individual is already employed. Perhaps the most significant finding of our work is the demonstration that aggressive and acting-out individuals can work competitively. The support of the job coach and the high staff-to-client ratio is necessary; but this type of support would be necessary in *any* good educational, therapeutic, or residential program. Why not provide such support, therefore, in a real work environment? The data presented herein, while not experimental in nature, are convincing in terms of the number of clients and diversity of challenging behaviors that have been encountered.

The key elements that have made our program successful are: (1) systematic behavioral training for clients, (2) a training program for staff which ensures compliance with program guidelines and competencies, and (3) a commitment to a model of supported employment which ensures job retention and integrated worksites. We put our resources into trained staff to work with challenging clients and not into large capital expenditures on buildings and equipment.

In sum, CSAAC has served as a model in the provision of supported employment to persons with severe handicaps. This model had demonstrated that persons with severe problems in behavior, communication, and intellect can maintain successful employment, provided that sufficient support is given. This demonstration has made the service delivery system more aware of the possibilities for persons with severe handicaps. More research and demonstration projects need to be conducted with this population. Service delivery systems seem to be serving persons with more severe handicaps than in the past. However, persons with severe handicaps such as autism are still not typically included by the service delivery system in such opportunities as supported employment.

CHAPTER 10

LOCAL IMPLEMENTATION OF SUPPORTED EMPLOYMENT
Three Programs Making It Work

*Rocco Cambria, Jeannine Strom Boyer,
John J. Miller, Janet Segrott, Daniel Rossi,
Ernest J. Markovic, Jr., Eileen Latimer,
Brian Sobczak, and Larry Naeve*

The local implementation of supported employment programs is perhaps *the* major challenge facing advocates of supported employment in the 1990s. As the research has shown, persons with mental retardation and other developmental disabilities can work competitively. Local service programs, however, are now working to meet the challenge of adapting and implementing this research in such a way as to make it relevant in their communities. The ability of local programs to meet this

Rocco Cambria, Jeannine Strom Boyer, John J. Miller, Janet Segrott, and Daniel Rossi ● Association for Habilitation and Employment of the Developmentally Disabled, Inc., Lemoyne, Pennsylvania.   *Ernest J. Markovic, Jr., Eileen Latimer, and Brian Sobczak* ● Central Adult Training Center, Cuyahoga County Board of Mental Retardation/Developmental Disabilities, Cleveland, Ohio.   *Larry Naeve* ● CITY Education and Employment Services, La Canada, California.

challenge is especially timely because supported employment has frequently been criticized as being manageable only in university settings.

In this chapter, three excellent local programs have been described to show the success of competitive and supported employment programs outside university settings. These programs clearly suggest that when strong values, good management and operations, and careful recording of client progress are present, supported employment can become a reality.

As editors of this book we are pleased to share the data which three model programs, AHEDD (Association for Habilitation and Employment of the Developmentally Disabled) (Lemoyne, Pennsylvania), the Central Adult Training Center (Cleveland, Ohio) and the CITY Program (Los Angeles, California) have collected. These programs are remarkable in many ways, but are especially noteworthy because of their longevity and the clarity of their missions. Each has shown incredible ability to build upon an already excellent historical foundation of vocational programs and to accommodate new research ideas. The examples that follow are detailed descriptions of the programs and the data they have presented.

AHEDD (ASSOCATION FOR HABILITATION AND EMPLOYMENT OF THE DEVELOPMENTALLY DISABLED)

AHEDD Incorporated is a private, nonprofit organization founded in 1977 to offer alternatives to traditional vocational training and employment programs. Through a cooperative partnership with business and industry and other community service organizations, AHEDD (Association for Habilitation and Employment of the Developmentally Disabled) assists persons who have a developmental disability to obtain competitive employment. By demonstrating new employment and training approaches, with involvement from the business community, AHEDD is working towards making positive changes in the vocational rehabilitation system. AHEDD's mission is to bring about the evolution of a vocational rehabilitation system whereby training and employment opportunities for persons with a disability are routinely carried out both in and by business and industry.

When AHEDD began, sheltered workshops and work activity centers represented the majority of vocational opportunities for individuals with a developmental disability. Since then, AHEDD has demonstrated that persons with a developmental disability can obtain competitive employment through industry-integrated training using an on-site training model (e.g., transitional, time-limited, and supported employment). AHEDD believes the best place to train a person for a job is directly *on* the job. Competitive employment in this case is defined as a job position within business and industry where pay is at least minimum wage.

All AHEDD programs are designed to be mutually beneficial to the business community and to the persons with a developmental disability. In addition to placing these individuals, AHEDD has been committed to demonstrating other types of industry-integrated models in order to enhance employment opportunities.

In 1980, AHEDD aligned itself with other businesses in the community to help organize a for-profit custodial company that is owned and operated by its employees, the majority of whom are people with a developmental disability. This business is designed to offer job security, attractive wages and benefits, and ownership that provides profit-sharing for its employees. The company has been operating successfully since its inception.

An employer-awareness concept was initiated by AHEDD for the purpose of increasing the interaction between persons with a disability and employers. The Volunteer Interview Network of Employers, VINE, as it is called, facilitates active employer involvement through a simulated interview approach. The program provides a learning experience for employers while providing job-seeking skill training for persons with a disability. The VINE currently has over 1,000 members nationwide, 900 of them in AHEDD's area of operation (Pennsylvania and Delaware).

AHEDD's experience and success with industry-integrated

programs has enabled the organization to develop education and training seminars, as well as provide technical assistance to employers and other vocational service providers. These training programs are designed so that rehabilitation professionals can assist employers to develop their knowledge and awareness regarding recruiting, screening, hiring, and training individuals who have a disability.

A decentralized organization, AHEDD has eight field offices providing services and demonstrating programs across Pennsylvania and Delaware. The organization receives program grants, fees, and performance payments through contracting with federal, state, and local government agencies and private foundations and companies.

INDUSTRY INTEGRATED PROGRAMS

Since 1977, AHEDD has placed over 1,800 persons who have a disability into competitive jobs. In developing job opportunities and by providing on-site training to the individual and respective company representatives, AHEDD does not use the traditional job-readiness model of train-and-then-place. AHEDD's private-sector based approach is to *place* and *then train*. This has enabled program participants to have access to real employment with competitive wages and has benefited over 1,100 businesses that have integrated such persons into their work force.

Using job development and marketing techniques, AHEDD's field staff survey the business community, contacting employers to identify their needs in recruitment and training. In entering into a partnership with a company, AHEDD has found success in exploring the needs and concerns of employers. After identifying needs, AHEDD staff are able to elaborate upon the services that may be appropriate and of benefit to an employer. Staff are trained to recognize that not all available services may benefit a particular employer.

SOURCE OF REFERRALS

Staff work with community-based service providers (e.g., schools, sheltered workshops, state vocational rehabilitation districts, group homes and community living arrangements, advocacy and support groups) in recruiting program participants. Through the referral agency, staff procure available psychological, medical, social, and vocational information to help determine the need for service, and develop the habilitation plan. This plan always reflects competitive employment and training from both AHEDD staff and company supervisors necessary to maintain employment.

Once a participant is placed on the job, AHEDD's employment specialist (also known as job trainer or job coach) is available to provide on-site skill training and counseling to facilitate learning and ensure proper job adaptation. Using training techniques based on principles of task analysis and behavior modification, the employment specialist analyzes a job, establishes a training plan, and teaches it to the participant. During intensive training, the employment specialist will monitor progress, keep records of the training, and coordinate accommodations as needed. In addition, the participant is guided in appropriate interactions with supervisors and coworkers, leading to successful integration in the work force.

As the individual demonstrates an ability to perform the job tasks with speed and accuracy levels which are acceptable to the employer without assistance or prompting, the employment specialist will begin to reduce involvement in the training situation. The reduction parallels an increased involvement on the part of the company's frontline supervisor. It is important that the employment specialist assist the supervisor in comprehending the change in roles and accepting the responsibility to coach and supervise the new employee.

Supported Competitive Employment

AHEDD's Industry Integrated Training model originally provided time-limited services which include up to 12 months of training and follow-up services. Over time it was found that some individuals with a severe disability have not been able to receive the ongoing support necessary to be independent and productive members of the community. In addition, many people were not even referred for competitive employment because the anticipated long-term training and support was not available for those individuals who might need it.

While demonstrating Industry Integrated Training, AHEDD has developed a program designed to meet the needs of persons with a severe disability who need ongoing support services. This program, called supported competitive employment, offers a new opportunity for some individuals with a severe disability to access and maintain competitive employment. The primary difference between AHEDD's time-limited service and the ongoing service of supported competitive employment is availability of staff time per participant. There are more staff available to provide extended training on the job and extended follow-up service for those persons receiving time-enduring services. The ratio of staff persons to participants, averaged over a 12-month period, was 1.13 for time-limited services versus 1:2 for supported competitive employment.

Supported competitive employment targets persons with a severe disability, including individuals labeled mentally retarded, chronically mentally ill, physically disabled, or visually impaired. Within this targeted group are persons with a severe disability who are transitioning from a special education program into a competitive work setting, and also persons who are currently being served in rehabilitation facilities. Also included are individuals from waiting lists and those who, for various reasons, have not previously been considered for vocational rehabilitation programming. As each individual with a severe disability is referred to AHEDD, staff determine whether the individual will need time-limited or ongoing support services based on their documented disability, record of work experience (both competitive or sheltered), record of past services received (i.e., training, counseling, hospitalization), and other available community resources for support of a competitive placement.

In Pennsylvania, supported employment began in 1986 through a statewide cooperative partnership (State Supported Employment Task Force). Stemming from this partnership of government in Pennsylvania, AHEDD developed a model to provide quality Supported Employment services to people with a severe disability. Through planning with numerous local agencies and businesses, AHEDD has been instrumental in the development of a consortium model for delivery of supported employment services (time-enduring service). In establishing this model, AHEDD trains staff of all provider agencies involved, oversees the project, and promotes cooperative efforts.

After the first year of service provision, the agencies involved in the consortium were able to deliver a quality placement service to persons severely disabled resulting in a job retention rate (persons remaining employed at initial job) of 94 percent. This model of cooperation between agencies is being adopted in other areas as supported employment expands throughout Pennsylvania and Delaware.

DETAIL OF RECENT DATA AND FINDINGS

As AHEDD continues to demonstrate the placement and training of persons with a developmental disability in competitive employment through Industry Integrated Training, data are being collected to inform others about this approach. AHEDD has developed a management information system in order to provide the most valuable information for all interested parties, including employers, funding sources, rehabilitation agencies, etc. In the earlier years of AHEDD, the focus was placed on developing and implementing training programs and the data collected were not tracked in the detail that it is today.

In January 1982 AHEDD was able to computerize placement records. From 1982 to 1987 AHEDD has recorded the placement of 1395 persons with a disability into 1754 jobs. This comes to an average number of 1.25 jobs per person during a 6½-year time period. During this same time frame, AHEDD placed and trained 210 persons who have a severe disability.

AHEDD has designed a new tracking system that follows all participants for at least 12 months of service. The system then follows up by tracking 2 to 5 years after the first job. In addition, the supported competitive employment program is using a specialized tracking program for Supported Employment Services (SEDS-Supported Employment Data System) developed by Dr. R. Timm Vogelsberg of Temple University. Through this system very detailed data are being collected and analyzed regarding services for persons with severe disabilities who receive ongoing support services.

Although AHEDD has been using both systems for a relatively short period of time, there are data available to compare and share with other provider agencies. Information that will be provided is the comparison of data on persons served through time-limited services and others served through supported employment services. Additionally, information is provided on persons with a severe disability who received time-limited services. Over time, more information will be available for cost-benefit analysis and program evaluation.

The following information is based on data taken from the time period of October 1, 1986 to June 30, 1987, and covers activity of AHEDD's Industry Integrated Training programs. During this time period, AHEDD placed 262 persons with disabilities (the majority of whom have a developmental disability) directly into competitive employment. The data will describe 247 people placed into 281 jobs through AHEDD's time-limited services (TLS) and 15 people, all with a severe disability, placed into 16 jobs through AHEDD's Supported Competitive Employment Program.

It should also be noted that in addition to the 15 people with a severe disability who are receiving Supported Competitive Employment Services, 47 other persons with a severe disability received employment and training services during this period through the time-limited service approach.

The primary disabilities of the participants were broken down into the following groups: Mentally Retarded (MR), Learning Disabled (LD), Mental Health (MH), Physical Disability (PHY) (excluding cerebral palsy and epilepsy), Cerebral Palsy (CP), Epilepsy (EP), and Other (OT) (e.g., head trauma, multiple sclerosis). The time-limited services targeted all disability groups, primarily developmental disabilities. Supported employment services targeted persons with severe disabilities, including mental retardation, chronic mental illness, or physical disabilities (including blindness or visual impairment).

Persons with a primary diagnosis of mental retardation received services through both approaches. Persons who received services through the supported competitive employment

Table 1. Wage Information

Hourly wage	Time limited	Time limited (severely disabled)	Supported employment
$3.35–$3.99	67%	71.5%	73%
$4.00–$4.99	21%	14.0%	20%
$5.00–$5.99	4%	2.5%	7%
$6.00 +	8%	12.0%	0%

model had an average IQ of 44. Persons who received services through time-limited services had an average IQ of 69.

For long-term support participants, the average wage at the time the individual was placed on the job was $3.97 per hour, ranging from minimum wage ($3.35 per hour) to over $10 per hour. In the supported competitive employment project the average wage was $3.68 per hour. (See Table 1.)

The time-limited group worked an average of 33 hours per week with the supported employment workers averaging 28 hours per week. The percentage of full-time employees was 66 percent and 34 percent for part-time employees for time-limited participants, with severely disabled persons from this group having 49 percent full-time and 51 percent part-time hours. Statistics for the same category in supported work were 47 percent full-time, and 53 percent part-time. Full-time employment is considered to be 30 or more hours of work per week. (See Table 2.)

The types of benefits that a participant receives from his employer are tracked for each job that they might have. The types are compared in Table 3: In time limited services, 58 percent of the participants received some type of benefit(s), 42 percent did not. For those receiving benefits, participants could

Table 2. Part- and Full-Time Status

	Time limited	Time limited (severely disabled)	Supported employment
Part-time	34%	51%	53%
Full-time	66%	49%	47%

Table 3. Percentage of Consumers Receiving Specific Fringe Benefits

	Time limited	Time limited (severely disabled)
Medical	15%	28%
Vacation/holiday	17%	11%
Paid sick	12%	11%
Pension	5%	5.5%
Other	22%	0%
None	29%	44.5%

receive more than one benefit. For example, a participant listed as receiving medical benefits could also be receiving vacation/holiday benefits. The "other" category includes items such as discounts, uniforms, free meals, and other items. Under the category for "none," it should be noted that some participants who are not currently receiving benefits will receive them after a specified time period (e.g., 90 days, 1 year, 2 years).

For all time-limited participants (including severely disabled persons) enrolled during fiscal year October 1, 1986 to June 30, 1987, the 3-month employment retention rate (i.e., still employed after 3 months) was 83 percent. For persons with a severe disability under time-limited services, the employment retention rate was 82 percent. Ninety-three percent of the persons with a severe disability served through supported employment were still employed at 3 months.

At 6 months, 71 percent of all time-limited services participants were still employed. Severely disabled persons served through time-limited services had the same employment retention rate for 6 months, while persons served through supported employment had an employment retention rate at 6 months of 93 percent. (See Table 4.)

A very important aspect of providing Industry Integrated Services to over 1,800 participants has been the building of partnerships with over 1,100 employers. Through hiring and training these individuals, employers have become aware of a valuable resource through the capabilities of these persons. Whether an individual can be independent within 12 months

Table 4. Percentage of Consumers Working 3 and 6 Months
after Placement

	Time limited	Time limited (severely disabled)	Supported employment
3 months	83%	82%	93%
6 months	71%	71%	93%

of service or will need time-enduring follow-along services, the
employer has been very willing to work together with vocational rehabilitation professionals to provide additional employment opportunties. The partnership has opened a door
for both business and persons with a disability.

THE CENTRAL ADULT TRAINING CENTER: CLEVELAND, OHIO

We now turn from the impressive data of the AHEDD
program to another program in a much larger city and area—
Cleveland, Ohio. Within this program, which provides an array
of different habilitation services, an excellent supported competitive employment program has been established. What follows below are detailed results and analyses which were developed and generated by the Central Adult Training Center in
Cleveland.

The Central Adult Training Center supported competitive
employment program has five staff who develop competitive
jobs and provide job training and continuous ongoing follow-up. The employment training specialist staff provide intensive detailed training to consumers until the employer's criteria
for job speed and responsibility are met. After that, follow-
along is provided to ensure job retention. Other supported employment programs provide direct referrals to the competitive
employment program. These consist of custodial and grounds
maintenance mobile work crews, industrial and hotel enclaves
and noninstructional teacher's aide workstations. These programs help in the transition from a sheltered workshop or
school setting into competitive employment.

The review of the data on the following pages assesses the history of competitive employment for 192 adults with mild, moderate, or severe mental retardation over an 8-year period (9/1/79–8/31/87). Included within this 8-year analysis are detailed 18-month data for 50 consumers (1/1/86–6/30/87) to determine whether employment outcomes significantly changed.

Demographic information includes sex, race, age, and functional level of the consumer and also entry-level job classifications. A Program Efficiency Index indicates how effective job placement services have been to consumer job retention and long-term effectiveness of the Job Placement Program. Finally, a Job Separation section gives the primary reason for each individual not remaining employed.

JOB PLACEMENT CONSUMER DEMOGRAPHIC INFORMATION ANALYSIS

There has been a consistent trend in the program over the 8 years to place six males to every four females entering competitive employment. Information received from the Ohio Bureau of Employment Services shows that service industry entry-level positions employ a generous number of females. The data further show that employment positions in manufacturing are predominantly held by males. It appears that stronger advocacy is needed to employ more females, especially in manufacturing jobs.

An analysis of the mental retardation functioning level shows individuals with severe and profound mental retardation to be an obviously underrepresented group in the demographics. This population will require greater initial training, job accommodations, and more frequent follow-up intervention. It is important to employ existing training technology and also conduct new research to improve placement of this group into competitive employment. Our data demonstrate that in 1985, 1986, and 1987, we have consistently increased the number of consumers with severe mental retardation employed in competitive employment.

Another trend between 1985 and 1988 has been a consistent increase in the number of mildly retarded individuals and a decrease in the number of moderately and severely retarded individuals employed competitively. It appears that the increase in the number of Bureau of Vocational Rehabilitation referrals, especially those with a dual diagnosis (mental retardation and a secondary handicapping condition), has resulted in individuals with a higher IQ but who function in the moderate range being placed competitively.

The average age of the consumer population over 8 years has remained relatively constant at 27 years. This ranged from an average of 25 in 1983 to 29 in 1987. With the development of a school-to-work transition program in our schools, we foresee that the average age will decrease, since consumers will find competitive employment directly out of school. (See Table 5.)

JOB PLACEMENT EMPLOYMENT INFORMATION ANALYSIS

In the Job Placement Program a successful employment experience is defined as retention on the job for a minimum of 6 months. Wehman and Hill (1985) established this 6 months variable because the work experience of nonhandicapped individuals beginning entry-level food service and janitorial positions was on average less than 6 months. Therefore, establishing a 6 month successful work history proved the individual could be successful and established a positive work history as a reference for other employment.

The mean starting wage of $3.97 for the 8-year study has been adjusted for inflation using a conservative annual present value discount rate of 2 percent. The mean starting wage over the 8-year period was 19 percent greater than the minimum wage.

The job classification analysis shows that 80 percent of the positions were in job categories classified in the service industry. During these 8 years, economists stated that 8 of every 10 jobs created were in the service sector. Therefore, the development of 20 percent manufacturing jobs appears to be consistent with national percentages for the nonhandicapped population.

Table 5. Consumer Demographic Information (Sex and Race of
Consumers Placed)

	8 years[a]		18 months[b]	
	N	Percentage	N	Percentage
Female	71	36.98%	21	42%
Male	121	63.02%	29	58%
Black	88	45.83%	24	48%
White	104	54.17%	24	48%
		Mean age		
		27.34		27.08
		Functional level		
Mean IQ		58.17		58.60
	N	Percentage	N	Percentage
Severe	8	4.17%	6	12%
Moderate	65	33.85%	9	18%
Mild	93	48.44%	29	58%
Borderline	26	13.54%	6	12%

[a] 8 years (9/1/79–8/31/87; $N = 192$).
[b] 18 months (1/1/86–6/30/87; $N = 50$).

Full-time employment status (defined as 30 hours or more
weekly) of trainees competitively placed was very high (69%).
However, in the 18-month study, it was significantly higher,
with 78 percent hired full-time and 22 percent hired part-time.
The 1981–1982 recession accounted for fewer full-time jobs in
the 8-year study. (See Table 6.)

PROGRAM EFFICIENCY INDEX

The purpose of the Program Efficiency Index (Table 7) is
to provide a means by which the Job Placement Department
can measure how effective services have been to the consumers. Specifically, the index demonstrates how well the program
has been able to maintain the employee in competitive employment during a 1-year period.

Table 6. Employment Information

	8 years[a]		18 months[b]	
	N	Percentage	N	Percentage
Food service	59	30.89%	19	38%
Janitorial	49	25.65%	13	26%
Industrial	40	20.19%	7	14%
Class aides	14	7.33%	7	14%
General laborers	19	9.95%	1	2%
Hskp/laundry	11	5.24%	3	6%
		Mean starting wage		
		$3.97		$4.12
		Retention rate		
More than 6 months		67.46%		70.97%
Less than 6 months		32.54%		29.03%
		Employment status		
Full-time		69.8%		78%
Part-time		30.2%		22%

[a] 8 years (9/1/79–8/31/87; $N = 192$).
[b] 18 months (1/1/86–6/30/87; $N = 50$).

The time period for each index is one calendar year and includes all consumers who begin work or have been working since January 1 of that year. In this way, the data are most sensitive to the long-term characteristics of the Job Placement Department. In combining the data from the index with information from other aspects of the study, the department was able to develop a more complete picture of the effectiveness of job placement.

The index is derived in a simple straightforward manner. It utilizes the number of months the employee actually worked during the year as compared with the potential number of months the employee could have worked during that same year. The potential amount of time is derived by using the date on which the consumer began competitive employment.

To put the above in the form of an equation:

Table 7. Program Efficiency Index—8-Year and 18-Month Studies
(9/1/79–8/31/87)

	8 years		
Year	Actual months worked	Potential months of work	Index
1979	49.00	50.25	97.51%
1980	158.25	178.00	88.90%
1981	322.25	383.50	84.03%
1982	372.75	393.50	94.73%
1983	382.00	431.50	88.53%
1984	443.75	497.50	89.20%
1985	595.50	661.25	90.06%
1986	704.05	828.00	85.03%
1987	488.50	516.50	94.58%

	18 months		
Year	Actual months worked	Potential months of work	Index
1986–1987	1192.25	1344.50	88.87%

A – The total actual time, in months, the consumer was maintained in competitive employment during a calendar year.

P – The potential time, in months, the consumer could have remained employed based on the date that consumer began competitive employment in that same calendar year.

A – Annual Program Efficiency Index (PEI).

As consumers are primarily placed in entry-level positions, it would be unreasonable to expect them to remain there forever. It is for this reason we use length of time employed rather than merely counting jobs. Consumers are not included in successive years if they withdraw from the program, as they are no longer eligible for the department's services.

JOB SEPARATION ANALYSIS

The principal cause of job separation (59 percent) was for consumer-related internal reasons. These reasons were skill deficits, attitudinal problems, and interfering behaviors. These internal reasons can be caused by many factors (Table 8), but demonstrate strongly the need for support during the consumer's initial employment by the job-coaching staff.

The external reasons for separation (41 percent) were strongly influenced by economic layoffs that occurred in the early 1980s, when unemployment was at record highs due to the recession. Also in the external category, job separation was caused by parental interference (1 percent). During the job development and job placement process, some parents may have objected to the competitive job, but were supportive when they realized the benefits to their son or daughter's independence and financial earnings. However, staff suggest that, in some instances, parental interference or lack of parental support was a secondary reason for job separation.

SUMMARY OF EMPLOYMENT OUTCOMES

In studying the demographic and employment information, we observed some changes between the population being competitively employed on the 8-year study versus those placed in the 18-month study. Most notable was the dramatic decrease in the percentage of moderately retarded persons competitively employed, with at the same time a significant increase of severely retarded persons getting jobs. While the percentage of mildly retarded people has increased, we do not think that this has the effect of decreasing the amount of time and effort needed to retain employment. On the contrary, secondary handicapping conditions indicate an increase in the needed amount of time for training and follow-up.

Another significant increase is in the percentage of those retaining their jobs longer than 6 months in the 18-month study. This reflects longer training and ongoing follow-up. We also find there has been a major shift away from industrial jobs to those in the service industry. This is not unique with our population but is a national trend. We are responding to the needs of the business community in expanding types of jobs offered to our consumers. Also, because more jobs will be available in the service industry, we foresee more part-time competitive jobs as the norm for the future.

Table 8. Causes of Job Separation Analysis

	8-year study			18-month study		
	N	Percentage	Mean IQ	N	Percentage	Mean IQ
A. Internal client skill deficits						
1. Low quality work	10	18.13	58.2	1	5.56	69.0
2. Too slow in work	10	8.13	56.2	2	11.11	59.5
3. Needed too much supervision	12	10.25	56.2	2	11.11	61.0
Total client skill deficits	32	26.51	56.9	5	27.78	63.16
B. Internal client attitudinal problems						
1. Choose to take nonmedical leave	1	.81	69	1	5.56	65
2. Does not want to work	4	3.25	58.75			
3. Does not "try"	2	1.62	78			
4. Poor attendance/tardiness	6	4.49	57.16			
5. Theft	4	3.25	58.25			
6. Wanted to return to workshop/social (peer influence)	4	3.24	63	2	11.11	72.5
Total client attitudinal problems	21	16.67	64.03	3	16.67	68.75
C. Client interfering behavior						
1. Insubordinate/aggressive	11	8.94	58.63	2	11.11	73.5
2. Aberrant behavior (peer influence)	8	6.50	61.5	3	16.67	65.6
Total client interfering behavior	19	15.44	60.07	5	69.55	69.55
D. External economic layoffs						
1. Legitimate layoff	22	17.88	62.69	1	5.56	60
2. Seasonal layoff, can return (peer influence)	2	1.62	59.59			
Total external economic layoffs	24	19.5	60.85	1	5.56	60

E. External parental interference						
1. Resigned due to parental pressure	1	.81	51	0	0	0
Total external parental interference	1	.81	59	0	0	0
F. External social-contextual reaction						
1. Supervisor/coworkers uncomfortable with client	1	.81	49			
2. Seasonal layoff, cannot return	1	1.62	59.5			
3. Appearance not appropriate for setting	0	0	0			
Total external social-contextual reaction	3	2.43	54.25	0	0	0
G. Other external causes						
1. Family moved	2	1.62	64			
2. Medical leave	0	0	0			
3. Financial aid interference	2	1.62	73			
4. Placed in better job	9	7.31	59.7	3	16.67	68.3
5. Transportation problems	2	1.62	59.5			
6. Died	3	2.43	56			
7. Management change	4	3.25	58.25	1	5.56	63
8. Quit—not enough work hours	1	.81	69			
Total other external causes	23	17.98	62.78	4	22.22	65.65
Total internal (client-related) causes	72	59.01	60.32	13	72.22	67.15
Total external (environmental) causes	51	41.41	57.22	5	27.78	62.83

The information from the job separation table displays shifts away from external causes to internal causes of separation. This might be related to more demands placed upon the consumer while on the job, which would suggest an increase in the intensity of training, the time spent in training, and more diligent follow-up efforts.

As we reviewed the Program Efficiency Index (PEI), there were no major changes. The program has remained consistent in its ability to help consumers retain employment.

In taking a global view of the data, we find that the Job Placement Department, with its limited personnel, has been doing a fine job overall. Still, there is a challenge to improve training techniques, initiate more frequent long-term follow-up, and intensify counseling with consumers, parents, and employers. Finally, we need to dedicate ourselves to increasing competitive employment for all functional levels of retardation and developmental disabilities. This population's lack of skills and the increased demands of the workplace are very important in determining the strategy of the Job Placement Department.

This study also shows the need for further research into community employment in general. More specifically, we see the need to form an analysis of how we use our work hours and how this compares with the outcomes achieved by participating consumers.

CITY EDUCATION AND EMPLOYMENT SERVICES

CITY Education and Employment Services began in 1982 as a public school's community-based educational program serving 9 students with severe disabilities. Today, CITY serves (at the time of publication) 47 students (16–22 years of age) with severe handicaps, 50 adults with developmental disabilities (ranging from mild to severe) and 400 other students who qualify for special education services. CITY is divided into three general service components: School-Age, Transition, and Adult Services. The School-Age and Transition components of the program are designed to serve all students with disabilities who are in need of specialized instruction and who attend the Burbank, Glendate, and La Canada school districts (Los Angeles area suburbs of approximately 350,000 in population). The Adult Component is designed to serve adults with developmental disabilities in need of supported employment services who reside in the greater Los Angeles area. Each component has been developed to provide individuals with the needed skills and experiences that may be required for them to be active, productive adults. Program participants receive individualized services that cover a wide variety of education, community and employment related training. Training for school-age and adult participants include:

   I. *Specialized Supported Employment Services*
     a. Assessment and job match;
     b. Intensive individualized on-job-site training;
     c. Consistent ongoing follow-up, counseling, and troubleshooting;
     d. Technical assistance provided to employers;
     e. Employment-related advocacy.
  II. *Specialized Year-Round Education Programming* that includes intensive community-based instruction through competency-based applied skills training in the areas of:
     a. Applied/functional academic skill instruction and generalization training;
     b. Integrated recreation and leisure participation;
     c. Mobility instruction;
     d. Self-advocacy training.

As CITY developed, it was found that at a system-level program options for individuals with handicaps required overall reform. Rather than suffering the illusion that individuals would move through the "Traditional System," CITY worked to develop a service delivery system that would allow individuals with disabilities to become active, contributing members in their home communities. CITY education and employment components were designed to meet the needs of individuals with handicaps by advocating *performance, accountability, productivity*, and *participation for everyone*.

A business must develop a basic philosophy of what it is all about—its mission that determines where it is going and how successful it will be. CITY, through its evolution, developed its mission: a quality service provider that provides the mechanism that will allow as many individuals as possible to participate (with appropriate support) in (1) employment, (2) recreational activities, and (3) community services settings within their home community. The program is driven by its vision of individuals with handicaps becoming active, productive citizens whose contributions are valued because of their *contribution*— not because of their handicaps. All individuals with disabilities deserve training that will enable them to earn money, to use leisure time appropriately, and to be as active and productive as possible. CITY's overriding goal became that of providing a training and support system that would assist participants in making meaningful contributions in their community environment.

EVALUATION

Education and human service programs do not traditionally view themselves as part of the service industry. Without a long-range look at their products, without market research into what services are needed, and without the view that they are ultimately accountable for their product, human service programs have difficulty measuring participant outcomes. CITY has, from its beginning, operated on the premise that it was a service provider acting as a business providing services to all of its customers (the participant), their parents and/or guardians, their center caseworkers, the employers, and involved community members. Like any business, CITY must meet the customer's needs today and be accountable in the future. As a service agency, CITY is constantly assessing its customers to meet their needs. To do this, a number of basic quality indicator benchmarks were developed which allow CITY's customers an avenue for giving meaningful input. Through CITY's data management system, quarterly evaluations are sent to the participant, employer, and regional center caseworker. The input data received are used to measure the quality of services provided. The benchmarks include:

1. *Employment*—With all the regular outcomes of having a job. Wages, working conditions, and job security are key considerations. The worker is given the status of being a member of the work force.
2. *Productivity*—Maximum/Optimal.
3. *Meaningful Interaction between Disabled and Nondisabled Coworkers*—Increased chances for interaction with nondisabled workers.
4. *Jobs, Not Service*—Programwide emphasis is on creating employment opportunities, rather than providing services to develop skills, or time-limited work experience. Assistance and support are comparable to normal provisions for any worker in a well-managed business.
5. *Social Interaction*—Social integration can occur at work with coworker, supervisors, and others. Contact and relationships with people without disabilities can occur near work during lunch, breaks, or nonwork hours as a result of wages earned.
6. *"Choice"*—Opportunity to choose in daily life through self-advocacy.

The measurement of these benchmarks is an important part of the management information system that has been established. Training staff collects data for each participant on prescribed time lines. Data is managed through the use of a CITY developed data-based management system. These data are used not only to evaluate and plan training but to gauge participant progress and outcomes. The areas of measurement are outlined in Table 9. The outcome, it is hoped, will not only be the success of our participants but a society that values each individual's contributions.

PROGRAM STRUCTURE

Divided into three components, CITY has an ability unique to most programs. CITY has the ability to provide services that transcend school-age programming into the world of adult services. It was felt that a school-based program whose focus was intensive integrated community-based instruction and supported employment training could successfully provide transi-

Table 9. Program Evaluation Benchmarks

Benchmark	Measurement
Employment environment	
Employment	Wages, benefits, variety of jobs
Productivity	Minimum wages, promotions
Integration	Integrated work setting, same work schedules as regular employees, etc.
Skill level	Learning marketable skills
Independence	Decreased direct and indirect training/supervisory instruction
Community—independence environment	
Mobility	Use of generic transportation or least restrictive mode of transportation
Social/recreation	Increase use of social/recreation options
Individual decision-making	Increased participant choices

tion and adult programming. The ability to have a consistent continuum of services will result in increased levels of positive outcomes for the individuals served.

The *Adult Services Component* is a non-facility-based program whose primary focus is the individual model of supported employment (CITY has operated one small work crew as a program option).

The *Transition Component* focuses on the development of a transition plan individually designed to meet each participant's needs in the areas of applied academics, community independence training, participation in integrated recreation/leisure programming, mobility instruction, and self-advocacy. This component also provides specialized supported employment services to individuals in needs of intensive initial training and ongoing follow-along services.

The *Secondary Special Education Program* included the development of an Employability Plan individually designed to meet each participant's needs involving vocational education, job-specific skills training, Regional Occupational Program classes, and literacy training in the areas of reading, writing, and mathematics. This program also provides specialized supported employment services as needed to individual participants.

The success of integrated programming and employment services must be based in hard data. It is important at a systems level to measure the effectiveness of the services being provided. But, more importantly, the measurement of individual outcomes is the measurement of effective services.

ADULT PROGRAM DATA

Data collected from the Adult Component has begun to show that (over the first year of operation) supported employment services have made a significant difference in the lives of individual participants and the System that provides adult services. Data from participant anecdotal records who increases in the movement of participants within their communities, using recreational and community facilities, and increased social interaction. Several trends have emerged through an analysis of employment outcome data:

1. Job retention rate for individuals with severe disabilities (12.67 months) is a much higher than the program average of 6.90 months.
2. The average starting wage for all program participants is $3.75 (California minimum wage $3.35).
3. There are a large number of individuals who were unemployed and not in a traditional program who have taken advantage of supported employment services and who are successfully employed. (See Figures 1 to 4.)

SCHOOL-AGE PROGRAM RESULTS

During the 1986–1987 school year the CITY Employment Project provided services to 484 students through WorkAbility funding. These students received a varying amount of employability-related services. Services included: (1) assessment; (2)

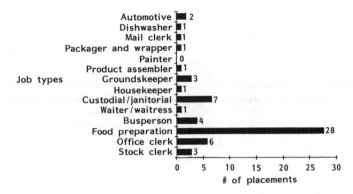

Figure 1. Placements by job type ($N = 50$; placements $= 59$).

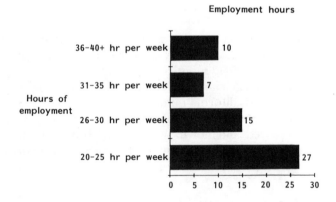

Figure 2. Hours worked per week ($N = 50$; placements $= 59$).

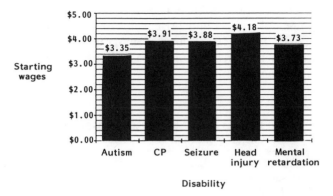

Figure 3. Comparison of starting wages and primary disability ($N = 50$; placements = 59).

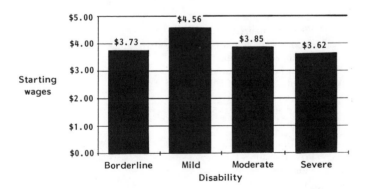

Figure 4. Comparison of starting wages and levels of retardation ($N = 40$; placements = 49).

support services; (3) employment preparation; (4) employment development planning; and (5) enrollment in vocational education class. Table 10 outlines demographic characteristics and employment outcomes of individuals participating in the school-age program.

Table 10. CITY School Age Program (Demographic Characteristics and Program Outcomes)

Education level
    Freshman—54
    Sophomore—164
    Junior—148
    Senior—118

Educational setting
    Special school or center—2
    Special day class—192
    Resource specialist program—248
    Regular class with specialized services—42

Handicapping conditions
    Mild mental retardation—41
    Hard of hearing—4
    Deaf—1
    Speech impaired—1
    Visually impaired—1
    Seriously emotionally disturbed—6
    Orthopedically impaired—2
    Other health impaired—3
    Specific learning disability—339
    Deaf and blind—0
    Multihandicapped—5
    "High risk"—39

Sector of employment
    Private sector—190
    Public sector—59

Wage provider
    Workability—9
    JPTA—42
    Department of rehabilitation—0
    Employer—197
    Employment development department—0
    Local education agency—1

Table 10 (Continued)

Project outcomes
  Work plan
    No job—no plan to seek employment—110
    Actively seeking employment—224
    Has subsidized employment—6
    Has unsubsidized employment/training site—130
    Has unsubsidized employment with other employer—13

  Education plan
    No plan to continue education—24
    Continuing high school education—404
    Enrolling in college—29
    Enrolling post secondary voc. tng. program—25
    Entering shelter workshop—0

SUMMARY

This chapter has described the results to date achieved by three exemplary supported employment programs. The programs vary widely in terms of the individuals served, the types of services provided, and the scope of their ongoing activity. What the programs share in common, however, is a strong philosophical basis for their program, extensive efforts to coordinate their services with other agencies and businesses in their communities, and a commitment to evaluate their effectiveness by analyzing the outcomes achieved by consumers participating in their programs. It is hoped that the efforts of these programs will serve as a model for other similar programs in the country, as they attempt to move supported employment from a university-based concept to an integral part of the ongoing community services for individuals with severe disabilities.

CHAPTER 11

SUPPORTED COMPETITIVE EMPLOYMENT IN NEW JERSEY

Thomas Major and Thomas Baffuto

Over the past 3 years, the Division of Developmental Disabilities (DDD) in New Jersey has implemented a plan to make competitive employment a realistic outcome for people with developmental disabilities. Without the benefit of Federal supported employment funding, New Jersey serves as an example of what can be accomplished when state officials are committed to redirecting existing funds to create a better system. The key figure in the New Jersey story is Eddie C. Moore, the Director of the Division of Developmental Disabilities. It was his conviction that severely disabled individuals could be competitively employed and his continued support that enabled supported competitive employment to develop in New Jersey at an unprecedented rate.

THE DEVELOPMENT OF A SUPPORTED EMPLOYMENT INITIATIVE IN NEW JERSEY

From its inception, supported employment developed in New Jersey as a top-down initiative of DDD. Formerly the Di-

Thomas Major ● Adult Services Program, New Jersey Division of Developmental Disabilities, Trenton, New Jersey. *Thomas Baffuto* ● Project HIRE, Association of Retarded Citizens of New Jersey, North Brunswick, New Jersey.

vision of Mental Retardation, DDD had good reason to become the lead agency in developing supported competitive employment in New Jersey. It was the agency that served the largest number of severely disabled individuals and had the most difficulty placing them into competitive employment.

Over the years, DDD had developed a rather extensive network of adult day programs to serve severely-to-moderately mentally retarded individuals in the community. These programs, called Adult Training Centers, now number over 100 and serve approximately 3,500 individuals. Although the intent of Adult Training had always been to move individuals into less restrictive programming as they progressed, staff reported difficulty in accomplishing this goal. Rehabilitation counselors viewed people who attended adult training as showing little or no potential for competitive employment and were, therefore, reluctant to recommend them for placement in sheltered workshops. The situation was complicated by the Division of Vocational Rehabilitation Services' (DVRS) 20 percent productivity criteria for funding individuals at sheltered workshops.

The lack of movement of individuals out of Adult Training programs was recognized as a problem as early as 1975. In that year, the Division began developing Crew Labor programs to serve the needs of the higher-functioning Adult Training population. This mobile crew model program was seen as an alternative to sheltered workshops, which accepted very few people from Adult Training Centers.

Only five Crew Labor programs were developed during the next several years, and their capacity to serve 120 persons did not begin to meet the needs of Adult Training participants whose functioning levels dictated less restrictive programming. Although the Crew Labor program offered individuals real work experiences, it was almost as costly as Adult Training, allowed only about 4 hours of work per day, and resulted in earnings far less than minimum wage. Furthermore, there was virtually no movement from Crew Labor into competitive employment.

This situation began to change in 1983 when DDD began to fund severely and moderately retarded individuals attending extended employment programs at sheltered workshops throughout the state. At that time, an interagency agreement was negotiated between DDD, DVRS, and the New Jersey Association of Rehabilitation Facilities. This agreement opened the doors for many severely and moderately retarded individuals to move from Adult Training programs into extended employment programs at sheltered workshops. These people generally functioned below the 20 percent productivity level which had been established as a minimum requirement for DVRS funding.

At that point, DDD appeared to have a continuum of services which would eventually lead to competitive employment. The theory was that an Adult Training program would prepare a person to move on to a sheltered workshop, where further vocational training would better equip the individual for eventual placement into competitive employment.

It was soon discovered, however, that although the workshops in New Jersey placed many individuals into competitive employment, severely retarded individuals were not usually selected for placement. Due to limited funding levels, the workshops concentrated their attention on individuals most likely to succeed in competitive employment; needless to say, these were not the most severely disabled.

With a rapidly expanding adult day program population, caused in part by a rather ambitious deinstitutionalization initiative and a lack of placements out of DDD-funded extended employment, the need to change the system became apparent. Given this set of circumstances, DDD issued a directive to establish an initiative designed to move Adult Training and DDD-funded extended employment clients into competitive employment. During the development phase, DDD staff consulted with the Rehabilitation Research and Training Center (RRTC) at Virginia Commonwealth University (referred to earlier in this volume as the individual placement model) and decided to adopt its direct placement supported employment model. The consensus among DDD staff was that the RRTC model had the best potential for producing the outcomes needed in New Jersey. A request for proposals was developed and the Association for Retarded Citizens/New Jersey (ARC/NJ) and the United Cerebral Palsy Associations of NJ

(UCPANJ) were selected as providers to implement what came to be known as Project HIRE (Handicapped Individuals Requiring Employment).

THE ORIGINS OF PROJECT HIRE

Project HIRE was funded by redirecting approximately $600,000 originally earmarked for Adult Training expansion. Although federal funding was applied for, it was never received. From the beginning, HIRE was designed to be a direct placement model, supported competitive employment initiative. Based on the RRTC model, on-the-job training by job coaches and continued follow-along support services were considered essential elements. DDD further stipulated that individuals must earn miminum wage or higher, employment should be full-time whenever possible, and jobs carrying benefits packages should be sought. The target population was defined as Adult Training and DDD-funded extended employment clients considered not placeable without on-the-job supports. Individuals were referred to the project by their case managers.

ARC/NJ and UCPANJ were selected to be the service providers because, as statewide organizations, they are not limited by geographical boundaries. Contracting with two agencies with statewide capability also seemed to be an effective means of minimizing administrative costs. The intention was to make the program available to individuals throughout the state as quickly as possible.

IMPLEMENTATION AND OUTCOMES

In July 1985 the first individuals were placed into competitive employment by the Project HIRE agencies. Within a year the two agencies had placed 135 individuals into competitive employment and 77 percent of them were still employed. Based on this success, the HIRE projects were expanded during the second year, and three additional providers were added. With the exception of Table 1, which represents 100 percent of the consumers placed, the following tables reflect

Table 1. Program Growth July 1985 to November 1987

Implementation period	Individuals placed	Still employed	Success rate
6 months	60	49	81%
12 months	135	104	77%
18 months	213	155	73%
24 months	322	234	72%
29 months	395	284	72%

the project outcomes for 86 percent of the consumers for whom computerized data are currently available. Table 1 illustrates the growth of the initiative during its first 29 months.

The overall placement data indicate that the success rate has remained stable over the past year, showing minor month-to-month fluctuations between 70 percent and 73 percent. All projects are evaluated on the basis of overall success, and a successful placement is defined as one where the consumer remains employed regardless of time. A total of 547 placements were made for the 395 consumers who obtained jobs. (See Table 2.)

The majority of individuals placed from sheltered workshops had been funded by DDD at those facilities because their production rates fell below the 20 percent productivity criteria required for DVRS funding. For the most part, individuals

Table 2. Consumer Demographics (N = 340)

Men = 60%	Women = 40%
Age range = 19–70	Range of IQ = 25–89
Median age = 33	Median IQ = 55
Average age = 44	Average IQ = 57

Intellectual functioning IQ of individuals placed:
70+ = 12%	40–54 = 23%
55–69 = 59%	20–39 = 6%

Day program prior to placement:
Sheltered workshop: 56%
Adult day program: 16%
No day program: 28%

Table 3. Types of Jobs Obtained (N = 340)

Maintenance/janitorial	37%	Cart handler	4%
Food services	32%	Clerical	2%
Assembler	10%	Laundry worker	2%
Stock clerk	7%	Packer	1%
Material handler	4%	Mailroom	1%

who were not in day programs prior to placement were either new referrals to DDD, were on waiting lists for day programs, or had dropped out of workshop programs.

For the most part, entry-level jobs with high turnover rates are targeted. At this time, projects report no difficulties in obtaining jobs for consumers, and they often locate more jobs than they can fill. This has led to more selectivity in finding jobs for consumers. (See Table 3.)

Employers generally express a high level of satisfaction with disabled employees, indicating that they are often more reliable than their nondisabled coworkers. (See Table 4.)

Projects are discouraged from placing individuals into part-time positions unless full-time employment is impractical for the consumer. All part-time positions are at least 20 hours per week, and none pay benefits.

The estimate that 88 percent of the consumers who work full-time receive benefits is conservative since it includes individuals employed for less than 3 months; this is often the time period before a new employee becomes eligible for company benefits. (See Table 5.)

With the exception of a few individuals who had some previous work experience, all consumers earned well below minimum wage ($3.35/hr.) prior to placement. During the first 6 months of the project, the average salary reported for the 60

Table 4. Consumer Employment Data (N = 340)

Employed full-time	75%
Employed part-time	25%
Receiving benefits:	88% of full-time
Average hours worked/week	32.23

Table 5. Consumer Earnings Data (N = 340)

Salary range	$3.35/hr.–$7.50/hr.
Average salary	$4.10/hr.
Cumulative earnings	$1,599,002
Cumulative taxes paid	$315,607

consumers placed was $3.74/hr. and the highest-paying job paid $5.63/hr. The average hourly wage has since shown a steady increase to $4.10/hr. and the highest-paying job obtained to date pays $7.50/hr.

ARC OF NEW JERSEY'S HIRE MODEL

The agency in New Jersey that has placed the greatest number of individuals (193) and maintains an exceptionally high success rate (79 percent) is ARC/NJ Project HIRE. This agency's placement methodology warrants closer examination, as it has become the standard by which all other projects in New Jersey are compared.

The staff of ARC/NJ undertook the task of implementing Project HIRE with a great deal of enthusiasm. Although not heavily involved in direct program services, the organization's statewide emphasis was considered necessary for the project.

Since supported employment was a brand-new concept in New Jersey, it was initially determined that the director of the project should not be attached to the rehabilitation community. In fact, this project is unique in that no one at the agency has a vocational rehabilitation background. Therefore, the staff hired to implement the project had few preconceived notions about the employability of disabled individuals and maintained the attitude that any disabled person who wanted to work could do so. Instead of evaluating why someone couldn't work, staff concentrated their efforts on getting people into jobs.

The ARC/NJ program developed a placement model that includes the use of both job developers and job coaches. The rationale was that job development (consumer/job matching) and job coaching (on-the-job training) are separate functions that require very specific skills and training. Job development requires a great deal of time to nurture prospective employers and develop contacts. Job coaching is also very time-consuming, and initially a coach has little time to do anything else. The continuity needed in the placement process can be lost when one person is responsible for all the tasks. Therefore, development and coaching evolved into two positions.

JOB DEVELOPMENT, CONSUMER ASSESSMENT, AND MATCHING

When a referral is made to the project, the job developer must make the vocational assessment, develop the appropriate job, arrange transportation, and establish a rapport with case managers, parents, residential counselors, guardians, and others involved with the consumer.

The most important concept stressed to all staff is that successful placements result from thorough preparation that matches the right consumer to the right job. The level and amount of training provided to the disabled employee is irrelevant if a poor job match is made. Experience indicates that the most talented job coach cannot salvage a poor match.

With the help of the National ARC On-The-Job Training Coordinator, the following four-step placement process was developed:

Step One stresses full knowledge and understanding of the consumer. The project staff spend several hours talking to consumers, their families, counselors, case managers, etc. Prior to placement, staff often visit the disabled individual three to five times in various settings, i.e., at home, at the training center, interacting with people on breaks or during leisure time. Finding the most appropriate position for an individual requires more than a superficial understanding of strengths and weaknesses.

Step Two emphasizes becoming familiar with the family's needs and concerns. Family, in this case, can mean parents, residential staff, sponsors, foster parents, and so on. It is well documented that if the family is not supportive, the placement will not be successful. The staff addresses each family's concerns and restrictions as well as practical issues such as SSI and transportation. Families need to feel comfortable with the project and the idea of competitive employment.

Step Three requires a thorough understanding of the job. The placement staff will not accept a job by hearing about it over the phone. They become familiar with it through on-site observation. They must know and observe the best worker, the worst worker, and the production rates of each. They must know the supervisor, the person who hires and fires, and the motives for hiring an individual with developmental disabilities. Staff will not accept a job created for a disabled individual, not only because these jobs represent charity, but because they are the first jobs to go during a budget crisis or a change in management. If the company wants a good, dependable employee who will get the job done up to production standards, then the staff can proceed.

Step Four entails investigating the transportation situation. To foster maximum independence, the project does not provide transportation but instead locates resources in the commuity and teaches the consumer to use them. Many individuals learn to use public transportation. Where this is not possible, the consumers travel by car pools, county transportation systems, rides with their families, bicycling, walking, or other means. Often job developers must become very creative in arranging transportation. In one instance a consumer was even placed on a job without a definite means of transportation established. However, since the job was perfect for this difficult-to-place individual, the developer took a chance that the company was large enough for a car pool to be developed. The job coach transported the consumer for 3 weeks until he was able to arrange a car pool.

Only after these four steps have been taken is the placement made and a job coach assigned.

DUTIES OF THE JOB COACH

Once the essential consumer/job match is accomplished, the success of the placement depends upon a well-trained, dedicated job coach to provide one-on-one training at the work site. The responsibilities of the job coach are numerous and varied. A coach must be versatile enough to fit in with white-collar employees of a major corporation one day and be equally comfortable with factory workers the following day.

The first responsibility of a job coach is travel training. The disabled employee must learn to travel to and from work and use backup transportation if necessary. When public transportation is used, the job coach initially rides the bus with the consumer and later follows the bus by car to make sure the individual gets off at the right stop. If the consumer walks, rides a bicycle, or uses any other form of transportation, the job coach makes certain it can be done without continual dependence on the project staff. In addition, it is imperative to teach the individual what to do if the primary transportation is unavailable, that is, during holidays or mechanical breakdowns. This might mean calling parents or residential staff, notifying a coworker, or contacting project staff.

The next responsibility is the actual job-task training. The coach must itemize the job duties and have the supervisor approve this list. Although the coaches are not required to do a formal task analysis, they must divide the job into easy-to-understand tasks. The first week or two the job coach actually performs the job along with the consumer. Gradually, the coach allows the consumer to assume responsibility for more of the job tasks, while constantly reinforcing appropriate work habits. It is important to note that the employer is guaranteed that the job will get done from Day One.

The job coach is also responsible for assisting in coworker socialization. Often this means "breaking the ice" for the disabled employee. The coach teaches the individual to interact appropriately during breaks and lunch, and assures inclusion in company social events. In addition, the coach often helps coworkers to understand the consumer's disability, addressing their misconceptions and prejudices and encouraging normalized interaction.

To help build a support network, the coach gives each consumer an ARC/NJ Project HIRE ID card. The card contains valuable information to help a consumer who gets lost, confused, or stranded at a job site or in the community.

At the job site, the coach utilizes a support network of

other personnel. This network is not designed to carry the consumer or mask any deficiencies, but rather to watch for any problems or changes in work patterns and alert the project staff. Often the job coach will befriend a secretary or receptionist who will report any potential problems. At a shopping mall, where a consumer worked at a maintenance position, a network of store owners would casually observe the individual and alert the coach to problems.

The job coach must teach appropriate work behavior. Because most consumers have never worked before, they are unfamiliar with company rules and regulations. They must learn what is not acceptable, such as working slowly when they wish to, talking loudly, or expecting to joke with the boss. They also need to learn how and when to use facilities such as bathrooms and break-rooms, how to treat company equipment, and what to do in case of inclement weather. On one occasion, many consumers went to work in a hurricane, not realizing the danger. Since companies were closed and public transportation stopped running, project staff had to transport the consumers home in the storm.

An important function of the job coach is to teach the employer and/or supervisor how to work with the disabled employee. Some individuals need a stern, businesslike supervisor while others react better to an exceptionally friendly one. It is the coach's responsibility to show each supervisor the best approach. In addition, the coach attempts to ensure that the employer will report any problems or changes in behavior, no matter how small. If called, the job coach offers to resolve the difficulty; otherwise minor problems often intensify and can eventually lead to termination of employment.

Once the consumer is working up to production standards, exhibiting appropriate work behavior and commuting unassisted by project staff, the coach gradually shifts into the follow-along support stage. Follow-along support consists of periodic site visits to make certain that the consumer is still meeting production standards, that the supervisor is satisfied, and that there are no problems. It is imperative that these visits take place on site because employers often will not relate problems over the phone but tend to discuss progress and/or problems more readily in person. Coaches are required to make at least two monthly follow-along visits to the work site during the consumer's first year on the job. Later, visitations vary according to the needs of the individual. In addition, coaches are trained to vary timing of follow-along visits to avoid the possibility of the consumer's working exceptionally hard because a visit is scheduled.

A job coach's responsibility does not end at the job site. Coaches are also required to assure the consumer has some social life outside of work, often by introducing the person to local recreation programs or other community activities. Consumers who established longstanding friendships at their day programs frequently report that they miss their friends after they begin working. This can lead to self-induced failure at the job site if not adequately addressed. Getting consumers involved in appropriate recreational programs allows them to see their friends and encourage others to try competitive employment. (See Table 6.)

This project's success rate of 79 percent is commendable in light of the number of consumers it has placed into competitive employment over the 29 months of its existence. The excellent

Table 6. ARC/NJ HIRE Outcome Data July 1985 to November 1987

Placement data:	
Total placements = 272	Consumers still employed = 152
Consumers placed = 193	Success rate = 79%
Demographics:	
Age range = 19–70	IQ range = 32–75
Median age = 31	
Average age = 44	Average IQ = 53
Intellectual functioning (IQ):	
70+ = 9%	40–54 = 26%
55–69 = 61%	20–39 = 4%
Employment/financial:	
Pay/hour: range = $3.35–$6.48	Average $4.03
Gross earnings = $980,125	Taxes paid: $195,586
Avg. hrs. wrk./wk. = 32.61	
Employed full-time = 80%	Receiving benefits = 96% of full-time
Employed part-time = 20%	

placement record of the project is attributed to the level of staff commitment, strict adherence to a sound methodology, and an efficient organizational structure. The project appears to be exceptionally selective in matching jobs and consumers.

The project staff spend considerable time dealing with the consumer's family members, which tends to intensify support for the consumer's employment situation. Job coaches are also willing to help individuals to connect with after-hours recreational activities, although this is usually considered the responsibility of a DDD case manager. This project becomes involved in every aspect of the consumer's life that has an effect on employability. Staff morale is extremely high and staff turnover is virtually nonexistent. This, coupled with the fact that the project provides consumers with more hours of service at a lower cost per consumer, warrants further study.

NEW JERSEY'S GOVERNOR'S INITIATIVE ON SUPPORTED EMPLOYMENT

At Governor Thomas H. Kean's request in January 1986, New Jersey was selected as one of eight states to participate in a Policy Academy process funded through a grant from the Administration on Developmental Disabilities in Washington, D.C. The Policy Academy process, designed to bring key state administrators together, led to the Governor's initiative. On discovering that many New Jersey citizens with developmental disabilities were unable to secure employment following graduation from high school, the Policy Academy selected this group as the initiative's target population. The supported employment approach was chosen based on the success of DDD's Project HIRE, which had demonstrated that severely disabled individuals could succeed in competitive employment with appropriate training and support.

In September 1986 the Policy Academy recommended to the Governor's Office a statewide supported employment initiative to assist developmentally disabled special education graduates in obtaining and maintaining jobs. The Governor formally endorsed the initiative on October 22, 1986 to representatives of 60 major New Jersey corporations at the Governor's Conference on Business and Rehabilitation.

In May 1987 three state divisions, Developmental Disabilities, Vocational Rehabilitation, and Special Education, signed an interagency agreement they had developed to implement the initiative. Three agencies were selected to become its service providers: Association for Retarded Citizens/New Jersey, United Cerebral Palsy Association of New Jersey, and the Monmouth Association for Retarded Citizens. The Division of Special Education (DSE) identified 50 education agencies in 14 counties to participate in the initial phase. The Division of Developmental Disabilities and the Division of Vocational Rehabilitation Services identified intake personnel in each county to assist in the initiative. Each education agency identified a case manager to coordinate activities and act as a liaison to local DDD and DVRS personnel. The division liaisons and Project HIRE representatives then conducted regional training sessions to familiarize participants with the implementation procedure.

The three divisions are committed to unprecedented levels of cooperation in order to assist developmentally disabled students to make a smooth transition into the work force. DSE identifies special-education students who have recently graduated or are about to graduate. This is accomplished locally by project case managers, who also work with families to assure their support. The local education agency case manager then makes a referral to DDD and DVRS intake staff on behalf of the student, who must be eligible for both agencies. To avoid unnecessary delays, presumptive eligibility determinations are made about 2 weeks based upon a review of the school records and personal interviews.

Once eligibility is established, DVRS authorizes the supported employment provider agency to seek an appropriate job for the individual. DVRS maintains responsibility for the case until the consumer completes the intensive training phase and is considered stable on the job. At that point, DVRS transfers responsibility for the case to DDD. The same provider agency is then funded by DDD to provide long-term support services for as long as necessary for the individual to maintain employment. If a person does not succeed in the job placement, participants from each agency meet to review the situation. If they conclude that an additional job placement would not be in the individual's best interests, an appropriate day program placement is identified. The goal of such a placement is to overcome difficulties and increase the individual's capacity to return to supported employment.

Although the initiative was ready for implementation in June 1987, it was delayed by the closing of school systems for summer vacation. A one-day conference was held in September to reorient the participants, and referrals began to trickle in during October. Outcome data on this initiative will become available when more of the referrals received have materialized into job placements.

Finally, liaison representatives have been designated by DDD, DVRS, and DSE to oversee the initiative and report on its progress to both the State Policy Academy and the Governor's Office.

JOINT FUNDING AGREEMENTS

DDD has signed joint funding agreements with DVRS and the Commission for the Blind and Visually Impaired. The impetus for both agreements was the receipt of federal vocational rehabilitation funds specifically earmarked for supported employment.

Both agreements are virtually identical in that they specify supported competitive employment methodology to be utilized to place targeted populations into competitive employment. Like the Governor's initiative agreement, the respective rehabilitation agency will fund intensive job coaching services and DDD will fund follow-along support. Unlike the previous agreement, however, the joint funding agreements specify criteria for developing new supported employment providers.

It is anticipated that these agreements will provide an opportunity for sheltered workshops to become supported employment providers. In fact, one such provider, Easter Seal Society of New Jersey, has already been funded to establish a supported employment component at three of its workshop facilities. The end result of these efforts could serve to institutionalize supported employment as a regular DVRS service available to more severely disabled consumers.

SUPPORTED EMPLOYMENT AND REHABILITATION ENGINEERING

New Jersey was selected by the National United Cerebral Palsy Association to participate in a federally funded national demonstration project which will combine supported employment with rehabilitation engineering technology to find competitive employment for severely physically disabled individuals. The service provider will be UCPANJ, which, in addition to being one of the original HIRE providers, has an outstanding rehabilitation engineering component which is also funded by DDD.

In the development phase in 1988, the project has DDD's philosophical and financial support. It is anticipated that a significant number of physically disabled individuals will become competitively employed as a result of this initiative.

CONCLUSION

Supported employment is alive and well in the state of New Jersey. Based on what has been accomplished over the past 3 years, it is anticipated that well over 1,000 individuals with developmental disabilities will benefit from supported competitive employment by the year 1990.

The future promises to enable many special education students to enter New Jersey's work force upon graduation. It is unlikely that the need for Adult Training programs and sheltered workshops will disappear in the immediate future; but some have already changed their orientation. The Division of Developmental Disabilities will continue to maintain a leadership role in the supported employment arena. A commitment has already been made; future employment prospects of individuals with developmental disabilities in New Jersey look better then ever.

ACKNOWLEDGMENTS. Special acknowledgment is given to Eddie C. Moore, Director of the New Jersey Division of Developmental Disabilities. Without his support the outcomes described here could not have been realized.

The authors would like to acknowledge the efforts of Sally DeVito-Beaumont, Director of UCPANJ's Project HIRE, for her development work on supported employment, as well as her continued collaboration on many of the issues presented.

Acknowledgment is also made to Loretta Bolger of DDD whose editorial skills were invaluable.

PART IV

TRANSITION
Research into Practice

CHAPTER 12

COMMUNITY INTEGRATION OF YOUNG ADULTS WITH MENTAL RETARDATION
Transition from School to Adulthood

John Kregel, Paul Wehman, John Seyfarth, and Kathleen Marshall

Assessing the degree of community integration of persons with mental retardation living in local communities is a difficult and complex task (Lakin, Bruininks, & Sigford, 1981). Many previous studies have taken a limited view of successful integration, considering only whether or not an individual is able to remain in the community, and not focusing on factors that indicate the quality of a person's life (Bercovici, 1981). Despite a shortage of reliable information, it is obvious that living in the community with relatives or in an alternative living arrangement does not guarantee a person with mental retardation a normal lifestyle. An individual's independent living and social activities

John Kregel, Paul Wehman, and Kathleen Marshall ● Rehabilitation Research and Training Center, Virginia Commonwealth University, Richmond, Virginia. *John Seyfarth* ● Division of Educational Studies, Virginia Commonwealth University, Richmond, Virginia.

should both be considered when evaluating the total community integration of persons with mental retardation.

Independent living skills refer to those activities that decrease an individual's dependence upon other people (e.g., grooming, cooking, and home management skills) as well as activities that allow the individual to use generic community services (e.g., mobility and shopping skills) (Vogelsberg, Williams, & Bellamy, 1982). Independent living skills identified as critical for successful community integration have included basic self-care, home management, independent mobility, and use of community facilities (Heal, Sigelman, & Switzky, 1978; Schalock, Harper, & Carver, 1981). Despite the importance of these skills, relatively little data presently exist that document the effectiveness of current attempts to equip individuals who are mentally retarded with independent living skills (Schalock, 1983).

It is obvious that there is a vast difference between living in a community and being socially integrated into the community. Unfortunately, many individuals with mental retardation are living in local community settings, yet are socially isolated within their homes and excluded from participation in the mainstream of community life (Baller, 1936; Bercovici, 1981; Charles, 1953; Edgerton & Bercovici, 1976; Edgerton, Bollinger, & Herr, 1984; Miller, 1965). Interaction with other community members and recreational activities should be examined to determine the social integration of persons with mental retardation.

The importance of interpersonal relationships in the community integration of persons with mental retardation has been widely explored (Reiter & Levi, 1980; Schalock, Harper, & Genung, 1981). In a comparison of mildly and moderately mentally retarded individuals, Landesman-Dwyer and Sulzbacher (1981) found that persons with severe handicaps spent more idle time within their residence, interacted less with others, and spent much less time outside the residence than persons with mild retardation. When individuals leave the residence, they rarely do so unaccompanied by caregivers (Scheerenberger & Felsenthal, 1977). These findings corroborate the results of earlier studies (Baker, Seltzer, & Seltzer, 1977; Gollay, Freedman, Wyngaarden, & Kurtz, 1978) which found that individuals living in community residential facilities generally did not develop friendships outside the faculty, did not visit others in the community, and rarely dated.

Engaging in active, community-based recreation activities is another powerful indicator of social integration. Current evidence (Salzberg & Langford, 1981; Wehman, Schleien, & Kiernan, 1980) indicates that many individuals spend leisure time inside their homes rather than participating in community-oriented recreation/leisure activities. Gollay and her colleagues (1978) found that individuals engaged primarily in passive recreation activities. Community recreation activities almost always occurred in programs designed exclusively for disabled individuals.

Many professionals recommend deriving the content of community integration training programs from an empirical analysis of the domestic, community, and recreational skills required for success in post-school environments (Snell, 1983; Wilcox & Bellamy, 1982). At the same time, little information presently exists to document the independent living and social activities of individuals with mental retardation who have recently exited public school special education programs. The purpose of this study was to investigate the community integration of a group of individuals with mental retardation who had exited public school programs from 1979 through 1983. Specific factors to be investigated included basic self-care, home management, community usage skills, use of free time and recreational/leisure activities, and personal satisfaction. The data presented are a part of a larger study which also investigated the vocational adjustment of persons with mental retardation.

METHOD

SAMPLE

Young adults who had been served in public school special education programs for individuals labeled mildly, moderately, or severely mentally retarded were selected for investigation. Survey participants were individuals from four communities in

Virginia who had exited school from 1978 through 1983. The
communities surveyed included a metropolitan inner city setting, an urban area, and a rural area. This final area revealed
so few special education students that four small school systems
were included for investigation. This classification system was
based on U.S. Census definitions (Bureau of the Census, 1981)
of rural, urban, and metropolitan areas.

A sample was constructed consisting of 444 individuals
who had exited special education programs for students with
mental retardation in the participating districts between 1978
and 1983. A professional in each of the locations who was
familiar with the schools and adult services in the area was
identified to conduct survey interviews. Each professional was
responsible for locating and interviewing the students. In instances where the student could not be contacted or interviewed directly, an individual such as parent or caregiver was
interviewed instead. Of the 444 students identified, 300 interviews were conducted with students who had exited programs
for individuals with mild mental retardation and 117 interviews
with students who had participated in programs for students
with moderate or severe mental retardation.

INSTRUMENT

A 60-item survey was generated which contained 35 items
addressing independent living and social integration activities. Questions were worded in either a forced choice yes–no
format or a multiple-choice format in order to expedite interviews. The items included were intended to determine the domestic, community, recreational, and social activities in which
an individual participated. The focus of the items was not on
whether the individual possessed the ability to perform the activities included in the survey, but rather whether the individual engaged in these activities as a part of his regular routine.

FIELD-TESTING

Once the survey was constructed, 15 mental retardation
professionals in academic and direct service circles in Virginia

were consulted to provide input and feedback. When this information had been gleaned and, where possible, integrated, several graduate students were trained and asked to survey individuals with mild, moderate, and severe mental retardation. Survey modifications were again made from this information.

INTERVIEWS

All four interviewers held bachelor's or master's degrees in the human services and were working as special education teachers, vocational placement specialists, or visiting teachers. All had lived and worked in their respective areas for at least 5 consecutive years. The interviewers were brought to a central location for 6 hours of training.

RESULTS

A total of exactly 300 individuals were contacted and responded to the survey. This total was divided into 31 percent metropolitan, 31 percent urban, and 38 percent rural residents. At the time of the interviews, 86 percent of the individuals surveyed lived at home with their natural family, and 8 percent lived independently. Six percent lived in some type of community-based alternative living arrangement.

Table 1 contains a breakdown of selected demographic data that profile key features of the group of individuals surveyed. As can be seen, 67 percent of the respondents were mothers. Males accounted for 57 percent of the individuals surveyed, and blacks and Caucasians each comprised 50 percent of the sample. Individuals ranged in age from 17 to 24, with a mean of 21.1 years.

INDEPENDENT LIVING

The independent living activities of the entire sample are summarized in Table 2. Over 90 percent of the individuals

Table 1. Summary of Demographic Characteristics

	Mildly retarded (*n* = 183)	Moderately/severely retarded (*n* = 117)	Total (*n* = 300)
Respondent			
Mother	108 (59%)	94 (80%)	202 (67%)
Father	29 (16%)	7 (6%)	36 (12%)
Client	18 (10%)	3 (3%)	21 (7%)
Other	28 (15%)	13 (11%)	41 (14%)
Sex			
Male	110 (60%)	62 (53%)	172 (57%)
Female	73 (40%)	55 (47%)	128 (43%)
Race			
Caucasian	85 (46%)	64 (54%)	149 (50%)
Black	98 (54%)	53 (46%)	151 (50%)
Age			
17–19	97 (53%)	5 (4%)	102 (34%)
20–21	63 (34%)	34 (29%)	97 (32%)
22–24	23 (13%)	78 (67%)	101 (34%)
Home location			
Rural	78 (43%)	35 (30%)	113 (38%)
Urban	61 (33%)	33 (28%)	94 (31%)
Metropolitan	44 (24%)	49 (42%)	93 (31%)
Residence			
Lives independently	21 (11%)	3 (3%)	24 (8%)
At home with parent	151 (83%)	108 (92%)	259 (86%)
Alternative living arrangement	11 (6%)	6 (5%)	17 (6%)

independently completed all basic self-care tasks (dressing, eating, toileting, bathing, and grooming). A majority of individuals participated in a variety of home management activities. Of those surveyed, 75 percent participated in cooking meals and/or snacks for themselves, 43 percent did their laundry, 24 percent sewed or mended their clothes, 80 percent cleaned their rooms, and 68 percent completed assigned household chores.

Participants displayed some degree of independent mobility and usage of community facilities. Seventy-five percent of those surveyed walked about their communities, 39 percent

Table 2. Summary of Independent Living Activities

Activity area	Percentage of individuals independently engaging in the activity		
	Mildly retarded	Moderately/severely retarded	Total
Basic self-care			
Dressing	177 (97%)	102 (87%)	279 (93%)
Eating	180 (98%)	107 (92%)	287 (96%)
Toileting	181 (99%)	111 (95%)	292 (97%)
Bathing	178 (97%)	97 (83%)	275 (92%)
Home management			
Prepare meals/snacks	159 (87%)	65 (56%)	224 (75%)
Laundry activities	99 (54%)	31 (27%)	130 (43%)
Sew or mend clothes	63 (34%)	10 (9%)	73 (24%)
Clean own room	155 (85%)	85 (73%)	239 (80%)
Complete household chores	123 (67%)	80 (68%)	203 (68%)
Mobility			
Walk about community	153 (84%)	72 (62%)	225 (75%)
Ride bicycle	78 (43%)	39 (33%)	117 (39%)
Drive a car	60 (33%)	1 (1%)	61 (21%)
Use public transportation	55 (30%)	22 (19%)	77 (26%)
Use of community facilities			
Restaurants	120 (66%)	20 (17%)	140 (47%)
Retail stores	149 (81%)	47 (40%)	196 (65%)
Post offices	73 (40%)	10 (9%)	83 (28%)
Banks	68 (37%)	8 (7%)	76 (25%)
Use of money			
Make purchases	173 (95%)	58 (50%)	231 (77%)
Make change	141 (77%)	15 (13%)	156 (52%)
Write checks	44 (24%)	2 (2%)	46 (15%)
Savings account	39 (21%)	13 (11%)	52 (17%)
Balance checkbook	30 (16%)	2 (2%)	32 (11%)

rode bicycles, 21 percent drove a car, and 25 percent used public transportation. Retail stores were frequented by 65 percent of the individuals, 47 percent utilized restaurants, 28 percent used the post office, and 25 percent used a bank. Over three-fourths of those surveyed used money to make purchases independently. Only 52 percent reported making change on their own. Banking activities were displayed by a smaller number of persons, with 15 percent writing checks, 11 percent balancing checkbooks, and 17 percent possessing savings accounts.

SOCIAL INTEGRATION

A majority of the social activities and interpersonal relationships reported by the respondents focused on passively oriented activities conducted within their own homes. As indicated in Table 3, a majority of individuals (60 percent) preferred spending free time with their families, 22 percent with friends, and 3 percent alone. Twenty percent of the individuals spent time only with their families. However, 59 percent of the individuals reported spending the vast majority of their free time with persons with no identified disabilities. A number of individuals reported some amount of time (more than one hour per week) engaging in social activities outside their homes, with 69 percent spending time in homes of friends, 28 percent in outdoor recreation facilities, and 29 percent in indoor recreation activities.

The individuals surveyed participated in a wide variety of recreational activities. Nearly all individuals (91 percent) reported watching television regularly, 90 percent listening to records and tapes, 27 percent playing card games, 19 percent playing table games, and 15 percent playing videogames. In contrast, considerably fewer individuals participated in sports-related activities. Less than a fourth of all those surveyed participated in activities such as jogging, swimming, cycling, bowling, basketball, or football. A greater number of individuals reported engaging in more passively oriented leisure activities, with 38 percent attending movies regularly. The area of recreational activities least frequently reported by respondents was that of membership and participation in social organizations or clubs. Only 14 percent reported participating in church activities such as chorus or clubs (46 percent reported attending church), and no more that 3 percent of the individuals partici-

Table 3. Summary of Social Integration Activities

Activity area	Percentage of individuals independently engaging in the activity		
	Mildly retarded	Moderately/severely retarded	Total
Individuals with whom free time is most frequently spent			
Family	100 (55%)	79 (68%)	179 (60%)
Friends	52 (28%)	15 (12%)	67 (22%)
In public	2 (1%)	1 (1%)	3 (1%)
Alone	4 (2%)	6 (5%)	10 (3%)
Equally	25 (14%)	16 (14%)	41 (14%)
Social activities outside the home			
In homes of friends	147 (80%)	59 (50%)	206 (69%)
Outdoor recreation activities	51 (28%)	32 (27%)	83 (28%)
Indoor recreation activities	53 (29%)	33 (28%)	86 (29%)
Recreation activities			
Watch television	166 (91%)	106 (91%)	272 (91%)
Listen to records or tapes	164 (90%)	104 (89%)	268 (90%)
Play card games	62 (17%)	18 (15%)	80 (27%)
Play table games	31 (17%)	25 (21%)	56 (19%)
Play video games	38 (21%)	8 (7%)	46 (15%)
Sports			
Jogging	39 (21%)	3 (3%)	42 (14%)
Swimming	41 (22%)	27 (23%)	68 (23%)
Cycling	49 (27%)	20 (17%)	69 (23%)
Bowling	21 (11%)	35 (30%)	56 (19%)
Basketball	15 (8%)	4 (3%)	19 (6%)
Football	5 (3%)	0 (0%)	5 (2%)
Events attended regularly			
Sporting events	86 (47%)	29 (25%)	115 (38%)
Concerts and plays	24 (13%)	13 (11%)	37 (12%)
Movies	91 (50%)	39 (33%)	130 (43%)
Fairs and festivals	22 (12%)	22 (19%)	44 (15%)
Social organizations and clubs			
Church-related activities	31 (17%)	11 (9%)	42 (14%)
YMCA/YWCA	1 (1%)	4 (3%)	5 (2%)
Scouting	3 (2%)	4 (3%)	7 (2%)
Exercise class	5 (3%)	2 (2%)	7 (2%)
Adult educational class	4 (2%)	5 (4%)	9 (3%)

Table 4. Summary of Personal Satisfaction with Present Situation

	Percentage of individuals independently engaging in the activity		
Activity area	Mildly retarded	Moderately/severely retarded	Total
Satisfaction with present situation			
Very satisfied	65 (36%)	44 (37%)	109 (36%)
Somewhat satisfied	80 (44%)	55 (47%)	135 (45%)
Somewhat dissatisfied	30 (16%)	15 (13%)	45 (15%)
Very dissatisfied	8 (4%)	3 (3%)	11 (4%)
Major identified problems			
Health problems	13 (7%)	17 (15%)	30 (10%)
Inappropriate behavior	15 (8%)	21 (7%)	36 (12%)
Transportation	39 (21%)	32 (27%)	71 (24%)
Making friends	20 (11%)	19 (16%)	39 (13%)
Lack of money	48 (26%)	18 (15%)	66 (22%)
Lack of work skills	42 (23%)	45 (39%)	87 (29%)
Lack of leisure activities	27 (15%)	21 (18%)	48 (16%)
Loneliness	24 (13%)	27 (23%)	51 (17%)

pated in a YMCA/YWCA, scouting program, or attended an adult education or exercise class.

The survey also attempted to assess the individuals' current satisfaction with their present situation and identify the significant problems faced by survey participants. Data summarizing these results are contained in Table 4. Over three-fourths of the individuals were reported as being very satisfied or somewhat satisfied with their lives. Only 15 percent were reported being somewhat dissatisfied and 4 percent very dissatisfied with their lives. A wide variety of problems were reported by the respondents. The most frequently reported problems included lack of work skills (29 percent of the individuals), transportation problems (24 percent), and lack of moeny (22 percent). Other less frequently cited problems included loneliness (17 percent), lack of leisure activities (16 percent), making friends (13 percent), inappropriate behavior (12 percent) and health problems (10 percent).

COMPARISON OF MILD AND MODERATE/SEVERE GROUPS

With few exceptions, the students who had exited programs for persons with mild mental retardation displayed greater proficiency in all areas of independent living skills. Mildly mentally retarded students were more likely to be mobile within their community, perform home management activities, frequent community facilities, and use money. Interestingly, students from programs for persons with moderate or severe mental retardation were equally likely to perform household chores (67 percent to 68 percent).

A comparison of the performance of the two groups in the area of social integration revealed more varied results. While mildly handicapped students were more likely to spend their free time in the homes of friends, the two groups were equally likely to participate in both indoor and outdoor recreation facilities. In terms of recreation activities, the two groups were just as likely to watch television, listen to records or tapes, and play table games, although the mildly mentally handicapped students reported a greater tendency to play video games (21 percent to 7 percent). Participation in sporting activities by the two groups were roughly equivalent in the areas of swimming, cycling, basketball, and football, with moderately and severely handicapped students being less likely to engage in jogging (3 percent to 21 percent) and more likely to engage in bowling (30 percent to 11 percent). Membership in social organizations and clubs was roughly equivalent between the groups.

The satisfaction of the individuals surveyed with their present situation showed no significant differences between the two groups. Eighty percent of the mildly handicapped group and 84 percent of the moderately and severely handicapped group reported being satisfied or very satisfied with their present lives. The group of individuals with moderate or severe mental retardation were more likely to report lack of work skills (39 percent to 23 percent), loneliness (23 percent to 13 percent), and health factors (15 percent to 7 percent) as major problems facing them at the present time. Lack of money was more frequently cited (26 percent to 18 percent) as a problem by persons with mild mental retardation.

DISCUSSION

The results of this study present a mixed picture of the community integration of young adults who have recently exited from special education programs for persons with mental retardation. The data presented should not be construed as reflecting the status of all adults with mental retardation in Virginia. The lack of a comprehensive representative sample, the reliance upon parental respondents, and the collection of data within only selected locations prevents generalized conclusions from being drawn. Results obtained are undoubtedly affected by the training provided in public school programs and the level of adult services available in the participating communities. However, the sample size of 300 is relatively large, and the use of trained interviewers appeared to increased the reliability of the data. Given the drawbacks in study design, a few significant trends emerged which may provide a basis for future investigations:

1. Almost all of the individuals investigated demonstrated some degree of competence in independent living skills. Nearly all possess basic self-care care skills, most participate in home management activities, and many possess some degree of independent mobility within their local community. Some individuals make significant use of community facilities, although environments such as restaurants, post offices, and banks are frequented by a relatively small number of individuals.

2. The individuals' participation in social activities reflected an emphasis on passively oriented activities conducted within their own homes. Well over half the individuals studied spend the vast majority of their free time with family members and 20 percent interact exclusively with members of their own family. The majority of recreational interests cited by respondents were passive, home-based activities. Relatively few individuals indicated participation in active, sports-related activities, and very few participated in any type of social organization or club.

3. Despite the lack of social interaction with other members of the community, the individuals surveyed appear quite

satisfied with their current life-style. Only 19 percent of the individuals expressed any degree of dissatisfaction with their current situation. However, a sizable number of individuals reported significant problems that inhibit their community integration. Lack of work skills, transportation, and lack of money were cited as problems by more than 20 percent of those surveyed.

The design and implementation of effective community integration training programs for persons with mental retardation presents a challenge to professionals in public schools and adult service programs. Successful community integration requires individuals to be independent within their homes and communities and to be socially integrated into all facets of community life. Although the majority of individuals surveyed engage in independent living activities and appear satisfied with their lives, many continued to be socially isolated in their homes and fail to engage in active, structured recreational or social activities. Further investigation is needed to determine the effects of factors such as type of school program, employment status, and level of retardation on community integration. Complete and accurate information on each of these factors is required to enable professionals to design training programs that maximize the community integration of individuals with mental retardation.

ACKNOWLEDGMENT. Reprinted from *Education and Training of the Mentally Retarded*, 1986, *21* (1), pp. 35–42, with permission.

REFERENCES

Baller, W. R. (1936). A study of present social status of a group of adults, who, when they were in elementary schools, were classified as mentally deficient. *Genetic Psychology Monographs, 18*, 165–244.

Baker, B., Seltzer, G., & Seltzer, M. (1977). *As close as possible*. Boston: Little, Brown and Company.

Bercovici, S. (1981). Qualitative methods and cultural perspectives in the study of deinstitutionalization. In R. H. Bruininks, C. E. Meyers, B. B. Sigford, & K. C. Lakin (Eds.), *Deinstitutionalization and community adjustment of mentally retarded people,* (pp. 131–144). Washington, D. C.: American Association of Mental Deficiency.

Bureau of the Census. (1981). *1980 Census of Population. Vol. 1, Characteristics of the Population.* Washington, D.C: U. S. Department of Commerce.

Charles, D. C. (1953). Ability and accomplishments of persons earlier judged mentally deficient. *Genetic Psychology Monographs, 47,* 3–71

Edgerton, R. B., & Bercovici, S.M. (1976). The cloak of competence: Years later. *American Journal of Mental Deficiency, 80,* 485–497.

Edgerton, R. B., Bollinger, M., & Herr, B. (1984). The cloak of competence: After two decades. *American Journal of Mental Deficiency, 80,* 345–351.

Gollay, E., Freedman, R., Wyngaarden, M., & Kurtz, N. (1978). *Coming back: The community experience of deinstitutionalized mentally retarded people.* Cambridge, MA: Abt Books.

Heal, L. W., Sigelman, C. K., & Switzky, H. N. (1978). Research on community residential alternatives for the mentally retarded. In N. R. Ellis (Eds.), *International Review of Research in Mental Retardation,* Vol. 9, pp. 210–250. New York: Academic Press.

Lakin, K. C. Bruininks, R. H., & Sigford, B. B. (1981). Deinstitutionalization and community-based residential adjustment: A summary of research and issues. In R. H. Bruininks, C. E. Meyers, B. B. Sigford, & K. C. Lakin (Eds.), Deinstitionalization and community-based residential adjustment: A summary of research and issues. In R. H. Bruininks, C. E. Meyers, B. B. Sigford, & K. C. Lakin (Eds.), *Deinstitionalization and community adjustment of mentally retarded people,* (pp. 382–412). Washington, D. C.: American Association of Mental Deficiency.

Landesman-Dwyer, S., & Sulzbacher, F. M. (1981). Residential placement and adaptation of severely and profoundly retarded individuals. In R. H. Bruininks, C. E., Myers, B. B., Sigfod, & K. C. Lain (Eds.), *Deinstitutionalization and community adjustment of mentally retarded people,* (pp. 182–194). Washington, D. C.: American Association on Mental Deficiency.

Miller, E. L. (1965). Ability and social adjustment at midlife of persons earlier judged mentally deficient. *Genetic Psychology Monographs, 72,* 139-198.

Reiter, S., & Levi, A. M. (1980). Factors affecting social integration of noninstitutionalized mentally retarded adults. *American Journal of Mental Deficiency, 85,* 25–30.

Salzberg, C. L., & Langford, C. A. (1981). Community integration of mentally retarded adults through leisure activity. *Mental Retardation, 19,* 127–131.

Schalock, R. (1983). *Services for developmentally disabled adults: Development, implementation and evaluation.* Baltimore: University Park Press.

Schalock, R., Harper, R., & Carver, G. (1981). Independent living placement: Five years later. *American Journal of Mental Deficiency, 86,* 170–177.

Schalock, R., Harper, R., & Genung, T. (1981). Community integration of mentally retarded adults: Community placement and program success. *American Journal of Mental Deficiency, 85,* 478–488.

Scheerenberger, R. C., & Felsenthal, D. (1977). Community settings for MR persons: Satisfaction and activities. *Mental Retardation, 15* (4), 3–7.

Snell, M. E. (Ed.) (1983). *Systematic instruction for students with moderate and severe handicaps* (2nd ed.). Columbus: Charles E. Merrill.

Vogelsberg, R. T., Williams, W., & Bellamy, G. T. (1982). Preparation for independent living. In B. Wilcox & G. T. Bellamy (Eds.), *Design of high school programs for severely handicapped students* (pp. 153–174).

Wehman, P., Schleien, S., & Kiernan, J. (1980). Age-appropriate recreation programs for severely handicapped individuals. *Journal of the Association for the Severely Handicapped, 5(4)*, 395–407.

Wilcox, B., & Bellamy, G. T. (1982). *Design of high school programs for severely handicapped students*. Baltimore, MD: Paul H. Brookes Publishing Company.

CHAPTER 13

PROJECTING THE SERVICE NEEDS OF TRANSITION-AGED YOUNG ADULTS EXITING PUBLIC SCHOOL PROGRAMS
A Statewide Analysis

Elizabeth Evans Getzel, John Kregel, and Linda C. Veldheer

Data collected on the service needs of individuals transitioning from school into work and adult life have usually occurred once these students have left the public schools. Follow-up studies on employment and residential adjustment (Hasazi, Gordon, & Roe, 1985; Hasazi, Gordon, Roe, Hull, Finck, & Salembier, 1985; Mithaug, Horiuchi, & Fanning, 1985; Wehman, Kregel, & Seyfarth, 1985) for special education students once they exit from schools have helped to focus attention on

Elizabeth Evans Getzel ● Community Services Assistance Center, Virginia Commonwealth University, Richmond, Virginia.   *John Kregel* ● Rehabilitation Research and Training Center, Virginia Commonwealth University, Richmond, Virginia.   *Linda C. Veldheer* ● Developmental Disabilities Program, Virginia Department of Mental Health, Mental Retardation, and Substance Abuse Services, Richmond, Virginia.

their service and support needs while living in the community. This type of needs assessment, however, is critical *prior to the students leaving school* so that better long-range service planning can be conducted.

The reauthorization of the Education for All Handicapped Children Act (P. L. 98–199) mandates the schools to assess the service needs of special education students before graduation. Such assessments are necessary, since without this information creation of adequate supports and resources for participation in the community cannot be sufficiently developed. Presently, future service needs of persons with developmental disabilities who are leaving school are not included in increased budget requests for community programs (McDonnell, Wilcox, & Boles, 1986).

It is all too common to find that students with disabilities face waiting lists for services and go for extended periods of time before receiving them once they are in the community (McDonnell, Wilcox, Boles, & Bellamy, 1985). It is not suggested that these problems will be alleviated by conducting assessments of service needs prior to students graduating from public schools. However, having data to project these needs can greatly assist in communicating to community programs what services will be needed for these individuals upon entering the adult service delivery network.

The following study was conducted to assess the service needs of students enrolled in secondary special education classes. The project was funded through Virginia's Developmental Disabilities Program. The data were collected to determine the prevalence, demographic characteristics, and future service needs of individuals with developmental disabilities in the state. Information obtained in the study was shared with the Planning Committee of the Board for Rights of the Disabled. This Committee comprises a variety of agencies serving persons with developmental disabilities, consumers, and advocacy organizations. The survey process represented a coordinated effort between agencies and organizations representing developmentally disabled populations and the Department of Education. The results were used by the Planning Committee in developing recommendations for future statewide activities and funding initiatives of the Developmental Disabilities Program.

METHOD

SAMPLE

The sample consisted of 1,066 students with developmental disabilities who were currently enrolled in Virginia public schools, including some persons residing in state residential training facilities. Thirty-three school districts were selected by a stratified random sampling procedure used by the Department of Education. The survey population represents one-fourth of all special education students enrolled in school between the ages of 18 and 21.

The students in the survey were identified as currently receiving special education services in accordance with state Department of Education regulations. Students with developmental disabilities were selected since, as a population, they present some of the most difficult challenges to overcome in developing transitional services.

It was determined that students 18 to 21 years of age would be used in the study. Students in this age group were closer to the actual time of transitioning from school into the community. The methodology employed in the study was modeled after the outstanding work of Smull, Sachs, and their colleagues in Maryland using 15-year-old special education students as the survey's target group (Sachs & Smull, 1983). Sachs and Smull sampled 15-year-olds in order to accurately estimate the prevalence of developmental disabilities in their state. The present study decided to sample students approaching the time of their graduation (18 to 21 years of age) to obtain a more accurate picture of their future service needs.

The participating school districts were representative of rural, urban, and metropolitan areas of the state. The districts were selected based upon the stratification factors of size of the school district, ethnicity of the population, and SES indicators. The proportional sample allowed for the generalization of the survey results to the remaining school districts in the state.

INSTRUMENT

A 28-item questionnaire was used to obtain the survey data. The Developmentally Disabled Persons Community Needs Survey (DDPCNS) was modified from a similar survey used by the service delivery network for persons with developmental disabilities in the state of Maryland (Sachs & Smull, 1983). Adaptations of the survey were made so that the information gathered would be more relevant to the organizational structure of the Department of Education in Virginia.

The survey is designed to address three different types of questions: (1) functional characteristics, (2) demographic characteristics, and (3) service needs. A number of the questions attempt to measure an individual's level of functioning, determine the demographic characteristics of the survey population that will influence future service planning, and identify the individual's current and future service needs.

PROCEDURE

A 1-day training session was conducted to instruct the participating school districts on how to distribute the forms and to answer any questions about the survey. Special education administrators were asked to attend since they were identified as playing a key role in disseminating the surveys in their districts.

The administrators were told to distribute the surveys to individuals who were most familiar with the students. It was presumed that a majority of the surveys would be completed by classroom teachers. Alternatively, the forms could be completed by a social worker, program supervisor, or other appropriate persons.

The training session discussed the purpose of the survey activity and how the data would be used. On the corner of each survey an agency code would appear to identify each participating school. Other identifying information was not required, unless the school district wished to provide it for its own purposes.

Information on how to contact the project staff for further

follow-up was provided. For school districts needing assistance, funds were made available to cover any costs for postage. After the initial dissemination of the surveys, a follow-up contact was made by the project staff with the participating school districts. The contact was made to answer any further questions or concerns by administrators since attending the training session.

RESULTS

DEMOGRAPHIC CHARACTERISTICS

Demographic characteristics were obtained from the survey items. Of the total student sample (1,066), 63 percent were male and 37 percent were female. Half of the population in the study was black, while 48 percent were white. The remaining 2 percent were identified as Hispanic, Asian, and other. Forty-six percent of the students were 18 and 19 years of age, with 54 percent representing 20- and 21-year-olds. The most frequently cited primary disabilities were mental retardation (58 percent), specific learning disability (25 percent), emotional handicaps (7 percent) and cerebral palsy (3 percent). Seventy-two percent of the sample were individuals living at home, 22 percent were in public institutions (i.e., mental health, mental retardation or private facility), and 4 percent were in residences such as a group home, licensed adult home, or nursing home. Key demographic characteristics of the sample are summarized in Table 1.

FUNCTIONAL CHARACTERISTICS

Survey respondents were asked to determine the level of supervision or assistance required by students on a daily basis. The range was from none to continuous 24-hour assistance. Of the total population surveyed, over two-thirds of the students require little or no supervision on a daily basis. Table 2 provides a breakdown of the results.

Respondents were asked to describe the students' mobility

Table 1. Summary of Key Demographics of
Student Population (N = 1,066)

Gender	Percentage
Male	63
Female	37
Race	
Black	50.4
White	47.7
Asian	0.5
Hispanic	0.9
Other	0.5
Age	
18–19 years	45.8
20–21 years	54.2
Student-identified disability (most frequently cited)	
Mental retardation	58
Specific learning disability	25
Emotional handicaps	7
Cerebral palsy	3
Residence	
Home	72
Public institution	22
Living independently	2
Other residences	4

needs. Human assistance was required by 21 percent of the students, with 7 percent needing mechanical aids and 3 percent needing a barrier-free environment. Seventy-one percent of the sample did not require any assistance for getting around in their daily activities.

Students were identified as utilizing a variety of independent living skills. Over half of the sample was able to tell time, use a telephone, perform routine chores, read safety words (i.e., stop, poisons), and stay at home safely while alone. Approximately half of the students could prepare meals, with less than half being able to shop for groceries, use public transportation, and manage their own money. Table 3 provides a summary of these results.

Table 2. Supervision or Assistance Required by Students (N = 1,066)

Level of supervision	Frequency	Percentage
None	337	31.0
Occasional monitoring	188	18.0
Minimal but daily supervision	211	20.0
Substantial daily supervision	106	10.0
Continuous waking supervision	62	6.0
Continuous 24-hour supervision	138	13.0
Missing value	24	2.0

The survey contained items on the behavior skills of the students. Respondents were asked to indicate whether a specific behavior occurred "Rarely/Never," "Occasionally," or "Frequently." The results indicate that overall disruptive behaviors are minimal among the students in the survey population. Those behaviors identified as rarely occurring were extreme mood changes (56 percent), injurious to others (82 percent), sexually agressive (73 percent), destroys nearby objects (82 percent), unusual fear of life events (67 percent), and overfriendliness to strangers (57 percent). The most cited behaviors that occasionally occur were extreme mood changes (32 percent), unusual fear of life events (19 percent), and over-friendliness to strangers (15 percent). Behaviors reported as occurring frequently were extreme mood changes (10 percent)

Table 3. Students' Level of Functioning for
Independent Living Skills (N = 1,066)

Skill	Percentage
Tells time	63
Uses telephone	67
Uses public transportation	46
Safely left at home alone	60
Manages own money to meet needs	43
Performs routine chores	67
Prepares meals	51
Reads safety words	68
Shops for groceries	44

Table 4. Students' Level of Functioning for Behavioral Skills (N = 1,066)

Students' behavioral skills	Rarely/never (percentage)	Occasionally (percentage)	Frequently (percentage)
Extreme mood changes	56	32	10
Physically injure others	82	7	2
Sexually aggressive	73	5	2
Destroys nearby objects	82	8	3
Unusual fear of life events	67	19	3
Overfriendliness to strangers	57	15	8

and overfriendliness (8 percent). Table 4 provides a complete breakdown of the responses to the items on students' behaviors.

Survey respondents were asked whether students were dependent on their caregivers. Fifty-six percent of the students dependent on a care-provider are living with a nonpaid provider. For those students dependent on a nonpaid caregiver, approximately two-thirds of the caregivers are between the ages of 40 and 59 years. Approximately 13 percent of the caregivers were reported as 60 or older. Table 5 provides further elaboration on the ages of these nonpaid care providers.

SERVICES

Survey questions dealing with the types of services required by students were divided into five main categories. Un-

Table 5. Caregiver Age for Students Reported as Dependent on Their Caregiver (N = 247)

Caregiver age	Frequency	Percentage
Under 30	6	2.4
30–39	42	17.0
40–49	101	41.0
50–59	67	27.1
60–69	23	9.3
Over 69	8	3.2

der each category heading, specific services were listed. The five main areas identified were residential, vocational, medical, mobility, and supportive services. Respondents completing the survey were asked to indicate the level of need for a specific service by placing a check in one of the three columns next to the service. The columns were identified as "Currently Receiving Services," "Needs Services Urgently," or "Needs Services in the Future." The two most frequently stated urgent needs were in the areas of vocational (13 percent) and supportive (12 percent) services. Future service needs were grouped around residential (21 percent), vocational (35 percent), and supportive (22 percent) services. Table 6 summarizes the results of the five main service areas listed on the survey.

Table 7 provides information on what specific services were identified as needed by the students. Employment services were the most frequently reported need, followed by support services including case management, independent living skills, and recreational services. Supervised residential placement was also indicated. The table lists the most frequent responses.

Survey respondents were also asked to determine the students' overall need for residential placements and support services. The survey items were constructed to obtain data on the urgency status of these services. Approximately 13 percent of those responding indicate their students are in urgent need of residential placements. Thirty-six percent believe there will be a need in the future. Table 8 summarizes the results for this survey item.

Concerning the urgency of need for day program/support services, half of the individuals answering this question indicate a future need for these services. Table 9 provides a breakdown of the responses.

DISCUSSION

Results of the study indicate that the majority of the 18- to 21-year-old student population with developmental disabilities exhibit a variety of independent living skills and are able to

Table 6. Students' Level of Need for Types of Services (N = 1,066)

Types of service	Currently receiving		Urgent need		Future need	
	Frequency	Percentage	Frequency	Percentage	Frequency	Percentage
Residential services	146	13.7	69	6.5	226	21.2
Vocational services	397	37.2	137	12.9	376	35.3
Medical services	389	36.5	45	4.2	69	6.5
Supportive services	571	53.6	129	12.1	236	22.1
Mobility services	189	17.7	37	3.5	89	8.3

Table 7. Expressed Need for Services (N = 1,066)

Services	Percentage
Supervised residential placement	22
Job skill training	27
Supported competitive employment	17
Sheltered employment	15
Case management	13
Independent living skills	15
Social/recreational services	11

Table 8. Expressed Urgency of Need for Residential Placement (N = 389)

Urgency status	Frequency	Percentage
Urgently needed	49	12.6
Wanted in the future	141	36.2
Present situation available indefinitely	103	26.5
Not sure, don't know	96	24.7

Table 9. Expressed Urgency of Need for Day Program/Support Services (N = 435)

Urgency status	Frequency	Percentage
Urgently needed	80	18.3
Wanted in the future	216	49.7
Not sure, don't know	139	32.0

function on a daily basis with little or no supervision. Seventy-one percent (71 percent) of the sample did not require any assistance to perform their routine activities; and other functional characteristics, such as disruptive behaviors, appear to be at a low incidence rate.

The most significant projected service needs for this population were in the areas of day program/support services and residential services. When reviewing the expressed need for future services, 68 percent of the sample was in need of day program/support services. Expressed need for residential services was 49 percent. Services such as supervised residential placement, job skill training, supported competitive employment, independent living skills, and case management are examples of the most frequently cited service needs.

When generalizing these results to the total statewide 18- to 21-year-old student population with disabilities, careful examination must be made concerning the appropriate day program/support services and residential services for this population as they transition into work and adult life. The appropriate mix of employment opportunities and residential facilities will be in high demand. These projected needs could be even higher as situations change in the lives of persons with disabilities. One example is the ages of the nonpaid care providers who have a person with disabilities dependent on them. Over a third of these care providers are 50 or older. Changes in the status of a care provider can increase the need for services in the community.

It is realized that this study only sampled those individuals currently enrolled in special education classes and did not include individuals who have already left the public school system. Thus, any projected statewide service needs assessment of 18- to 21-year-old persons with developmental disabilities is a conservative estimate. However, the data show definite trends of what the service needs are for individuals with disabilities as they prepare to leave high school.

It is important that efforts to assess the projected needs of students as they prepare to leave school be conducted in a design similar to the one used in this study. It is essential that the data collection activity be performed with the complete cooperation of the key agencies and organizations in the service delivery system. Because of the cooperation between the Department of Education and the Planning Committee for Virginia's Board for Rights of the Disabled, this study was designed so that the results could be shared with all agencies concerned. Projected service needs were evaluated by professionals in the public schools as they developed transitional service plans. In addition, these needs were shared with organizations in the adult service delivery system, helping to increase their awareness of the needs of this population as they transition into the community.

Another key element of the survey process was providing agencies and organizations demographics and functional characteristics of the sample population. These data provide specific information so that appropriate vocational programs, residential facilities, and support services can be targeted. With information on the functioning levels and characteristics of the population, an effective match between consumers and available services can be made. Projected service needs can also assist in the planning and developing of new programs in preparation for a higher demand for these services.

Assessing the needs of persons with developmental disabilities and the effectiveness of services received has been given increased emphasis in the reauthorization of the Developmental Disabilities Act (P. L. 100–146). Data collection activities will be further developed to better determine the numbers of individuals requiring services and the degree to which these services are provided. To assist in the planning process, a projection of the service needs of individuals prior to entering the community is essential. It is believed that such projections will impact the monies spent for services, the types of services available and the effectiveness of the transition process for students with developmental disabilities. Follow-up measures are important for determining how well persons with disabilities are adjusting after the transition process. However, it is equally important to assess their needs prior to leaving school so that the necessary supports and services are available to plan for their futures.

REFERENCES

Hasazi, S. B., Gordon, L. R., & Roe, C. A. (1985). Factors associated with the employment status of handicapped youth exiting high school from 1979 to 1983. *Exceptional Children, 51*(6), 455–469.

Hasazi, S. B., Gordon, L. R., Roe, C. A., Hull, M. Finck, K., & Salembier, G. (1985). A statewide follow-up on post high school employment and residential status of students labeled "Mentally Retarded." *Education and Training of the Mentally Retarded, 20*(4), 222–234.

McDonnell, J., Wilcox, B., & Boles, S. M. (1986). Do we know enough to plan for transition? A national survey of state agencies responsible for services to persons with severe handicaps. *The Journal of the Association for Persons with Severe Handicaps, 11*(1), 53–60.

McDonnell, J. J., Wilcox, B., Boles, S. M., & Bellamy, G. T. (1985). Transition issues facing youth with severe disabilities: Parents' perspective. *The Journal of the Association for Persons with Severe Handicaps, 10*(1), 61–65.

Mithaug, D. E., Horiuchi, C. N., & Fanning, P. N. (1985). A report on the Colorado statewide follow-up survey of special education students. *Exceptional Children, 51*(5), 397–404.

Sachs, M. L., & Smull, M. W. (1983). *Persons with developmental disabilities— Report No. 2: Development of prevalence estimates using available Maryland and national data bases.* Baltimore: University of Maryland School of Medicine.

Wehman, P., Kregel, J., & Seyfarth, J. (1985). Employment outlook for young adults with mental retardation. *Rehabilitation Counseling Bulletin, 29*(2), 90–99.

CHAPTER 14

AN ANALYSIS OF THE EMPLOYMENT OUTCOMES OF YOUNG ADULTS WITH MENTAL RETARDATION

John Kregel and Paul Wehman

Along with supported employment, transition has been one of the major priorities of the Office of Special Education and Rehabilitative Services during the 1980s (Will, 1984). The major focus of the transition movement has been on bringing together multiple agencies and disciplines who work cooperatively to bring about meaningful employment as an outcome for students exiting special education programs. The federal transition focus has had a positive effect to date in that more and more states and local programs are attending to the necessity of locating employment for students with severe disabilities before school is over and also initiating transition planning for individual students at a much earlier age. For example, the state of New Jersey has recently changed the transition planning age from 21 to 14. Many other states have developed comprehensive statewide planning systems (Wehman, Moon, Everson, Wood, & Barcus, 1988).

Early transition activities have focused primarily on devel-

John Kregel and Paul Wehman ● Rehabilitation Research and Training Center, Virginia Commonwealth University, Richmond, Virginia.

oping interagency agreements that define roles of various
agencies in a state or community and mechanisms for designing individual transition plans. A more recent activity has been
the establishment of supported employment placement programs within secondary special education programs to place
students with moderate and severe disabilities into competitive
employment *before* the student exits public school and enters
the adult service system.

This approach is based upon several assumptions. First,
the lengthy waiting lists for adult service programs that exist in
many states often mean that students who have participated in
preemployment programs in public schools will face a 2- or
3-year wait before entering an adult employment program. It
is feared that this gap in services may lead to individuals losing
many of the vocational skills they have acquired in their secondary programs, and subsequently lower the employment expectations of the individuals and their families. Second, placement into competitive employment will allow adult service
agencies to be responsible for only the long-term follow-along
component of the individual placement model. This will significantly lower the costs of serving these individuals within the
adult service system and thereby maximize the number of individuals who may be accommodated in the system.

ISSUES RELATED TO SERVICE DELIVERY

Competitive employment for severely disabled adults previously excluded from integrated work environments, as em-
bodied in the supported employment initiative, is a very new
concept. Empirical evidence demonstrating the efficacy of supported employment programs, such as those described in previous chapters, are just emerging in the professional literature.
It is not clear whether adolescents between the ages of 18 and
21 will also be able to be successfully employed through supported employment services. The new emphasis on placing
secondary students with moderate and severe disabilities into
competitive employment leads to several currently unanswered
concerns. For example, the results of recent follow-up studies

(e.g., Wehman, Kregel, & Seyfarth, 1985) document extremely high unemployment rates of individuals who have exited public school programs. It has been hypothesized (Rusch & Chadsey-Rusch, 1985; Wehman, Kregel, & Barcus, 1985) that these high unemployment rates are due in large part to a lack of functional curricula, community-based training programs, and integrated service delivery models within secondary special education programs. However, widespread research data do not presently exist to document that public school special education programs can effectively implement supported employment service delivery models.

A second concern relates to the lack of previous work experience on the part of the adolescents participating in the programs. Many students with moderate and severe disabilities may reach the latter stages of their secondary program without ever having the opportunity to gain work experience in integrated work environments. These students may well have not acquired the formal and informal work experience obtained by their nonhandicapped counterparts, who may have worked in a variety of jobs during their final years in school. This lack of experience may negatively affect their chances for successful employment in at least two ways. First, students may require a much longer period of initial training and far more follow-along services when they are placed into integrated, community-based employment settings. Second, students who lack previous work experience have no experiential basis from which to make informed employment choices. This may result in individuals being placed into positions that they do not enjoy and that are not of their own choosing, a situation that will adversely affect their long-term employment retention.

A final concern relates to the perceived role of parents within the supported employment process. Parental support has been previously identified as a crucial component of employment success (Goodall, Wehman, & Cleveland, 1983). A frequently expressed concern, whether real or imagined, is that parents of adolescents with moderate or severe disabilities may be more hesitant to allow their son or daughter to participate in competitive employment programs than the parents of adult-aged individuals. It is feared that parents of adolescents will be less likely to agree to supported employment placement, may interfere with the employment process, or may be more likely to terminate employment when the results of the program do not meet their expectations.

The remainder of this chapter summarizes the results of a large-scale effort to place individuals under the age of 22 into paid employment in integrated work setting through supported employment programs in Virginia. The outcomes achieved by a group of individuals will be described and then compared to the results achieved by a similar group of adults in the same state. Finally, the results achieved by the supported employment programs will be discussed in relation to the concerns relating to the implementation of supported employment programs for adolescents aged 18 to 22 described above.

RESULTS OF SUPPORTED EMPLOYMENT ACTIVITIES

The results presented below address the outcomes achieved by a number of both public school and nonprofit community service programs providing supported employment services to adolescents aged 18 to 21. The public school programs involved represent five large metropolitan school districts in three major geographical areas of the state that have placed 52 students into supported employment since 1985. The districts initiated placement activities in cooperation with a federal project implemented for the purpose of demonstrating successful approaches to improving the vocational transition of students with moderate and severe disabilities. The outcomes of these programs have been previously described in Wehman, Moon, Everson, Wood, and Barcus (1988). The community service programs represented have placed 134 individuals into competitive employment.

The data reported in this section were collected by professional staff directly responsible for providing supported employment services to the participating consumers. Virginia has developed a centralized supported employment management information system (RRTC, 1987). The data management system collects individual data (as opposed to aggregated group data) on over 200 demographic and employment outcome variables throughout the course of an individual's employment. This uniform system provides a standardized data set that allows the direct comparison of the individuals served and the outcomes achieved across various programs.

Selected Consumer Demographic Data

A total of 186 adolescents and young adults are represented in this analysis. All individuals were placed into their first job prior to the age of 22. Over two-thirds of the consumers were male (68 percent). The primary disability of the overwhelming majority of consumers (93 percent) had been previously identified as mental retardation. Other primary disabilities were reported for a small number of individuals, including autism, long-term mental illness, and neurological impairments. The average IQ score for all individuals for whom mental retardation was identified as the primary disability was 52. Significantly, the average IQ score for individuals placed through the public school programs was 44, whereas the consumers placed by the community-based programs had a mean IQ score of 55. Most of the individuals were reported to be functioning in the mild (38 percent) and moderate (47 percent) range of mental retardation. Sixty-nine of the 186 consumers had diagnosed secondary disabilities. Major categories of secondary disabilities included cerebral palsy (9 individuals), convulsive disorders (13 individuals), language impairments (30 individuals), and visual impairments (12 individuals).

Selected Employment Outcome Data

The 186 individuals have been placed into 264 positions, and average of 1.4 positions per consumer. Nearly all individuals (96 percent) were placed into a supported competitive employment situation. Only four percent of the consumers were placed into group employment options such as work crews or enclaves. The group of individuals worked an average of 27 hours per week, with 55 percent of the individuals working less than 30 hours weekly. (See Table 1.) The types of jobs held by

Table 1. Number of Hours per Week
in Position

Hours worked per week	Cumulative percentage
Less than 20 hours	26.1%,
20 to 29 hours	28.4%
30 to 40 hours	45.1%
More than 40 hours	0.4%

consumers reflect the entry-level service occupation positions that are characteristic of supported employment participants, with 47 percent working in food service positions and 32 percent employed in janitorial/custodial positions.

The average hourly wage of all consumers was $3.66 per hour, slightly above the federal minimum wage during the time period. The average consumer had worked a cumulative total of 77 weeks across one or more positions, and had earned $7,896 throughout their employment. Sixty-two percent of the individuals reported receiving some type of fringe benefits, ranging from medical insurance to employee discounts. Table 2 outlines the percentage of individuals reported as receiving a variety of fringe benefits.

Little difference was evident between students placed by the five public school programs and the individuals placed by community service agencies in terms of employment retention.

Table 2. Fringe Benefits of Job Placements

Fringe benefits	Percentage of reported consumers receiving benefits
Sick leave	32.9%
Paid vacation	39.9%
Medical insurance	31.6%
Dental insurance	7.0%
Employee discounts	12.3%
Free/reduced meals	18.9%
Other benefits	8.3%
No fringe benefits	38.2%

Table 3. Reasons for Separation from Employment

Reason for separation	Percentage
Transportation problem	2.5%
Moved away	1.9%
Does not want to work	15.6%
Parent/guardian initiated	8.1%
Economic situation	10.0%
Slow work	3.1%
Low-quality work	5.0%
Poor attendance/tardiness	6.3%
Insubordinate behavior	5.0%
Aberrant behavior	1.9%
Parental interference	0.6%
Poor work attitude	4.4%
Employer uncomfortable	8.7%
Income maintenance interference	0.6%
Need for continual prompting	1.9%
Medical/health problems	1.9%
Poor job match	2.5%
Seasonal layoff	3.7%
Took better job	9.4%
Criminal behavior	3.7%
Deceased	0.6%
Other reason	2.5%

Exactly 55 percent of both groups remained employed as of January 1, 1988. For those individuals who were separated from employment, the most frequently cited reasons for separation were (in rank order): (1) the individual does not want to work; (2) the individual was laid off due to local economic conditions; (3) the individual resigned to take a better job; and (4) the employer felt uncomfortable working with the consumer. A complete listing of all reasons for employment separation is provided in Table 3.

IMPLICATIONS

The results of the supported employment activities described above clearly demonstrate the ability of adolescents and young adults with moderate and severe disabilities to obtain competitive employment in integrated community settings. The similarity of the employment outcomes achieved by the participating individuals to those achieved by the adult consumers employed by the Rehabilitation Research and Training Center and described in detail in the chapter by Wehman and Kregel is quite striking. The adolescents and young adults achieved outcomes roughly equivalent to the adults in terms of types of jobs, hours worked per week, wages earned and benefits received, and reasons for and rate of separation from employment. That individuals between the ages of 18 and 21 can successfully obtain competitive employment working at or above minimum wage is a significant finding that lends support to the concept that public schools in particular have an important role to play in placing individuals in competitive employment *prior* to their graduation from secondary special education programs.

The results also address the previously stated concern that public schools themselves may be ill-equipped to provide the intensive job placement and training services required by the supported competitive employment model. Very few differences were found between the results obtained by individuals placed by the five school districts and those placed by the community service agencies. One key difference that was discovered was that the five school districts involved worked with a significantly lower functioning population. The average IQ score of individuals placed through public school programs was 44, compared to an average IQ score of 55 among individuals placed by community service agencies. The ability of public school personnel to work effectively with individuals with limited previous work experience and significant skill deficits is one of the most encouraging findings of the present analysis.

The success of the public school programs clearly indicates the benefits of initiating transition planning activities at an early age. School personnel were able to identify student needs, involve parents in the transition process, and provide intensive training to individuals still in school. One of the key elements of the successful public school programs was that each program was able to develop a cooperative agreement with local adult service agencies to provide ongoing support for students placed into employment after the individuals had graduated from school and had been removed from the public school caseload (Wehman *et al.*, 1988). These agreements guaranteed that these individuals would bypass existing waiting lists for services and receive the ongoing support required to maximize their chances to remain successfully employed.

Another trend emerging from the data that should be addressed is the disproportionate representation of males (68 percent male to 32 percent female) in the population of placed consumers. The overrepresentation of males in supported employment programs is a finding that has been reported and discussed elsewhere (Wehman & Hill, 1985). However, the fact that this occurs even in programs serving adolescents and young adults prior to the age of 22 is disturbing. It would be hoped that a more proportional representation of females would occur in transition programs for public school students. Service providers at all levels remain challenged to discover the reasons for this lack of participation on the part of females and develop methods to maximize their successful participation in supported employment programs.

The results also indirectly address the role of parents in the supported employment process. Some professionals have feared that parents of adolescents may be "overprotective" and not be overly supportive of supported employment activities on behalf of their son or daughter. Anecdotal data from the public school programs indicate that some parents expressed initial concerns about the purpose of the program and low expectations for success. After placement, however, public school staff reported significant changes in parental expectations as the students participated in integrated employment settings. These changes may have been the direct result of a concerted effort to involve parents at all stages of the transition process.

A final comment should be made regarding the employment retention of the consumers participating in the programs. A significant number of individuals were able to retain employment for 6 to 12 months after placement. However, only 55 percent of the individuals remain currently employed. This may be due to numerous factors. For example, the lack of prior work experience on the part of the consumers may have led to their being placed into positions not of their own choosing, which ultimately led to their dissatisfication with their employment situation. Perhaps participation in an array of career exploration activities at an earlier age would result in greater employment stability. Another potential factor may be the difficulty involved in adult service agencies attempting to provide ongoing support services in employment settings where they were not involved in the initial job placement and training activities. Effectively coordinating placement, training, and ongoing support functions across cooperating agencies remains one of the greatest challenges to effective local transition programs.

SUMMARY

The ability of adolescents and young adults with moderate and severe disabilities to obtain competitive employment in integrated community settings was clearly demonstrated through the results achieved by both public school and community-based service programs. Consumers were able to achieve employment outcomes equivalent to those achieved by adults with disabilities in supported employment programs. The results indicate the crucial role that public school programs may play in the employment process. Job placement and training activities conducted prior to individuals leaving school will prevent them from facing lengthy waiting lists for adult service programs and will ultimately be a cost-effective approach to maximizing the number of individuals participating in local supported employment activities. An analysis of the outcomes achieved by the programs also raises several challenges for service providers, including the need to increase the number of females participating in competitive employment placement and training programs and the need to coordinate services between cooperating agencies to maximize each individual's chances to maintain employment over a lengthy period of time.

REFERENCES

Goodall, P., Wehman, P., & Cleveland, P. (1983). Job placement for mentally retarded individuals. *Education and Training of the Mentally Retarded, 18*(4), 271–278.

RRTC. (1987). *Data management system operations manual.* Richmond: Rehabilitation Research and Training Center, Virginia Commonwealth University.

Rusch, F.R. & Chadsey-Rusch, J. (1985). Employment for persons with severe handicaps: Curriculum development and coordination of services. *Focus on Exceptional Children, 17*(9), 1-8.

Wehman, P., & Hill, J. (1985). *Competitive employment for persons with mental retardation: From research to practice (Vol. I).* Richmond: Rehabilitation Research and Training Center, Virginia Commonwealth University.

Wehman, P., Kregel, J., & Barcus, J.M. (1985). From school to work: A vocational transition model for handicapped students. *Exceptional Children, 52*(1), 25–37.

Wehman, P., Kregel, J., & Seyfarth, J. (1985). Employment outlook for young adults with mental retardation. *Rehabilitation Counseling Bulletin, 29*(2), 91–99.

Wehman, P., Moon, M.S., Everson, J.M., Wood, W., & Barcus, J.M. (1988). *Transition for school to work: New challenges for youth with severe disabilities.* Baltimore: Paul H. Brookes.

Will, M.C. (1984). *OSERS programming for the transition of youth with disabilities: Bridges from school to working life.* Washington, D.C.: Office of Special Education and Rehabilitative Services, U.S. Department of Education.

INDEX